FROM THE OUTSIDE IN

From the Outside In

Suburban Elites, Third-Sector Organizations, and the Reshaping of Philadelphia

Carolyn T. Adams

Cornell University Press

Ithaca and London

First published 2014 by Cornell University Press

Printed in the United States of America

Library of Congress Cataloging-in-Publication Data

Adams, Carolyn Teich, author.
   From the outside in : suburban elites, third-sector organizations,
and the reshaping of Philadelphia / Carolyn T. Adams.
      pages cm
   Includes bibliographical references and index.
   ISBN 978-0-8014-5162-1 (cloth : alk. paper) —
   ISBN 978-0-8014-7998-4 (pbk. : alk. paper)
   1. Regionalism—Pennsylvania—Philadelphia Metropolitan
Area.   2. Nonprofit organizations—Pennsylvania—Philadelphia
Metropolitan Area.   3. City planning—Pennsylvania—Philadelphia
Metropolitan Area.   4. Urban renewal—Pennsylvania—Philadelphia
Metropolitan Area.   5. Philadelphia Suburban Area (Pa.)—Politics and
government.   I. Title.
   HN80.P5A33 2014
   307.1'160974811—dc23
                                                            2014016073

Cornell University Press strives to use environmentally responsible
suppliers and materials to the fullest extent possible in the publishing
of its books. Such materials include vegetable-based, low-VOC inks and
acid-free papers that are recycled, totally chlorine-free, or partly
composed of nonwood fibers. For further information, visit our website
at www.cornellpress.cornell.edu.

Cloth printing   10   9   8   7   6   5   4   3   2   1
Paperback printing   10   9   8   7   6   5   4   3   2   1

Contents

ACKNOWLEDGMENTS

This book draws upon previous books and articles I have published over several decades of research devoted to my city. It reflects thirty years of personal experience in the city's nonprofit world, where I have served as either board member or board chair for a college, a foundation, and a number of public interest nonprofits, as well as a researcher and consultant to additional civic groups and governmental agencies. It is also based on a wide range of sources, including annual reports, land use plans, analysis by consultants, funding proposals, enabling legislation, and press coverage. I supplemented that documentary information with personal interviews of two dozen knowledgeable respondents who serve as board members or professional leaders of major civic institutions. Although I am bound by my promise to keep their identities confidential, I want them to know how much their open and candid interviews helped me understand both facts and perspectives about their work.

One particular respondent deserves special mention. At different times in his life, Bernard Watson has served as academic vice president of Temple

University, both vice chair and chair of the Pennsylvania Convention Center Authority Board, chair of the Board of Philadelphia's Avenue of the Arts, president and CEO of the William Penn Foundation, and chair of the board of the Barnes Foundation, among many other positions of civic responsibility. He knows as much as any Philadelphian about the workings of the city's major Third-Sector institutions, and his willingness to share that knowledge helped me immeasurably. Neither he nor any of the respondents who devoted their time to answer my questions is responsible for any errors of interpretation they may find in these pages. That responsibility is mine.

At Temple University my colleagues David Bartelt and David Elesh, with whom I have worked on many projects large and small over two decades, have taught me a great deal about our shared city. Some of those many lessons are reflected in this book. I am also indebted to the members of my 2013 graduate seminar, who carefully read and critiqued drafts of the manuscript: Ritwika Biswas, Charlotte Castle, Kwesi Daniels, Clint Davis, Nicole Hall, Yoonhee Jung, Dan Mina, Karen Pezzetti, Christian Przybylek, Alisa Shockley, and Sarah Stinard-Kiel. Temple University deserves my thanks for providing a sabbatical that allowed me to draft this manuscript. In addition the College of Liberal Arts generously contributed to the book production. At a time when every dollar in academic budgets is precious, I am delighted to acknowledge this strong support from my institution.

I am grateful to Mark Mattson of CARTONOVA Web Software not only for designing the figures for this volume but also for teaching me many lessons over the years about visualizing data.

Several anonymous reviewers spent their precious time at different stages of the manuscript to strengthen the project with thoughtful and constructive suggestions, which I gladly accepted. I appreciate their help and encouragement more than I can say, and I hope they feel that the finished product justifies their investment in it. Finally, I owe special thanks to my editor, Michael McGandy, whose professionalism, perception, and guidance have helped shape the manuscript and kept the project moving. Michael knows just when to press an author and when to relent, which he proved at one important point in the process by assuring me, "I am pushing, but I am not crazy." Indeed you are not, Michael. Thank you for all your support.

FROM THE OUTSIDE IN

Introduction

Regionalism and the Third Sector

Metropolitan regions represent critically important economic and social units for which the United States possesses no adequate governmental framework. This is an enormous problem for the nation, which is why urbanists continue to think and write about the prospects for consolidating suburbs with cities, despite almost universal pessimism about the likelihood of creating formal institutions of government at the metropolitan scale. Except for the constantly cited exception of Portland, Oregon, we have scant evidence that states, cities, and suburbs possess either the will or the ability to establish metropolitan governments. That has led advocates for metropolitan cooperation to shift their sights away from governmental consolidation and toward the informal coalitions, alliances, and networks that weave together nongovernmental actors with existing units of government in metropolitan areas. Regionalists now focus less on formal *government* than on *governance* through special-purpose authorities, quasi-governmental bodies, and nonprofit corporations—that is, networks of institutions that constitute a Third Sector alongside the private profit-making sector and the governmental sector.

Proponents of metropolitan planning look to progressive mayors to weave these networks together, as Chicago's mayor Richard J. Daley did when he convened the Metropolitan Mayors Caucus, to engage suburban municipalities in strategizing about the region's economic health, or as Denver's mayor Federico Peña did when he reached out to suburban officials to collaborate on airport development, an initiative that ultimately spawned the Metro Mayors Caucus of greater Denver (Katz & Bradley 2013, chapter 2). We think of regionalism as an impulse that emanates from central cities reaching out to surrounding suburbs. A former mayor of Albuquerque, David Rusk, has spent two decades traveling across the nation to urge big city mayors to move beyond their city limits to form alliances with suburban political and business interests. Rusk argues that dealing successfully with population outflow from inner cities, sprawling development of suburban land, racial segregation, and poverty requires city leaders to play an "outside game." They must build regional alliances that can ultimately change the rules of the game that are creating systematic disadvantages for central cities (Rusk 1999, 2013).

The Philadelphia experience suggests that while mayors work to perfect their "outside game," they need to be attentive to an "inside game" being played within the bounds of their cities by outsiders. A kind of stealth regionalism has emerged in greater Philadelphia, increasingly incorporating outside interests into the process of restructuring the city. While this book focuses on one city region, readers who live elsewhere will recognize parallel patterns in their own regions. Suburban towns and counties continue to resist formally coordinating investments and services with each other, much less with central cities. While this resistance continues, a new form of regionalism is evolving, practiced from the outside in. This incorporation of outside influences into the central city confirms a theoretical point made near the end of the 1990s by two adherents of postmodern urbanism when they posited a new "re-territorialization of the urban process in which hinterland organizes the center." Previous models of urban growth had envisioned the city as "an organic accretion around a central, organizing core." In contrast, these scholars identified "a postmodern urban process in which the urban periphery organizes the center within the context of a globalizing capitalism" (Dear & Flusty 1998, 65). This book describes how that outside influence is being exerted to restructure one central city.

I argue against a long-standing premise that the suburbs have turned their back on central cities. As long ago as the early 1970s urban observers were lamenting that economic and political elites in our major metropolitan areas were not merely moving their residences to the suburbs but ceasing to be concerned about what happened to the cities. "It is not exploitation that the [urban] core areas must fear; it is indifference and abandonment," predicted George Sternlieb (1971, 15). That grim vision from the 1970s has proven to be wrong. Many suburbanites have recognized that cities serve critical economic functions in the twenty-first century and cannot be allowed to decline in ways that jeopardize the region's future and therefore their own. The recognition that cities are too important to fail has prompted outsiders to take an increasingly active hand in shaping the city's future. This book presents evidence from greater Philadelphia to show how outside actors from the suburbs and from state government have intervened during the past fifteen years to redevelop the central city in ways that bolster the region. Taken together, these interventions constitute a kind of de facto regionalism that brings outside money and influence into the city to help restructure urban land and services. While they increase resources, however, these interventions exacerbate the problems of transparency and accountability facing the citizens of the city. And they prompt the question: Do initiatives that strengthen the region necessarily help city residents?

The City-Suburban Divide in Greater Philadelphia

In many respects the relationship of Philadelphia to its suburbs resembles that of other old cities in the northeastern and midwestern United States. The city grew as a manufacturing center during the nineteenth century, with industrial districts composed of factories, warehouses, rail yards, and worker housing spreading outward from the central business district. Slightly farther from the center, leafy streetcar suburbs sprang up on the north and west sides of the city to house families whose workers commuted daily to downtown businesses. The city's industrial decline during the second half of the twentieth century closed a devastating share of its manufacturing plants, leaving whole neighborhoods without their traditional economic base and forcing the city to rely primarily on its downtown offices and accompanying commercial and service economy to generate the jobs and tax revenues that support the municipal budget. Like most downtowns, central Philadelphia faces constant challenges from multiplying office complexes in the suburbs. The most prominent is the massive agglomeration of offices and shopping malls in King of Prussia, which sits west of the city at the intersection of routes 202, 422, I-76, and the Pennsylvania Turnpike. The growth generated by that vast commercial concentration has created some of the best paying white-collar jobs in the region, particularly in finance and insurance. Downtown Philadelphia also competes against the Route 1 corridor in New Jersey between Princeton and New Brunswick, where high-tech firms have clustered, particularly those connected to the region's pharmaceutical industry. While the suburbs have spawned many high-paying jobs, the city is burdened with disproportionate poverty. Over 28 percent of city residents live below the poverty line, bringing the city's median income down to one of the lowest among major cities in the United States (Philadelphia Research Initiative 2013a, 6).

This brief sketch of city-suburban relationships will sound familiar to students of U.S. cities, but Philadelphia is unusual in the degree of separation between city and suburbs because of the way governmental services are organized and boundary lines are drawn. Unlike most U.S. cities, Philadelphia functions as both a city and a county rather than being nested within a larger county. In 1854, when the city acquired its current boundaries, the easiest way to create a governmental unit that covered the existing urban economy was to consolidate into a single municipality all thirteen townships, six boroughs, and nine districts that were then located in one county. Ever since then the government of Philadelphia has served simultaneously as a county and a city with identical boundaries. Readers might assume that dual role confers advantages on Philadelphia, particularly readers who favor city-county consolidation as a way to achieve regional solutions to metropolitan problems. But in fact that dual role as county and city has created significant fiscal problems for Philadelphia's government.

City-county consolidation may bring benefits to cities when the county boundaries encompass affluent suburbs whose resources can help meet the heavier service burden that falls on central cities because they house a poorer population and a disproportionate share of the region's infrastructure, including ports, airports, and higher education and cultural facilities. But because city-county consolidation here took place a hundred years before the great migration to the suburbs started in the mid-twentieth century, the higher income households that abandoned the city to seek a suburban lifestyle were taking their resources across the county line.

Since it is not nested within a larger county, as many U.S. cities are, Philadelphia shares virtually none of its service burden with surrounding suburban communities. City, county, and school functions must all be supported by the city's tax base. That places an unusually heavy burden on the city's taxpayers. A study in the late 1990s compared the tax burden on the citizens of Philadelphia to that of Pittsburgh, which is nested within the larger jurisdiction of Allegheny County. The study found that if Philadelphians were financially responsible for county-level functions (such as child welfare, public health, prisons, homeless shelters, the court system) only to the extent that Pittsburgh taxpayers were accountable for their share of Allegheny County expenditures, then Philadelphia could shift close to a half-billion dollars from county services into its schools without increasing its local tax effort (Landis 1998, iii). The separation of the city and its suburbs into separate counties means there is less motivation and structural opportunity for city and suburbs to cooperate on providing services.

An additional barrier to coordination arises because the metropolitan area spans the Delaware River to include communities in New Jersey as well as Pennsylvania. Figure 1 shows the collection of counties spanning two states that together constitute the Philadelphia metropolitan area. On the western side, three Pennsylvania counties (Bucks, Montgomery, and Delaware) directly adjoin the city, while a fourth (Chester County) is closely linked historically and economically to the city even though it does not share a border with Philadelphia. Multiple bridges crossing the Delaware River make it possible for residents in southern New Jersey to commute into Philadelphia, linking four New Jersey counties (shaded in gray on figure 1) more closely to Philadelphia than to metropolitan areas within their own state. This bifurcation of the region means that suburban communities on the two sides of the river respond to different constitutional and political frameworks, a fact that complicates efforts to cooperate. In this book I focus on Pennsylvania when analyzing the role of government in metropolitan

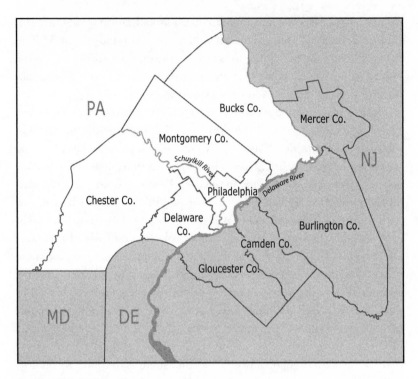

Figure 1. Philadelphia and eight surrounding counties.

affairs because Philadelphia's mandates and resources come from the Pennsylvania capital, Harrisburg.

Cities Are Too Important to Fail

Older urban centers have surprised pessimists who had predicted, if not their complete demise, then certainly their continuing decline. Contrary to that bleak outlook, cities are more important than ever in the global economy of the twenty-first century because they are strategic places where entire regions intersect with wider world forces. They house collections of business services (insurance, accounting, law, marketing, etc.) for which there is growing demand. Companies now operate in ever-expanding markets across the globe—markets whose conditions, regulations, and business requirements vary tremendously. To navigate that variety of environments, companies that operate internationally rely heavily on business services. And those business services enjoy advantages by clustering together in central cities. Being in cities matters the most to the most globalized sectors of the economy (Sassen 2009). Making a related point, Edward Glaeser says that cities remain viable because they attract highly-educated, innovative people and provide places for them to work collaboratively. Cities, in his view, "magnify human strengths" by attracting talent and sharpening it through competition (Glaeser 2011, 15). Talented people feed on each other's ideas, as proximity makes them more inventive.

Cities provide services and infrastructure that support globally competitive concerns, especially transportation and education (Rondinelli et al. 1998). Central cities are typically the transportation hubs of metropolitan areas, where ports, railroads, and airports converge, transporting local people and products to distant places while bringing visitors and freight into the region. Philadelphia plays that role in southeastern Pennsylvania. Its port on the Delaware River handles imports of fruit, cocoa, wood pulp, and forest products, as well as consumer goods for about three hundred regional distribution centers ranging from IKEA and Office Depot to Porsche North America and Harley-Davidson Motorcycles. It handles exports manufactured by regional companies, notably chemicals and pharmaceuticals. The city's airport serves over 30 million passengers annually, including about 4 million international passengers. The city's 30th Street Station, a major stop on Amtrak's Northeast Corridor connecting Philadelphia to Washington, New York, and Boston, ranks as the third busiest station in the Amtrak system.

The city's value to the region also hinges on its concentration of universities and hospitals. In a global economy that places a premium on knowledge, technology, and innovation, central cities are sites of innovation, research, and development, particularly cities like Philadelphia that contain strong health centers, universities, and research institutions, a constellation known as "meds and eds." In this realm, as well as the arts, the city contains the institutions that connect southeastern Pennsylvania to broader national and international trends. In effect the central city "brands" the region, creating its identity in the eyes of the world.

Since the global economy puts a premium on education and innovation, regions thrive by attracting and retaining a talented workforce. Here Philadelphia serves the region less well. One might imagine that the presence of dozens of colleges and universities in greater Philadelphia signals an inexhaustible supply of well-educated workers. One would be wrong. The city is home to twenty colleges and universities yet has one of the lower rates of college attainment among U.S. cities. Of the young adults (ages eighteen to thirty-four) living in the city, fewer than half are enrolled or hold a college degree. Much of the college problem is attributable to a devastatingly high dropout rate in the city's public school system. The high school graduation rate is only 64 percent. Without improving the education of the city's children in kindergarten through high school, college attainment will remain illusory for young Philadelphians despite the presence of an impressive higher education establishment.

Location decisions made by businesses also depend on other aspects of a region's quality of life besides education, including cultural, recreational, and entertainment resources. In this realm Philadelphia unquestionably remains the center of the region, especially after the substantial investments the city has made since the 1990s. As will become apparent in subsequent chapters, in the 1990s the city began to significantly reshape its cultural, retail, and restaurant offerings and continues working to upgrade its two riverfronts along with its parks. Proponents of this strategy see those investments as achieving multiple goals simultaneously: they enhance the city's image as a tourist and convention destination, attracting outsiders who spend dollars in the local economy and may form a connection to the region; regional visitors come into the city for its parks, zoos, museums, concerts, and sporting events; and these amenities enhance the region's appeal to firms and people considering a move from other parts of the country.

The View from the Outside

It is true that politicians outside the city and their constituents have shown little appetite for permanently tying their governmental and fiscal future to the central city. But that does not mean they remain indifferent to the city's fate. For more than fifteen years residents of the Philadelphia suburbs have been periodically surveyed about how they regard the city. The findings released by the first such poll, taken in 1995, surprised the editors of the *Philadelphia Inquirer*, who wrote, "From a bunch of folks who supposedly don't give a hoot whether Philadelphia disappears down a sinkhole, this is amazing stuff: suburbanites saying their future is linked inextricably with the city's" (Editorial Board 1995). In annual surveys taken between 1995 and 2000 an average of 81 percent of suburban residents thought that the business and social conditions inside the city of Philadelphia were either very important or somewhat important to them. When that question was asked again in a poll taken in 2010, 78 percent of suburban respondents chose those options, a result that was statistically equivalent to the earlier result. A similar percentage of suburban respondents said that Philadelphia's economic condition is somewhat or very important to the economy of the region (Philadelphia Research Initiative 2010).

Given such widespread recognition of the city's importance to the region, including the suburbs, it is not surprising that suburban residents with resources and access have invested in reshaping Philadelphia for the new century. This book argues that outsiders have recognized the city as the region's main point of intersection with global forces. Whether or not they frame it in the economistic terms used by scholars, many leaders in the suburbs and in state government regard the future of the city as critical to the region and therefore deserving of their attention and investment. Outsiders have not engaged mainly through the city's traditional political processes, which many of them regard as unsavory, inefficient, hidebound, and patronage-ridden. That is hardly surprising since regional news media offer suburban dwellers a constant stream of Philadelphia stories featuring deficit budgets, uncollected taxes, sweetheart deals for connected individuals, and corrupt politicians going to jail. It is the rare suburban resident who participates in city affairs through electoral campaigns, city council hearings, or ward politics of the traditional kind. Outsiders are daunted by the complicated race and class dimensions of city politics, by the power of public employee unions, and by bureaucratic complexity and rigidity. Rather than trying to reform or remake city government, they are engaging in city affairs through Third-Sector vehicles. By assuming leadership positions in nonprofit institutions, public corporations, and quasi-public authorities, they are influencing the future development of the city—especially land development in the central core and the future direction of its school system.

The proliferation of such Third-Sector entities for city development is contributing to a general blurring of the boundaries between the public and private sectors in American civic life. To construct and manage urban infrastructure, city managers are increasingly turning to private investors to help finance roadways, bridges, and other public facilities through a variety of new contracting and ownership models (Perry 2003). While many other commentators have observed this emerging mix of public and private sector contributions to urban infrastructure, my purpose is to draw attention to the blurring of geographical boundaries in producing that infrastructure. In previous eras urban public works were largely planned and managed by local officials, although admittedly with financial contributions from federal and state agencies. Indeed local politicians have often been judged by their success in bringing outside resources to support local initiatives. They get credit from constituents and the media for mobilizing resources that are used by local government to provide public services and facilities. However, this book highlights the extent to which actors whose home base is outside the city now take substantial responsibility for financing, planning, and building public infrastructure that is reshaping the central city. I argue that the geographical shift in influence is directly related to the shift in sectoral boundaries; it is the proliferation of Third-Sector entities blending private and public resources that has made possible the expanding influence exerted by outsiders on the city's infrastructure.

As the coming chapters will show, suburban participants gravitate toward very particular types of urban assets that advance the region's fortunes rather than investing their resources, talent, and time to improve the general welfare of the city. Two critical policy domains in which suburban and state interests have played an expanding role are land development and public education—areas of deep concern to outsiders looking at the current state of the city. State and suburban actors have sought to influence these domains even though American political tradition places both land development and education squarely under local control. In fact these are among the most jealously guarded prerogatives of local citizens. As long ago as the early 1970s a scholar studying the Philadelphia metropolitan area singled out education and land use as two domains of local policy that were *least* likely ever to be assigned to regional authorities because suburban communities would never relinquish local control over them (Williams 1971). Both types of policy touch "salient lifestyle concerns" that citizens typically defend against external influence: "Educational policy . . . defines who will come together in a socio-spatial unit called a school. . . . Land use policies are similarly life style policies in that they place limits on who is likely to interact with whom" (89).

Local prerogatives allow residents to mold their communities to attract some kinds of households and businesses and discourage others. In fact some observers have concluded that suburbs were incorporated in the first place in order to give outlying residents control over their own land development (Briffault 1996; Fischel 2004) and schools (Bishoff 2008; Meyer 2010). Over the years local self-determination has become "the rallying cry of Americans, and this has meant that each fragment of the metropolis would enjoy the right to govern itself and decide its destiny" (Teaford 1979, 6). With respect to land development and education even more than other local policies, citizens living and voting in each community have controlled their local decisions and investments. State legislatures and courts have traditionally deferred to locally elected bodies, which can generally be expected to resist any efforts to shift land development or school management outside the community boundaries.

Ironically, while they jealously guard these local prerogatives in their own communities, suburban dwellers are exerting growing influence over these developmental priorities for Philadelphia. Their participation in these domains is made possible by Third-Sector institutions whose role in urban development warrants more attention than it gets. The literature on urban land redevelopment is rich with commentary and case studies showing how profit-seeking developers have influenced cities' built environment, sometimes in concert with political leaders and sometimes in opposition to the wishes of both residents and their political representatives (Dahl 1961; Salisbury 1964; Wolfinger 1974; Mollenkopf 1983; Frieden & Sagalyn 1991; Hannigan 1998; Fainstein 2001). Yet only a small emerging literature exists about the influence of Third-Sector developers on the physical restructuring of cities. A recent spate of commentaries about "anchor institutions" appears largely hortatory—calling upon universities and health care institutions to work more cooperatively with neighboring residents and businesses—rather than providing a critical account of the collective impact of anchor institutions across urban landscapes.

The projects and institutions I examine in this book are restructuring Philadelphia by creating new development districts beyond the traditional boundaries of the downtown area (which locals call "Center City"). This expanding definition of downtown has parallels elsewhere, as many cities have invested in meds and eds, hospitality, and culture and entertainment districts. In Philadelphia as elsewhere the restructuring of the urban landscape serves a dual purpose. First, it accommodates a growing number of residents who are choosing to live downtown (Birch 2009, 149–50). The professional classes employed by business service firms have gentrified urban neighborhoods and fueled an expanding cultural and entertainment sector. The Urban Land Institute's 2011 forecast of real estate trends waxed optimistic about continuing housing demand in central cities, predicting that "the influx of Generation Y, now in their teens through early thirties, will change housing demand. They are comfortable with smaller homes and will happily trade living space for an easier commute and better lifestyle" (Kirk 2011). Second, this restructuring equips the city with infrastructure that serves the needs of outsiders, from cargo shippers to conventioneers, business location consultants, prospective college students, patients seeking high-end medical treatments, and suburban consumers of the city's culture and entertainment.

This book offers a critical analysis of the advantages and drawbacks of the expanding role played by Third-Sector institutions. These institutions have enhanced the influence of outside decision makers in the city's Third Sector, while diluting the control that democratically elected officials exercise over their own city's development. In ways that will become apparent in the chapters to come, city officials have traded off much of their ability to pursue a comprehensive, coordinated planning agenda in exchange for other strategic advantages that the Third Sector offers. This subject has received limited public attention, possibly because it is hard for citizens to recognize Third-Sector organizations as distinct from government. After all, our society defines nonprofit organizations partly by their pursuit of public interest rather than private gain. It should not surprise us that many citizens assume organizations pursuing public purposes represent government, especially when they use government funds. Third-Sector institutions, however, are *not* the same as government. They differ in fundamental ways from government. Outlining those differences is one of the purposes of this book. A second purpose is to illustrate through the Philadelphia case how their distinctive characteristics are shaping the city's development. Further, this study highlights the substantial influence that outsiders wield in the Third Sector. Viewed in the most positive light, these vehicles promote regionalism; viewed negatively, they reduce the city's control over its own development and therefore its own destiny.

The Crucial Third Sector

An article published in 2012 asks, "Can nonprofits run cities?" (Clark 2012). It describes the crucial role played by Midtown Detroit, Inc., a nonprofit corporation working since 1976 to revitalize a district just north of downtown Detroit where Wayne State University, the Detroit Institute of Arts, and the Detroit Medical Center are all located. Since this location is regarded as the centerpiece of Detroit's renewal, it is significant that the renewal effort is being led by a nonprofit organization rather than city government. The writer uses the term "curating development" to describe Midtown's process of seeding over forty development projects chosen because they are expected to be mutually reinforcing. Midtown's urban planning and redevelopment efforts have earned the nonprofit a reputation for being "better at performing the role of government than government itself" (Clark 2012). The Detroit case is not unique. A comparable organization, University Circle, Inc., takes even broader responsibility for an area on the east side of Cleveland that contains Case Western Reserve University, the Cleveland Orchestra, and the University Hospitals system. In addition to promoting $3 billion in development projects, University Circle, Inc. employs a security force for the area and operates a bus line (Clark 2012).

Those local development corporations in Detroit and Cleveland are examples of a variety of different kinds of nonprofit, nongovernmental organizations grouped under the heading of "Third Sector." The size of that sector has expanded considerably since 1980, as government has privatized an increasing number of its functions that citizens want but are reluctant to have government provide directly. Most of the commentary about this trend toward privatization has focused on government contracting for public services (Salamon 1987, 1995; Kettl 2009). But nonprofit organizations are not only service providers; they are also investors whose physical facilities shape our cities—a reality that puts them at the center of urban politics: "The battlefield of city politics is not flat but is tilted toward an alliance of public officials and land interests" (Elkin 1987, 100).

Admittedly the Third Sector is the smallest of the three sectors in the U.S. economy, accounting for only 9 percent of jobs and 5 percent of GDP. But it is the fastest growing sector, adding jobs in recent years while the business and governmental sectors shed them. From 2001 to 2011 the number of nonprofits increased by an amazing 25 percent. The sector is composed of independent organizations that are voluntary, self-governing, and of public benefit and distribute no profits to any shareholders or owners (Roeger et al. 2012). Most people think of Third-Sector organizations as depending largely on charitable contributions for their support. While it is true that philanthropy makes a significant contribution to these organizations, charitable donations represent a smaller share of nonprofit revenue than is generally recognized. Actually nonprofit institutions get the largest share of their income from fees and charges, with government supplying the second-largest component of their budgets. Experts who study nonprofits identify government support as the single most important factor accounting for the growth of the sector (Salamon 2012, 5) and draw attention to the changing form of government support during recent years.

Rather than granting funds to nonprofit institutions, government has shifted more of its aid to support consumers of nonprofit services, for example, supplying insurance for medical patients or tuition aid for college students instead of allocating government funds directly to hospitals and universities (Gronbjerg & Salamon 2012). That shift has prompted nonprofits to market their services more assertively and constantly seek broader audiences. Another indirect tool used by governments to support nonprofits is tax breaks for donors and investors who help finance nonprofits. Here too nonprofits compete to find donors and investors who can assist them while benefiting from tax concessions. As we will see, the growing pressure to compete for audiences and investors has shaped the development strategies that nonprofit institutions employ and thereby helped shape the city.

For this Philadelphia study, I have not limited my definition of the Third Sector to institutions normally classified as charitable organizations by the federal Internal Revenue Service, such as colleges, hospitals, museums, and theaters. For my purposes the Third Sector also includes quasi-public organizations, that is, independent organizations established by acts of government to serve a public purpose. They are normally created to finance, construct, and maintain facilities that serve the public. A number of the organizations I describe fit this designation, including the Southeastern Pennsylvania Transportation Authority, the Pennsylvania Convention Center Authority, and the Delaware River Port Authority.

Such organizations share crucial characteristics with traditional nonprofits. Both types of institutions serve as major developers of urban space. Both occupy a middle ground between government and the for-profit sector.

Pennsylvania allows municipalities wide latitude to create special-purpose authorities, while cautioning local officials that when they do so, they cannot regard those entities as government departments. The new entity "coordinates its actions with local government, but it is not controlled by that government" (Governor's Center for Local Government Services 2002, 11). Once established, they operate as independent corporations governed by their own boards of directors. Like nonprofits, special-purpose authorities are prohibited from distributing profits to any shareholders, as for-profit corporate boards must do in order to stay in favor with investors. Both nonprofit and quasi-governmental institutions manage large-scale, complicated development projects that are changing the face of Philadelphia. To do so they borrow funds, which they repay with revenues earned by charging fees to users in the form of rents, tolls, charges, or assessments of some kind. In that way they place a significant share of the cost of projects on those who directly use the facilities or infrastructure. Nonetheless both types of institutions receive major infusions of money from government because their operating revenues are seldom sufficient to cover their costs.

The similarities between these two types of organizations have been acknowledged by the federal IRS, which allows quasi-governmental organizations to apply for 501(c)3 status if they can demonstrate that they operate separately from state or municipal government and they accomplish one or more exempt purposes (McCray & Friedlander 2004). When granted, that designation confers on quasi-governmental organizations the same important tax benefits that it confers on traditional nonprofits: they are exempted from paying taxes, and they can accept donations from contributors who enjoy a tax deduction for making those donations.

Earlier than other U.S. cities, Philadelphia attracted notice for its reliance on nongovernmental organizations to accomplish public purposes. The urban historian Sam Bass Warner traced this tendency all the way back to the early 1800s. He titled his influential history of Philadelphia *The Private City* (1987) because city leaders so often relied on voluntary associations to address civic problems. An early example was the Fairmount Water Works. At the turn of the nineteenth century the city constructed a waterworks that could furnish clean water from the Schuylkill River to replace the foul water that residents were drawing from contaminated backyard wells. The city council turned to a watering committee composed of prominent merchants who "arranged their own financing without state aid. Despite setbacks in construction and periodic shortages of funds, which the committee sometimes met by the members' advancing money out of their own pockets, they pushed the project through to completion" (Warner 1987, 104). As further examples of the city's historic dependence on private solutions for public problems, Warner cites schooling, policing, and firefighting—all organized as voluntary nongovernmental initiatives that only gradually came under the aegis of government when privatized efforts proved incapable of handling the expanding needs of a growing manufacturing town. Although Warner wrote specifically about Philadelphia, his interpretation of urban culture has widely influenced scholarship about American cities. His observation that U.S. cities have tried whenever feasible to address public challenges through private actions and institutions, although written almost fifty years ago, seems directly applicable to twenty-first-century cities.

Not just scholars but urban practitioners as well have recognized Philadelphia as a forerunner in the use of nonprofit, nongovernmental organizations for civic purposes. A fascinating book written in 1973 tells the story of how Philadelphia's mayors in the middle of the twentieth century became trailblazers in the practice of deploying nonprofit corporations to reconstruct a city that needed to reequip its nineteenth-century manufacturing landscape to support the postindustrial service economy (Petshek 1973). The author, an insider who was trained as a Harvard economist and employed as a Philadelphia civil servant during the 1950s and 1960s, describes the evolution and eventual proliferation of nonprofit corporations and explains how, "through this device, largely untried at the time," reform mayors launched and oversaw a broad program of urban revitalization (87). The Philadelphia Industrial Development Corporation attracted new jobs to the city. The Old Philadelphia Development Corporation renovated downtown residential neighborhoods. The Food Distribution Corporation moved the city's overcrowded and unsanitary wholesale food market out of the historic colonial district to an industrial park in South Philadelphia. In creating an ever-increasing number of quasi-public entities, officials were motivated by a reformist impulse to remove important projects from the influence of machine politicians who were corrupt and ineffective at managing major initiatives. While each organization had an assigned task, the overall vision and coordination remained within the mayor's office. In fact several mayors in a row relied on the same individual, a famously competent civil servant named William Rafsky, to coordinate the work of these steadily multiplying organizations and to avoid "projectitis," a tendency to see each development project as important on its own rather than tied to the overall development program (92). Over time, however, as the number of Third-Sector organizations multiplied, they were less closely guided by the city's elected leadership. Subsequent chapters will show that at present Third-Sector organizations often operate independently, even when they are established by governments. Philadelphia offers an example of David Perry's (2003, 19) observation that the language of city builders has changed in recent times, replacing "public works" with "infrastructure," a term that does not necessarily connote governmental responsibility and that acknowledges growing reliance on nongovernmental investors and operators.

State Government Addresses Regionalism through the Third Sector

David Rusk (1999) argues that the suburbs will ultimately be brought around to cooperate with the city within the framework of state governments. He counsels city leaders, "Where it's at is state legislatures." The battle to achieve equity across metropolitan regions must be fought in statehouses (325). Why? Because state legislatures set the rules by which communities control land use, housing, zoning, and taxation in their borders. States set allocation formulas for school funding and decide whether and how those formulas recognize that it costs more to educate children in poverty than to educate children from middle-class backgrounds. They decide how much emphasis allocation formulas for state water and sewer funds place on new construction versus maintenance. Such "rules of the game" often confer advantages on newer, wealthier communities, while they impose costs on older central cities. To change them, mayors and other city leaders must cultivate supporters in statehouses, Rusk counsels. Another forceful voice arguing in the 1990s for changing the rules of the game was that of Myron Orfield, a one-time legislator in the Minnesota state senate. In his books of 1997 and 2002, Orfield advises state legislators representing older urban centers to form legislative coalitions to enact sweeping state policies to alter formulas for revenue-sharing among local governments, strengthen regional fair-share housing obligations, and change water and sewer funding and other allocation systems that reinforce urban disadvantage.

Rusk and Orfield gained credibility during the 1990s because of their personal experience as state legislators. Both men traveled across the country to speak in many of our major metropolitan centers, focusing attention on the state as the level of government with the resources and constitutional power to influence metropolitan development patterns. Yet two decades after they sounded that call there is little evidence that state legislatures responded with any measures that systematically altered the rules of the game. Few legislatures enacted the changes in state allocation formulas they advocated. Still fewer built any metropolitan institutions to weave together the multitude of local governments sitting side by side within urban regions. Rarest of all were agreements by local governments to share their tax bases.

Instead of those sweeping reforms, state governments have continued a pattern that is many decades old: the proliferation of special-purpose authorities, commissions, and districts for narrowly defined purposes. Those purposes often involve making large-scale investments within central cities that are intended to serve the interests of entire regions. Typical examples are transportation infrastructure like ports, bridges, and tunnels, regional park systems, and major convention centers. State legislatures in virtually every part of the United States have established such single-purpose entities, granting them the ability to collect fees, tolls, or rents from users and also to borrow money to maintain and improve the facilities they operate. Their governing boards are usually appointed by state and city officials. So ubiquitous are these arrangements that a Chicago study concluded, "Without state government aid and states' willingness to create special-purpose authorities, much of the money used to rebuild America's downtowns would have been unavailable to political actors" (Smith 2010, 430). Many such development projects serve the interests of the entire metropolitan area; in that sense they advance regional goals. For state governments, this approach to regionalism is far easier than restructuring the rules of the game.

Why the Third Sector Is Becoming a Development Engine

While the Third Sector sits outside of government, it produces many services of a public nature. These are public goods not simply in the sense that they generate benefits for individual members of the public; they also enhance the quality of life for the city and the metropolitan area as a whole. The public as a whole benefits from the presence of cultural, medical, research, and higher education institutions, ports, bridges, and other infrastructure built and maintained by the Third Sector. Economic development professionals across the nation acknowledge that these assets attract residents and firms, strengthening the regional economy. Consequently the responsibility for supporting these institutions should not be left to the marketplace.

Yet government is unlikely to assume all those functions. In a period of governmental austerity and political antagonism toward big government, we expect to see fewer civic assets managed by government. Many citizens would argue that the investments managed by Third-Sector organizations should not be the government's responsibility because they produce services that are not universally consumed or equally desired by all citizens, so universal taxation is not the fairest way to fund them. Nevertheless governments recognize the value of these assets by conferring on them the special benefit of tax exemption and also by channeling substantial grant funds to support their operations and investments. However, they maintain independence from government, even when they have been established by acts of government, as is the case for quasi-governmental authorities, and even when they receive substantial sums from government. Once created, they escape direct government control and can often use that latitude to operate independently, especially if they derive significant portions of their revenue from entry fees, tolls, tuitions, patient charges, ticket sales, and other revenue sources. Their boards of directors devise plans for them that may actually put them in contention with government. Chapter 2 offers the example of the Center City District (CCD), a nonprofit business improvement district whose leader has been dubbed "the king of Center City" in recognition of his organization's outsize influence. At a 2010 public hearing where the CCD leader was testifying about his organization's plans to reconstruct land adjacent to city hall, the president of the city council complained that the proposal would virtually transfer a public space to private hands: "I mean, we [the city council] have minimal influence over what you do" (council president Darrell Clarke quoted in Thompson 2011, 12). Yet the council ultimately accepted the CCD proposal because it promised to mobilize outside funding to make public improvements.

Philadelphia city government extends help to nongovernmental institutions in many different forms, ranging from changing traffic patterns and closing streets to adapting parking regulations, coordinating city policing with institutional security forces, and helping these institutions gain access to tax-exempt borrowing. When establishing independent quasi-governmental authorities, both city and state governments have on occasion granted them mandates to raise their own revenues by charging fees, tolls, or assessments. The city's zoning code includes a special designation called an Institutional Development District that allows major institutions to negotiate the standards the city requires before it issues building permits. As early as the 1960s the city council approved such zoning districts for university campuses located in North and West Philadelphia (Petshek 1973, 249). In these and other ways the city government has encouraged the expansion of the Third Sector. The chapters that follow will show that state and city officials continue to assign critical initiatives and projects to the Third Sector.

Why do governments at both state and local levels encourage the proliferation of these nongovernmental institutions? The most common explanation offered by public officials is their desire to ensure proper management of major projects by assigning them to nongovernmental entities whose work focuses on a single well-defined mission. Another advantage they cite is that those organizations are unhampered by inefficiencies built into government operations by regulations and rules that apply to such activities as procurement and civil service hiring. Unhampered by those strictures, the Third Sector can act more quickly to respond to opportunities and threats in the environment.

Nongovernmental organizations are not subject to the same debt ceiling that constrains the city government. This was the feature that prompted President Franklin Roosevelt's administration during the Depression to encourage cities to create independent corporations so they could build public infrastructure without running afoul of restrictions in most state constitutions that limited borrowing by local governments. While FDR may have seen this as a temporary expedient, it turned into a permanent fixture of local governments (Perry 1995, 217–18). Starting with the Municipal Authorities Act in 1935, Pennsylvania's legislature allowed local governments to create new institutions that were not burdened by the substantial debt that local governments were already carrying. For example, Philadelphia's borrowing limit is set by the Pennsylvania state constitution at no more than 13.5 percent of the value of all property in the city. The city circumvents that debt limit by assigning major development projects to organizations outside of city government whose borrowing does not count against the limit.

Lenders are willing to finance Third-Sector projects provided that the sponsoring organization can show it has the revenues to repay its debts, often earned by charging fees to users. Nonprofits are sometimes criticized for being so focused on such revenue streams that they behave indistinguishably from for-profit businesses. That is because they operate in the same capital market as for-profit enterprises and must guarantee lenders that they will generate revenues to pay their debts. Museums promote "blockbuster" exhibits; hospitals maximize patient revenues; universities raise tuition; various transportation authorities levy charges on travelers to spread the cost of bridges, tunnels, and ports. Since city officials themselves have gradually relied more heavily on user fees as citizens resist higher taxes, they see Third-Sector institutions as consistent with this broader trend (Pagano & Perry 2008, 24). Asking users to pay is an especially attractive option for facilities that serve visitors, like convention centers and tourist attractions, because it brings external resources into the city economy. However, it rarely results in the services being completely self-financing; they usually rely on government subsidies as well to balance their budget (Leigland 1995, 158).

City leaders value Third-Sector institutions because they can attract private wealth in the form of philanthropic contributions to help support important public-serving institutions. Although it is legal for citizens to make tax-deductible charitable contributions to government agencies, in practice that rarely happens. Nonprofit institutions, on the other hand, have garnered impressive contributions from wealthy individuals and foundations. In an economy where wealth is disproportionately accumulating in the hands of the so-called 1 percent, the Third Sector represents a vehicle to tap some of that wealth for public purposes.

Even if City Hall possessed sufficient resources to undertake large-scale development projects on its own, elected officials would still probably rely on Third-Sector developers because they lack the political will to concentrate the city's capital spending on large projects in one or a small number of locations. Politicians generally prefer to distribute dollars and services more broadly. It is virtually impossible for the city council to agree to target development dollars in only a few locations because that shortchanges other areas. Spending plans must spread dollars across the city to satisfy multiple constituencies. Government needs Third-Sector institutions because elected officials do not have the political will to concentrate investment in a single project over several years. Nongovernmental organizations can insulate large projects from public protest about costs and impacts, for example, from property owners whose land is taken by eminent domain, or from nearby neighborhoods affected by the construction and the permanent presence of a major facility. Separated from democratic politics, project managers can "make decisions without worrying about maintaining an electoral coalition" (Judd & Simpson 2003, 1061). For anyone concerned about democratic process, this feature carries obvious drawbacks along with benefits. Governor Mario Cuomo of New York famously remarked about the Third Sector, "The big advantage: free from the control the people have. The big disadvantage: free from control the people have" (quoted in Bang-Jensen 1984, 4).

Third-Sector organizations have the advantage that they can furnish strong, clear, consistent leadership of projects, which a University of Chicago study of cultural building projects cited as a primary determinant of project success (Woronkowicz et al. 2012, 3). Major building projects take years, sometimes decades, to move from plans to completion. Although elected officials may encourage such initiatives, they cannot hope to maintain the long-term focus across elections that is required to bring the starting vision to bricks and mortar. The longer time horizon of Third-Sector organizations, compared to elected politicians, equips them to plan for entire development districts as well as particular facilities.

Midtown Detroit, Inc. offers one example of the impact that a long-term, geographically focused nonprofit can have in revitalizing one section of the city. The coming chapters offer numerous other instances of Third-Sector organizations playing this role, among them the Delaware River Waterfront Corporation, Avenue of the Arts Initiative, Center City District, Parkway Council, and University City District. The concentrated long-term focus they bring to a single city district is unlikely to be provided by city government, which has many neighborhoods and different constituencies clamoring for attention and resources.

Public officials, the media, and urban scholars have identified all of the reasons above for the proliferation of Third-Sector organizations leading urban development projects. Yet there is another dimension of this trend that has received little attention from urban observers. That is the opportunity that Third-Sector organizations offer to outsiders who desire a role in reshaping the central city because they recognize that the suburbs have a stake in the redevelopment of the metropolitan center. As already noted, suburban respondents outside Philadelphia tell pollsters they recognize that the city's future affects them. But lacking any framework for regional government, suburbanites have no broad, general-purpose institutions within which to act on their stake in the city. The suburbs are highly fragmented, making it difficult to muster any common position on projects and agendas affecting the central city. Lacking collective structures to influence the city's future development, suburbanites are choosing to engage with the city through particular institutions. They are influencing the city's future via the growing variety of quasi-public corporations, authorities, commissions, districts, and nonprofit institutions that are driving the redevelopment agenda. In this way suburban residents play an important part in managing substantial city assets.

Chapter 1

STATES CREATE TRANSPORTATION AUTHORITIES TO CROSS LOCAL BOUNDARIES

If state and regional elites are conscious that the city's viability affects the entire region's competitive position, where do we find evidence that regional priorities are influencing the redevelopment of central Philadelphia? One might assume that the most likely place to look would be the organizations that bring together representatives from the city and suburbs to form regional boards, commissions, authorities, compacts, and councils. Special-purpose authorities that build and manage infrastructure systems crossing local government boundaries are the most common type of organization that state governments have used to develop metropolitan regions. Such organizations, which often take responsibility for infrastructure such as water and sewer systems, ports, bridges, and tunnels, are widely recognized by urbanists as the main substitute for governmental consolidation in metropolitan areas. Local residents can comfortably assign these kinds of infrastructure to regional bodies, even while they jealously guard local control over other kinds of services. That is because, unlike schooling or policing, the management of infrastructure is seen as requiring largely technocratic decisions such as how to borrow funds at the lowest possible interest rates, how to calculate cost-benefit ratios, and how to estimate return on investment (Nunn 1990; Williams 1967; Norris et al. 2009). Rosentraub and al-Habil (2009, 41) are referring to such arrangements when they assert, "There is far more regionalism taking place in the governance of urban regions than advocates for consolidation want to acknowledge."

Among the most common regional authorities are those that plan and operate transportation systems. All planners recognize the potential of transportation to influence land development. Transportation systems are clearly regional in scope, serving populations from the center to the periphery and everywhere in between. So it makes intuitive sense to look at transportation planning for signs that state and suburban leaders see their fate as tied to that of the central city. That means examining the working of the region's metropolitan planning organization (MPO), a type of special-purpose regional authority commonly found in U.S. metropolitan areas, along with the leading regional operators of transit services.

Before the 1960s little transportation planning was carried out below the state level. It was in the 1960s that Congress began requiring all urbanized areas to plan their transportation expenditures cooperatively with state governments, and in 1973 Congress required that each urban region establish an MPO as a condition for receiving federal transportation funds. From then on, every highway investment in urbanized areas had to be based on a *regional* transportation planning process. As a result MPOs quickly came into being in regions across the country. During the 1980s their role waned, as the Reagan administration reduced federal scrutiny of lower level governments. However, the 1991 Intermodal Surface Transportation Efficiency Act (ISTEA), followed by the 1998 Transportation Equity Act for the 21st Century, gave new vitality to MPOs. Those bills directed additional federal funding to MPOs, including for freight planning, expanded their authority to select projects, and mandated new metropolitan planning initiatives. ISTEA provided greater flexibility in the use of funds, allowing regions to use previously restricted highway funds for transit development, and it encouraged MPOs to employ modally mixed strategies for greater system efficiency, mobility, and access.

Significantly ISTEA began requiring MPOs to conduct "fiscally constrained planning" in order to ensure that transportation plans take into account the fiscal constraints prevailing in each region. Regional plans and programs may not include more projects than can reasonably be expected to receive funding through existing or projected sources of revenues. This new requirement imposed fiscal discipline on planners, requiring them to make difficult choices among competing needs. In short the federal government used its power of the purse to press local governments within metropolitan areas to take a regional approach to making transportation investments.

The MPOs established in different parts of the nation vary significantly in their structure and operation and have adopted different labels. Many are called either regional or metropolitan transportation authorities, while others choose to be identified as transportation planning boards, commissions, or even regional mobility authorities. Their governing boards allocate seats by different methods, but in general they assign seats in ways that under-represent central cities and racial minorities while overrepresenting white suburbs (Sanchez 2006; Benjamin et al. 1994; Nelson et al. 2004). In only a few regions, such as Orlando and Washington, DC, do MPOs allocate city and suburban seats in alignment with their share of regional population.

The geographic scope of some MPOs encompasses more than one major city. For example, both Dallas and Fort Worth are members of the North Central Texas Council of Governments. The Metropolitan Transportation Commission in the Bay Area of northern California encompasses San Francisco, Oakland, and San Jose. Not only their scope of territory but also their scope of functions can vary. Most MPOs serve as planning and allocation bodies, but some are also transportation operators. The Metropolitan Council serving as the MPO for Minneapolis and St. Paul not only plans transportation investments but also operates transit services. Despite these variations in name and scope, all of these MPOs must forge a consensus on both short-term and long-term investment of transportation dollars in their region. If they do not, they can lose a portion of their federal funds.

This chapter focuses on the MPO operating within the greater Philadelphia region, the Delaware Valley Regional Planning Commission (DVRPC), along with two other regional authorities that dominate transportation planning and investment in greater Philadelphia: the Southeastern Pennsylvania Transportation Authority (SEPTA), which operates regional rail lines and subway and bus transit for Philadelphia and its suburbs, and the Delaware River Port Authority (DRPA), which has responsibility for bridges crossing the Delaware River and also for a high-speed rail line linking Philadelphia to New Jersey suburbs. These organizations were created by decision makers at the state level to achieve greater coherence in building the region's transportation infrastructure. Their creators were pursuing the same goals that have animated regional authorities across the United States: fostering greater unity in the balkanized landscape of the state's most important metropolitan area as well as greater rationality and equity in financing and delivering transportation assets and services.

Do these organizations offer the suburbs a vehicle for reshaping central cities in ways that promote regional priorities? In the opening years of the twenty-first century, have these organizations demonstrated a will and a capacity to use transportation investments to reshape the city to advance regional goals? The answer to both questions is no. Instead of serving as vehicles for the suburbs to pursue an agenda for Philadelphia, we see these transportation authorities allocating their substantial resources mainly to reinforce already existing patterns of public investment. Rather than reshaping the regional territory through bold new investments, they are reinforcing the transportation and land-use patterns established over preceding decades. This was not always the case. In the twentieth century regional planners did try to use large-scale transportation investments to reshape the downtown area.

Regional Priorities versus Community Preferences

During the second half of the twentieth century it looked as though the interests of suburban commuters would dominate transportation planning for the city. In Philadelphia's 1960 Comprehensive Plan, city planners proposed over a hundred miles of new highways crisscrossing the region "to move people and goods quickly, cheaply and conveniently" (PCPC 1960). In that era of ambitious urban renewal and highway building, the city's official plan proposed twelve concentric and radial expressways radiating out from downtown, the majority of which were never built (see figure 2). From a regional perspective, the crucial elements of that 1960 highway plan were two crosstown expressways allowing easy travel from east to west through the central city. While Philadelphia has long had major expressways running from south to north, it has lacked limited-access highways running from east to west.

Both crosstown expressways encountered stiff resistance from city residents on grounds of community dislocation and environmental impacts.

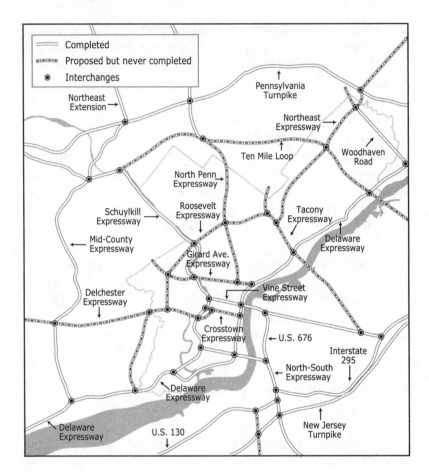

Figure 2. Expressways as proposed in 1960.

Although opponents defeated one of them, they succeeded only in delaying the other. Opponents of the Crosstown Expressway, proposed in 1960 for the southern edge of downtown, maneuvered legally and politically to delay the plan for a decade, only to find it revived on an even grander scale. In its 1972 incarnation the expressway would have been flanked by a massive corridor of new housing, offices, shops, and parking facilities that planners were calling Southbridge. The project would have dislocated about two thousand households, including both long-established African American residents and recent white arrivals who were beginning to return to urban neighborhoods. Opponents managed to enlist allies on the editorial boards of major newspapers and in the governor's office. Ultimately the plan was dropped (Weiler 1974, 145–46) and has not been resurrected.

Planners had greater success with the Vine Street Expressway to carry east-west travelers quickly across what was then the northern edge of downtown. That essential corridor was intended to connect the Schuylkill Expressway on the west to Interstate 95 and the Delaware River on the east, accommodating both crosstown motorists and trucks hauling freight through the region. As early as 1959 a four-block section of that route was completed (between 18th Street and Broad Street). In 1973 a new environmental impact statement was required because previous studies had ignored air and noise as well as other secondary impacts. A combination of community concerns and environmental reviews stalled the extension well into the 1980s. Finally, Governor Robert Casey revived the project in 1986. By 1991 suburban interests were strong enough to enable the construction of the Vine Street Expressway at a cost of $225 million.

The Vine Street Expressway offers a classic example of infrastructure that serves the region's interests at the expense of city dwellers who live nearby. The initial proposal for eight lanes along the entire length of the expressway would have eliminated a Catholic church and school that served as crucial institutions in Chinatown. Community activists protested, and the builders reduced the width of the project to six lanes only for that length of roadway. While the church and school remained standing, the highway nonetheless separated the heart of the commercial and residential community from those important community institutions that sit in isolation on the north side of the highway. One of the founders of the Philadelphia Chinatown Development Coalition described the situation this way: "I think we saw it as a plan to get rid of Chinatown. The church and school was the only thing good in Chinatown at the time. We thought it was a fight for survival" (Cecilia Yep quoted in *AsianWeek* Staff 2000).

The politics surrounding these large highway projects frequently pitted neighborhoods against traffic engineers working for the state highway department and against the city's mayor. Philadelphia mayors in the 1960s and 1970s favored the crosstown expressway projects, including the massive Southbridge commercial development that was ultimately defeated. They recognized that the number of construction jobs generated by such megaprojects would translate into labor union support, an irresistible prize for mayors and other local officials. Up against a combination of state-level and regional interests, and even their own mayor, the community activists who stalled and even defeated one of these highway plans achieved amazing results.

In the late 1970s community protests were not as effective in defeating the last great mass-transit project built in downtown Philadelphia, the underground tunnel connecting the Reading Railroad station east of City Hall with the Pennsylvania Railroad station west of City Hall. Called the Commuter Tunnel, it closed a four-block gap between the two rail systems, doubling the reach of suburban rail passengers. Suburban commuters could ride between the northern and western suburbs without changing trains. Mayor Frank Rizzo strongly supported the project, arguing that it would create up to three thousand well-paid construction jobs that would last for four to five years. Regional leaders championed it through the Delaware Valley Regional Planning Commission, whose board assigned it the highest priority of all transportation projects in the region at that time. Their priority designation meant that over 90 percent of the project's cost was paid by a combination of state and federal funds.

The tunnel was vociferously opposed by a coalition of the city's community groups called Stop the Tunnel and Improve Neighborhood Transportation (STINT). They saw the tunnel as a project to serve suburban commuters and feared that cost overruns would be paid by city taxpayers. STINT filed a lawsuit against the project on multiple grounds, including a complaint that the city's fiscal crisis and cash-flow problems would prevent it from bearing the financial burden of constructing the tunnel, that the environmental impact statement was inadequate, and that the DVRPC acted improperly in assigning the project its highest priority because the largest portion of the mass-transit allocation for the entire construction period would have to be used for the tunnel, depriving other worthy transportation projects of needed funds. In 1977 a federal judge dismissed the lawsuit, opening the way for the huge project to begin in 1978 (*Philadelphia Council of Neighborhood Organizations v. William T. Coleman* 1977). In 1984, at a cost of $325 million, the tunnel was completed. Both city and suburban commuters who used either of the two lines gained access to the entire network of rail lines covering the region. It spurred important redevelopment along a shopworn stretch of Market Street, where the Gallery shopping mall expanded and the Reading Terminal head house and train shed were eventually transformed into the Pennsylvania Convention Center (discussed in chapter 2).

Diminished Government Funding for Megaprojects

In Philadelphia today no transportation projects on a comparable scale are planned, not because of community opposition and not for lack of big ideas but simply for lack of money. For example, many regional planners and leaders would love to consider covering the entire stretch of Interstate 95 that runs through downtown alongside the Delaware River. But city officials are publicly dismissive of the idea of burying the expressway. Asked to comment, Philadelphia's deputy mayor for transportation compared the proposal to Boston's experience with the Big Dig: "That $14.8 billion project ran so far over budget, and required so much additional money from the state, that it nearly bankrupted Massachusetts' highway authority. . . . With the focus in Washington on spending less and less, we'd be hard-pressed to get anyone to consider funding to bury the highway" (Rina Cutler quoted in Saffron 2012).

Another large-scale project in central Philadelphia is a light rail line along the Delaware River to help revitalize the waterfront, as light rail systems have done for Toronto, Portland, and Baltimore. Planners predict light rail would attract new development and enliven the area by reducing the automobile's dominance of the I-95 corridor. Again there is no prospect of funding for that project. Nor is there money to build a mile-and-a-half addition to the main north-south subway line along Broad Street to extend as far south as the Navy Yard, an emerging regional employment center (discussed in chapter 2). Without access to mass transit, that thousand-acre site at the southern tip of Philadelphia could become severely congested by auto traffic as it adds jobs. Yet the project to extend the subway line is stalled for lack of funds (DVRPC 2012, 22).

An even bigger project proposed by Amtrak and city officials is a ten-mile tunnel linking a new high-speed rail station near City Hall to the airport. That tunnel would allow high-speed trains to avoid slowing down as they make their way into downtown, helping to meet a goal of thirty-seven-minute train trips between Philadelphia and New York by 2040. As yet no funds are in place to implement the idea, which is estimated to cost $3 billion or more.

Not even transportation projects intended to help the suburbs have garnered the resources needed to fund them. One example is an ambitious proposal hatched in the early 2000s to build a light rail line sixty-two miles long between Philadelphia and Reading, Pennsylvania. It would have stopped at over thirty suburban towns, linking them together and spurring development along its route. Running along the Schuylkill River, it was intended to relieve some of the traffic load on the overcrowded Schuylkill Expressway. The massive project carried an equally massive price tag of $2 billion. The suburban backers of that Schuylkill Valley Metro Project initially had high hopes that Pennsylvania's veteran U.S. senator Arlen Specter could secure the needed federal funds. And in fact Specter was able to earmark over $40 million to support the project over a number of years, but ultimately the Federal Transit Administration dealt it a fatal blow by assigning it "not recommended status" because too little matching money could be mustered at local and state levels.

The region's business leaders are unhappy with the seeming inability of transportation authorities to undertake major game-changing initiatives. They want to see greater investment in large-scale transportation projects, and they fear their region is woefully behind other regions. In 2006 they expressed their collective frustration in a report published by the CEO Council for Growth (2006, 10), a corporate leadership group within the regional chamber of commerce: "Our regional leaders have become complacent about thinking big in order to make major regional infrastructure investments a reality."

That business coalition championed user fees such as the tolls being proposed for highway improvements, and they urged transportation planners to consider joint ventures with private-sector organizations, sometimes labeled "public-private partnerships" (PPP). These arrangements are increasingly common across the United States as governments are pressed to meet demands for public infrastructure. Private-sector partners are sometimes willing to invest directly in projects or to lend money to governments with unusual arrangements for repayment. For example, a state or local government might sell long-term bonds to fund projects eligible for federal aid, with debt service payable from the federal grants expected in future years, or government might grant a long-term lease or franchise to a private company for the construction and operation of a transit facility, allowing the private company to collect tolls or fares (subject to public regulation of the rates). In fact the only big new transit project to appear in the greater Philadelphia region in two decades was built in just this way. The New Jersey River Line is a thirty-four-mile light rail that began carrying passengers between Camden and Trenton in 2004. That billion-dollar project was developed under an operating contract with a partnership formed by two corporations, Bechtel and Bombardier. In exchange for taking responsibility for building and operating the line, the private companies received payments from the state and recovered a portion of operating costs from fares. Not until 2012 was it legal in Pennsylvania for state or local public entities to enter into PPPs. It was the obvious inadequacy of public funds to finance any large new transportation initiatives that convinced the legislature to make this option available to local and state governments as an alternative.

Emphasis on Repair and Maintenance

The absence of large-scale transportation projects in this region does not mean that it lacks transportation funding altogether. In fact this region spends over a billion dollars a year on transportation infrastructure. Like all other regions in the United States, this one receives annual allocations of federal and state funds to invest in highways, mass transit, bicycling, walking, and other modes of transportation. The federal funds come from the Highway Trust Fund, created by Congress to collect proceeds from a federal tax levied on every gallon of gasoline. The Trust Fund was intended to help build the nation's interstate highway system (Puentes & Prince 2003); its funds are allocated annually to every state government based on miles of roadway, vehicle miles traveled, gas tax revenues paid into the Fund, and other factors. Unfortunately the value of this federal support has diminished steadily since the beginning of the twenty-first century, as Congress has resolutely refused to increase the federal gas tax above 18.4 cents per gallon. That constant rate of taxation provides states and localities with declining purchasing power to maintain the nation's transportation infrastructure. This has proven especially problematic since 2007, the year the vehicle miles traveled in the United States peaked, causing gas tax revenues to level off.

In addition to receiving federal dollars, state governments raise their own funds for transportation by imposing additional taxes on gasoline purchases within their borders and tapping other revenue sources such as tolls, bond proceeds, and fees for drivers' licenses and vehicle registration. Many states, including Pennsylvania and New Jersey, generate more transportation dollars from their own sources than they receive from the federal government.

For example, most states tax gasoline at a higher rate than does the federal government. The state departments of transportation then allocate transportation dollars downward to local levels based on distribution formulas that typically take into account population size, number of registered vehicles, and miles of highway located within community boundaries.

In the greater Philadelphia region those federal and state dollars are allocated to the Delaware Valley Regional Planning Commission. DVRPC was formed as a two-state compact through legislation passed by the Pennsylvania legislature in 1965 and by the New Jersey legislature in a series of conforming acts between 1966 and 1974. Its voting members are the governments of Philadelphia and three small cities in the region, plus the four suburban counties on the Pennsylvania side of the Delaware River and four on the New Jersey side. The voting members also include six state-level representatives divided evenly between Pennsylvania and New Jersey. DVRPC assigns federal and state funds to transportation projects through its annual Transportation Improvement Plan. The TIP, which is updated on a two-year cycle, is a list of priority projects throughout the member counties that are expected to be supported by federal, state, and local funds. The federal government requires DVRPC to construct the TIP as a way of deciding how transportation funds will be assigned to projects throughout the region. Congress imposed the requirement in order to force metropolitan regions to coordinate their planning for transportation.

Since states raise a significant portion of transportation funding through gas taxes, it is not surprising that state departments of transportation exert considerable influence in planning and building transportation infrastructure for metropolitan America (Puentes & Bailey 2005, 143; Sciara and Wachs 2007; Mallett 2010). The process used in Pennsylvania brings to the table the state's fourteen MPOs and ten organizations representing rural counties to discuss the shares of federal and state funds to be assigned to each of their areas. For example, in the transportation plan designed for the years 2011–14, the state proposed to turn over 71 percent of combined federal and state funds for highways and bridges to regional organizations, as well as 99 percent of federal and state funds for transit (DVRPC 2009b). Even though Pennsylvania's Department of Transportation passed these funds down to the regions, it nevertheless continued to exercise significant influence. The reality is that all spending plans devised by MPOs in the region must gain the approval and signature of the governor and must fit into the state-level transportation plan.

The state has exercised its influence by directing MPOs across the state to give priority to existing infrastructure as opposed to spending funds on new projects. With its motto of "Fix It First," the state has instructed MPOs to give highest priority to system preservation, defined as "extending the life of existing facilities and their associated equipment," and to system management, defined as "improving the reliability, safety, traffic flow, and security of existing facilities." The state specifically recommends that "at a minimum, at least 90% of any MPO's program resources be dedicated to system preservation," meaning repaving roads, rebuilding bridges, replacing railroad tracks, buying new buses and rail cars, and generally sustaining and upgrading the existing transportation network (PADOT 2009, 2).

DVRPC's 2012 plan, "Connections 2040," reflects this emphasis on repair and maintenance. Looking forward over several decades, it foresees spending a mere 10 percent of highway investments on new capacity. For mass transportation, it proposes spending only 9.3 percent of the total transit dollars in Pennsylvania for new capacity (DVRPC 2012, 5). The "Connections 2040" report looks at how three different spending levels will affect the region's transportation system over three decades. The skeptical regional reporter who covered the presentation of these different scenarios for the *Philadelphia Inquirer* opined, "The funding scenarios are labeled low, medium, and high, but they might as well be: 'could happen,' 'dream on,' and 'hell freezes over'" (Nussbaum 2012b). Even the "high" scenario, or best case, forecasts some decline in current road and bridge conditions, although it achieves a state of good repair for the region's transit system. In the "medium" scenario, road and bridge conditions would worsen considerably, while conditions for mass-transit infrastructure would hold steady. The "low" or worst scenario would see road and bridge conditions declining substantially between 2012 and 2040, with a hundred state-maintained bridges closing due to lack of funding and the transit services compromised by the repair backlog. It is a bleak picture.

Why this overwhelming emphasis on repair and maintenance? The simple answer is that the region's repair needs are urgent, massive, and growing by the month. The region's major roadways, built during the fifty years since the Highway Trust Fund was established, were mostly designed for a life expectancy of only forty years. The states and counties have been unable to keep up with pavement maintenance and repair. According to the DVR-PC's estimate, the region needs to resurface about nineteen thousand lane miles and reconstruct more than 3,300 lane miles between 2014 and 2040, at a cost of over $19 billion. In addition the region needs to replace or rehabilitate nearly 2,200 bridges at an estimated cost of $58.4 billion over that same period (DVRPC 2012, 7–8). The prospect of addressing that backlog is politically daunting. Consider that Pennsylvania's governor had to wage an all-out, year-long campaign during 2013 to convince the legislature to pass a bill that gradually increases the state's annual commitment for repairing roads and bridges over five years until finally, by 2018, Pennsylvania will be spending $2.3 billion more each year *for the whole state.* Just to gain this relatively meager increase (in proportion to transportation needs), the governor and his supporters struggled against widespread popular resistance to the higher gas taxes necessary to fund it (Nussbaum 2013).

The infrastructure for mass transit is in equally dire condition. The Federal Transit Administration (FTA 2010) estimated in 2010 that the Southeastern Pennsylvania Transportation Authority had a $4 billion backlog of repairs to make in order to bring the system up to standard. The rail portion of SEPTA is responsible for much of that need, as are rail lines in other U.S. cities. In 2009 the FTA reported on massive repair backlogs in the country's largest rail transit systems serving the metropolitan areas of Chicago, Boston, New York, Philadelphia, Washington, and San Francisco. The FTA reported that in this group of older rail systems, fully one-third of the infrastructure was near or had already exceeded its expected useful life. For the rest of the nation's rail infrastructure, the share of infrastructure in similarly dire condition was only one-fifth. That large difference shows that the older rail systems have substantially greater reinvestment needs than the rest of the transit industry (FTA 2009).

One obvious reason for the poor condition of older rail systems is that they have withstood longer and more intensive use than newer transit systems. Even when SEPTA was created in 1964, the new regional authority inherited a collection of separate transit companies whose operations were already in poor condition as a result of underinvestment during the Depression, World War II, and the rise of the automobile in the 1950s. Indeed a major rationale for SEPTA's formation was to rescue those crumbling transportation lines. Having taken over a system in disrepair, SEPTA struggled from its inception to invest enough money to stay ahead of the system's advancing age.

That struggle continues. A 2007 state-level study of SEPTA bluntly described the difficulty of planning ahead in a system that requires urgent repairs: "Rather than placing emphasis on a coordinated long range planning process, the majority of the agency's focus is placed on the availability of funds in the annual capital budget and the requirements of operating the existing service." As proof of how completely repair and maintenance dominate the agenda, the report cited SEPTA's action in 2006 to move the agency's planning function into the budget office (Commonwealth of Pennsylvania Transportation Funding and Reform Commission 2007, 16, 10). Henceforth all future planning would be dominated by budget constraints.

Philadelphia is over three hundred years old and indisputably contains the region's largest and oldest concentration of roads, bridges, tracks, access roads, off-ramps, tunnels, and other transportation infrastructure. In an era when the primary consideration is shoring up existing infrastructure, one would expect the region's historic core to command disproportionate annual shares of investment. That has not been the case in recent years, as we shall see.

Rational Planning versus Territorial Politics

A fundamental issue for all MPOs nationally is whether to adopt a centralized decision-making model or serve as an aggregator of decisions made by the constituent governments: "Is the MPO to be a central priority-setting body? Or is it to be an umbrella organization with some functions devolved to the counties?" (Lewis & Sprague 1997). The answer varies from one MPO to another. An example of the "umbrella" approach is the San Francisco Bay Area Metropolitan Transportation Commission, which delegates significant discretion downward to member counties to identify transportation priorities for their own jurisdictions (Barbour 2002; Chai 2002). One study of San Francisco described a process that distributed resources to key players "to induce them to support the overall package," an approach that "assured that all key players received benefits, but made it difficult for region-wide solutions to emerge" (Innes & Gruber 2005, 181). At the other end of the spectrum, the Twin Cities' Metropolitan Council occupies a strong position relative to local governments; if local plans are not consistent with the regional plan, the Met Council can require that they be changed. One reason for the relative strength and unity of the Met Council is that its seventeen members, although chosen to represent geographic districts, are appointed by the state governor.

The MPO for greater Philadelphia sits between these two extremes. DVRPC has drafted a unified long-range plan that calls for directing future development into a hierarchy of existing centers as a way to save money on infrastructure costs and energy, as well as preserve natural resources and open space. This vision of a region organized into centers for concentrated development prescribes different levels and types of infrastructure spending in different areas (DVRPC 2009a). Considering this comprehensive, forward-looking vision of transportation and land use in the region, one might expect to see that plan driving the priorities assigned to investments. But in fact the criterion for including particular projects in the TIP is that they must be *consistent* with DVRPC's regional plan, not in conflict with it. In other words, the plan helps rule out certain proposals but does not dictate in what order the multitude of accepted projects should be completed.

Setting priorities among eligible proposals is as much about balancing the preferences of the constituent counties as it is about executing a unified regional plan. The TIP is constructed by soliciting proposals from each of the eight suburban counties plus Philadelphia. The counties may consult with local officials, but ultimately the county governments decide which projects to submit. Although the process includes opportunities for all members of the regional body to comment on each other's proposals, the TIP is essentially an aggregation of individual county plans. To see how Philadelphia fares in the distribution of transportation investments, consider the allocation of highway funding. Table 1 shows the shares of federal, state, and local highway dollars assigned to projects in the Pennsylvania counties across three succeeding TIP exercises (2009, 2011, 2013). (The table excludes transportation dollars invested in mass transit, which I consider separately below.) Each of the three TIPs included in table 1 projected investments to be made out of highway funds over a four-year period, so the percentage shares listed in the table represent more than just one-year amounts. The four-year dollar amounts allocated to each county may shift significantly after the TIP is adopted, as costs are adjusted. Therefore no TIP document can be regarded as more than an estimate at a single moment in time of costs for the projects included. For our purposes, however, what is important is the share of funds assigned to each county in the three TIPs. The table allows us to compare each county's share of the funds with its share of the population living in that county.

Table 1. Shares of population and transportation dollars in regional TIPs

	Population share of 5-county total	Share of Highway $ in 2009 TIP	Share of Highway $ in 2011 TIP	Share of Highway $ in 2013 TIP
Bucks County	15.5%	16.0%	13.5%	30.5%
Chester County	12.5	21.0	27.0	18.0
Delaware County	14.0	8.0	8.0	8.5
Montgomery County	20.0	23.0	16.5	19.5
Philadelphia	38.0	32.0	35.0	23.0

Sources: U.S. Census Bureau, Population Division, 2012, http://factfinder2.census.gov/faces /tableservices/jsf/pages/productview.xhtml?src=bkmk; DVRPC, Transportation Improvement Programs for Pennsylvania, FY 2009, FY 2011, FY 2013, http://www.dvrpc.org/tip/.

Note: The shares of highway dollars represent the percentage of total investments assigned to projects within each county. The calculation excludes dollars assigned to projects that cross several counties, which DVRPC reports separately.

Table 1 shows that those three TIPs consistently assigned Philadelphia less than its share of total dollars, if we measure shares by the size of the population living within each jurisdiction. By that same measure, Delaware County also consistently received less than its share. That is surprising, given that those two jurisdictions contain larger numbers of older communities than the other suburban counties. As observed earlier, one would have expected the priority on repairing and maintaining existing infrastructure to privilege these older places. Yet it has been observed across the United States that TIPs generally underfund central cities relative to their population size (Nelson et al. 2004). Why does this happen? It is not because suburban members conspire against the city. Rather it results from an institutional structure that gives equal standing to each member county, setting up a framework of expectation that available resources will be broadly shared across all the members. Philadelphia occupies no more than one seat—the same voting representation as each suburban county—even though the city has a far larger population than any of those counties.

Turning from roads to mass transit, we find a distribution that is more favorable to the city. Consider the capital program of SEPTA, the region's largest transportation operator, with responsibility for bus, trolley, subway, and commuter rail services in the city and four suburban counties. SEPTA plays the primary role in deciding how funds for mass transit will be invested in the region. Many capital dollars are spent to purchase rolling stock (rail cars, buses, etc.), dispatching systems, and other inventory whose benefits spread across the entire system. However, other investments in fixed infrastructure are divided among the counties. I analyzed a series of SEPTA reports on the fixed capital projects completed from 2000 to 2008 in the city of Philadelphia (http://www.septa.org/reports/pdf/phila12-08.pdf), in Bucks County (http://www.septa.org/reports/pdf/bucks12-08.pdf), in Chester County (http://www.septa.org/reports/pdf/chester12-08.pdf), in Delaware County (http://www.septa.org/reports/pdf/delaware12-08.pdf), and in Montgomery County (http://www.septa.org/reports/pdf/montgomery12-08.pdf). I included only projects completed from 2000 to 2008, not projects proposed for the future. I excluded systemwide purchases of radio dispatching equipment, audiovisual display equipment, computing technology, and other acquisitions to improve logistics for the system as a whole. I also excluded two major projects that improved Suburban Station and 30th Street Station because they serve as hubs for both the city division and regional rails. In these documents SEPTA reported that it had made 70 percent of its fixed investments within the city of Philadelphia and 30 percent in the Pennsylvania suburbs. That might seem like a highly favorable ratio for the city, until you consider that fully 80 percent of SEPTA's ridership uses the city division; the rail lines serving the suburbs carry only 20 percent of SEPTA's passengers.

Just as DVRPC's governing board underrepresents the city's share of the regional population, SEPTA's governing board underrepresents the city's share of riders. SEPTA is governed by a board that gives two votes to Philadelphia and two votes to each of the four participating counties, along with five more votes exercised by appointees of the governor and legislative leaders in the upper and lower state houses. That means that of the ten locally appointed board members, 80 percent are there to represent suburban areas that altogether generate only about 20 percent of the ridership. Those suburban counties as a group contribute only 20 percent of the local funding for SEPTA, and yet they far outnumber the city's representatives (Pennsylvania Transportation Funding and Reform Commission 2006, 77).

Given the suburbs' dominance of the SEPTA board, they could in theory choose to use transportation dollars from the federal and state government to reconfigure Philadelphia in ways that promote regional competitiveness. But that is not the pattern we see. The system's need for repairs leaves only about 1 percent of SEPTA's capital budget in recent years for new initiatives. Even if its suburban-dominated board were inclined to use transportation investments to help reshape central Philadelphia, it has had no opportunity to do so. There is no dearth of ideas for game-changing transit projects, such as the extension of the Broad Street subway to the Navy Yard or a new light rail line along the Delaware River. But such large-scale projects are impossible to consider when virtually all of SEPTA's capital dollars are used to repair and replace parts of the existing SEPTA system.

In sum, the planning process in these two regional authorities (DVRPC and SEPTA) focuses on maintaining the legacy of past patterns rather than forging new patterns, and it depends on a governance structure in which county governments are the constituent members. The result is a geographic distribution of resources that is driven more by local concerns than by regional plans. Myron Orfield lamented this pattern in MPOs around the United States, concluding that "the divided loyalties of board members who are local representatives hurt metropolitan areas." Orfield would fix that problem by "appointing more board members from state or regional agencies. While this does not guarantee that regional interests will prevail, it nevertheless curbs the parochialism of local representative-dominated governance" (Orfield & Gumus-Dawes 2009). Robert Puentes (2011, 2) at the Brookings Institution put it more colloquially when he asserted that MPOs typically make investment choices based on "logrolling where funds are spread around like peanut butter rather than on prioritization." That fragmented process, which ends up aggregating the plans of separate counties, does not offer regional leaders the leverage we might have imagined to reshape central Philadelphia.

The Port Authority

Another regional authority with major responsibility for transportation infrastructure is the Delaware River Port Authority, a bistate authority that operates bridges across the Delaware River and manages the PATCO high-speed rail line that carries riders from the New Jersey suburbs into and out of Philadelphia. In 1951 the U.S. government formally recognized a long-standing cooperative arrangement between the states for bridge building by constituting DRPA as a federal interstate compact to operate bridges and transit lines. In 1991 that compact was amended to grant DRPA the ability to engage in economic development efforts to improve and develop the port district.

DRPA earns a constant revenue stream by collecting a toll for each round trip across the bridges. The revenue stream makes it easy for DRPA to borrow funds, since the authority can always assure lenders there will be a constant source of revenues to pay them back. DRPA has used that advantage to fund new initiatives in central Philadelphia and Camden at a time when DVRPC and SEPTA were primarily focused on preserving existing infrastructure. In doing so DRPA was following the well-known example of Robert Moses, whose control of revenues from bridge tolls helped him expand his influence over the development of New York City (e.g., by building Lincoln Center) and its surrounding regional network of expressways, bridges, tunnels, and parks (Caro 1974).

Unlike the regional transportation authorities discussed earlier, DRPA's constituent members are state officials rather than representatives of county and city governments. The board is entirely composed of commissioners appointed by the two governors, plus two Pennsylvania state officials who sit on the DRPA board ex officio. The governor of New Jersey appoints eight commissioners, the governor of Pennsylvania appoints six commissioners, and the Pennsylvania state treasurer and auditor general automatically take seats on the authority. That equal division of votes between the two states has led to a decision-making process that tends to occur primarily within the state caucuses rather than in full board meetings. Before each public meeting the commissioners from each of the two states meet separately in private. They have operated by an unwritten agreement that spending is divided evenly between the states and that neither state will challenge the other's proposals so long as those proposals are within reason (Brown 2009, 188–89). Notwithstanding these informal rules of engagement, DRPA has sometimes served as a stage for epic battles between the two states.

The most dramatic example occurred in 2005; this was a highly contested dredging project favored by Pennsylvania and opposed by New Jersey. The combined ports of Philadelphia and Camden play a critical role in the economy of the wider region by connecting to national and international trade networks, especially with the growth in international consumer goods flowing into U.S. markets. The Vine Street Expressway is a critical artery for freight traveling to and from the west side of the region to Interstate 95 and the port of Philadelphia. Knowing that the Panama Canal would be widened by 2014, Pennsylvania's governor was determined that Philadelphia's port should be upgraded to accommodate larger ships from Asia. That meant deepening the ship channel in the Delaware River to forty-five feet. The governor fought hard for the project, recognizing that the entire state had an economic stake in the viability of the port. New Jersey's governor was equally adamant that the project should *not* go forward. Officials in his state feared the dredging would endanger an aquifer supplying drinking water to southern New Jersey and that the toxic sediment from the river bottom would be dumped in New Jersey. DRPA was deadlocked to such an extent that the chair refused to call a meeting of the board for seventeen months, from autumn 2005 to spring 2007. The public spectacle of a paralyzed regional institution dragged on until a deal was finally reached. New Jersey agreed to support the project if Pennsylvania would furnish all the local funding required for dredging, would accept all the dredge spoils on its land, and would secure an updated environmental impact study from the U.S. Army Corps of Engineers.

That deal did not satisfy citizen environmentalists in the region, who continued to oppose the dredging. But they could not gain a foothold in the debate because DRPA does not answer to constituents within the region; it reflects the interest of state political leaders. Unable to reach DRPA through the structures of democratic politics, environmentalists brought a lawsuit to stop the dredging. In the end they lost in the Pennsylvania courts, and the dredging project moved ahead. The simple fact is that Pennsylvania state leaders and their appointed commissioners saw this major investment as critical to their state's prosperity, and the institutional framework of port governance allowed them to pursue the project despite local opposition.

That same insulation from democratic politics cushioned the port authority when it began to use its resources for purposes beyond the bridges and the port. Even as DVRPC was shifting its transportation emphasis toward repair and maintenance of existing facilities, DRPA's leaders invoked the 1991 amendment to their compact, which charged them with improving and developing the port district. They began to invest in economic development projects near the waterfront that would reinforce the port. Their amended compact gave DRPA a broad mandate to invest in a wide variety of projects that promised to strengthen central Philadelphia and Camden, even projects unrelated to transportation. And invest they did. From 1992 to 2010 DRPA borrowed about $500 million, to be repaid from bridge tolls, and used the proceeds to support a variety of initiatives, the majority of which focused on the tourism, convention, and entertainment economy. DRPA's chief executive officer explained, "This was a niche not being filled by any other agency" (Paul Drayton quoted in Ung 2003).

On the Camden side of the Delaware River, DRPA's investments clustered on the waterfront, helping to build a minor league baseball stadium and a children's garden adjacent to a waterfront aquarium and restoring the battleship *New Jersey* as a waterfront attraction. On the Philadelphia side, the grants spread from the waterfront to locations in other parts of the city. For waterfront development, DRPA made grants totaling $22 million to support initiatives by the Penn's Landing Corporation. Other grants farther removed from the water went to initiatives at the Sports Stadium Complex in South Philadelphia ($14 million), the National Constitution Center ($11.5 million), Independence Visitors Center ($4 million), and President's House Memorial ($3.5 million) in the historic district; the Pennsylvania Convention Center in the heart of downtown ($2.5 million); the Kimmel Center for the Performing Arts, anchoring the Avenue of the Arts ($3.6 million); and the Philadelphia Zoo ($750,000).

An investigative report issued by the New Jersey comptroller's office concluded that many of these grants were made through an informal approval process that sometimes did not even require an official proposal. They sometimes reflected the personal choices of commissioners, "relying in large part on personal relationships" (New Jersey State Comptroller 2012, 45). Even though the original bistate compact that had created DRPA required the agency to regularly update its master plan to include any new economic development projects it funded, no updating was done after 2005. That meant that dozens of projects were funded without any reference to the master plan, which theoretically should have guided those expenditures (50–51).

This pattern of spending drew heavy criticism from motorists who insisted they paid tolls to maintain the bridges, not to subsidize development initiatives in Philadelphia and Camden. DRPA was fiercely criticized for borrowing funds to bankroll a wide variety of projects seemingly unrelated to the bridges. But the bistate authority was slow to heed public criticism even when state-level officials began to question these economic development expenditures. In fall 2010 members of Pennsylvania's legislature introduced bills in the upper and lower houses to impose more oversight on DRPA, and by early 2011 the governors of both states took the position that DRPA's long-standing practice of economic development spending should end. Even with major state officials standing against this program of economic development spending, it took a year after both state governors demanded changes before the bistate authority brought an end to its practice of distributing dollars to fund economic development projects. The final such grants were approved in December 2011. DRPA also took its time responding to both governors' insistence on more open records, new ethics policies, and procedures to reduce patronage and insider dealing. Although DRPA's board drafted such rules in 2010, it took more than two years to implement them (Nussbaum 2012a).

Even the U.S. government, which established the interstate compact and wrote its charter, could not always exert authority over a body it created. When the U.S. Government Accountability Office (GAO) set out to examine the extent of transparency and accountability in four bistate authorities, its auditors encountered resistance from DRPA. GAO staff members were following up on congressional concerns that had earlier forced DRPA to establish an inspector general to monitor the way it spent money and accounted for the expenditures. But DRPA refused to allow GAO investigators to meet privately with that inspector general. Not surprisingly the auditors concluded that DRPA's inspector general lacked independence needed to do a proper job (USGAO 2013, 30–31).

How do we explain that the DRPA board was able to stonewall for so long before responding to the governors and other, higher level officials to whom they were formally accountable? The explanation is suggested by Peter Hendee Brown (2009), who compared DRPA to three of the nation's other port authorities. He concluded that DRPA has greater autonomy from state supervision than other port authorities because it is accountable to two state governments instead of one. Whenever either state government tries to intervene in its operation to impose unwanted directives, the other state must be persuaded to agree. If governing board members choose to do so, they can maneuver to complicate the issue and discourage the two sides from agreeing (186).

The New Jersey commissioners were especially determined to get their fair share of economic development grants before the program ceased, because they regarded the authority's revenue stream as largely produced by

New Jersey. In their view these economic development grants redistributed dollars that were mainly collected from New Jersey motorists who use the bridges to commute to Pennsylvania. It was their job to ensure that New Jersey got its rightful allocation.

Sharing the Wealth

In the introduction I argued that in order to flourish in the era of globalization, metropolitan areas must equip their central cities to connect the regional economy to the wider world. Should we expect intergovernmental regional authorities like the ones described in this chapter to take the lead in reshaping the central core to serve the region's interests? Probably not. Although they were created to forge an integrated regional approach to building the transportation network, these institutions operate mostly as allocation mechanisms for dividing up available resources among member governments. For the foreseeable future they are unlikely to pool their respective shares in order to undertake large-scale initiatives that can significantly change the course of the region's development.

This chapter showed that in an earlier period, large-scale projects like the downtown commuter tunnel and the Crosstown Expressway on Vine Street *were* undertaken when they were seen to both benefit suburban travelers and simultaneously create value for many city residents (although it is worth reiterating that they damaged properties and dispossessed owners and renters in their paths). Since the quasi-governmental authorities described in this chapter operate on a regional scale, they might be expected to serve as the locus for planning and launching such large-scale transportation investments that fundamentally reconfigure urban space to benefit the region as a whole. But they do not. These regional bodies are not the main actors advancing regional priorities to reshape central Philadelphia. Why? The account in this chapter suggested two explanations.

One reason is that in an era of scarce resources for big initiatives, their expenditures are almost exclusively focused on repairing and upgrading existing infrastructure. The major regional transportation authorities, DVRPC and SEPTA, are struggling just to maintain an existing transportation network. Even with an infusion of a billion dollars a year in federal and state transportation funds, the dollars are not being used in ways that substantially reshape development patterns. Instead of big projects, the funds are being spent to maintain older roads, bridges, and transit lines. Using annual budgets to salvage ailing infrastructure means perpetuating already existing patterns of development, not reshaping land-use patterns. The Delaware River Port Authority presents a slightly different case. That organization borrowed a half billion dollars to spend over fifteen years specifically to strengthen central Philadelphia and Camden. It made investments that affected areas of the central city focused on the arts, history, and tourism, helping to build cultural districts. But DRPA spent those funds without a comprehensive plan, doling out investments one by one, often based on personal requests by board members.

An even more important reason for the lack of game-changing initiatives to reshape Philadelphia is the structure of these quasi-governmental bodies: they are controlled by board members who represent governmental jurisdictions. In two of them the constituent units are counties, while the third organization is composed of the state governments of Pennsylvania and New Jersey. All three authorities in this chapter were designed by state government to be steered by boards that allocate seats among the member jurisdictions. Together they illustrate the distributional pattern inherent in organizations that bring together multiple governments within a metropolitan area to forge coordinated, strategic plans and investments. When governments are members, the decision-making process seldom leads to large-scale game-changing projects because the dynamics favor dividing up the resources, not concentrating investments. Although the purpose of such intergovernmental authorities is to get member governments to see their home areas in a broader regional context, ironically the arrangements encourage members to focus their efforts on bringing home the dollars to their own jurisdiction. Precisely because board members represent their jurisdiction, they feel compelled to capture an appropriate share of the spoils for their constituents.

As we will see, *nongovernmental* actors are playing a larger role than *intergovernmental* organizations in shaping central Philadelphia's development patterns. The Third-Sector organizations discussed in the next chapter have made significant contributions to reterritorializing the city to advance regional interests. They have become important vehicles for state and suburban interests to express their vision of how central Philadelphia should change. While a number of them have benefited from the largesse of the DRPA to build and refurbish their buildings and expand their programs, those investments have not been guided by a comprehensive plan for central Philadelphia but by the decisions of numerous independent organizations. In the next chapter we will see how land development decisions taken by some major institutions over the past fifteen years have influenced the city center.

Chapter 2

Third-Sector Organizations
Reshape Central Cities

In chapter 1 I explored how intergovernmental authorities carry out their responsibility for transportation systems that link the city to the suburbs across municipal boundaries. I explained why the suburban representatives who dominate these intergovernmental authorities are unlikely to use their power over transportation investments as a tool to alter land-use patterns in the city. In contrast, this chapter documents significant suburban influence in city institutions that are redeveloping urban spaces and, in the process, building new centers of gravity within the city. In the past twenty years Third-Sector organizations have played key roles in retrofitting the traditional downtown for new functions. As in other U.S. cities, in Philadelphia they have built a convention center, a regional performing arts center, and other facilities that are transforming downtown to serve visitors. They have also anchored development in other parts of the city, establishing new employment centers and visitor destinations. They have made massive dollar investments to advance their own institutional goals and, in the process, have reshaped land-use patterns in central cities.

Philadelphia was one of the earliest cities to adopt Third-Sector vehicles for urban redevelopment. The creation of a web of nonprofit institutions was born of a reform impulse that swept through Philadelphia in the 1950s. Long seen as politically "corrupt and contented" (Steffens 1903), the city threw off its oppressive Republican machine in the late 1940s and early 1950s, adopting a new Home Rule Charter that restructured local government. Voters elected Democrats to modernize the administration of the city. When Philadelphians elected their second reform Democratic mayor in 1956, he worked with business leaders to create a series of nongovernmental, nonprofit corporations to undertake virtually every crucial development project in the mid-twentieth century. These organizations diffused power across an ever more crowded and complex network of independent organizations. Although in the early years of urban renewal the mayor served as the pivotal decision maker, broker, and negotiator, his control diminished as the number of nongovernmental organizations grew. A book written by Kirk Petshek (1973) about urban renewal in that period described the government's relationship to the nonprofit corporations as one of virtual equals. Petshek contrasted Philadelphia with the strong mayoral control over New Haven's redevelopment that Robert Dahl famously described in his book *Who Governs* (1961). In Philadelphia, Petshek (1973, 88) observed, "civic leaders exerted an important influence on the content of the programs even where programs were totally financed by a public body. Conversely, if financing was principally private, but public involvement was essential . . . the public voice was heeded. Such a reciprocal relationship could not easily have occurred in a situation where, as in Dahl's New Haven, the mayor takes central control."

This chapter shows how firmly entrenched Third-Sector organizations had become by the turn of the twenty-first century. I provide a tour of major development districts that have emerged, highlighting the critical roles played by Third-Sector organizations. Those districts are portrayed by the shaded areas on the map in figure 3; the circled numbers identify the institutions featured in the chapter. In every one of these cases, Third-Sector actors have taken primary responsibility not just for building major institutions but for redeveloping *whole districts*. In twentieth-century Philadelphia place building had been shared by the two sectors. While private investors were expected to build businesses that would employ workers and pay taxes, city planners had been expected to think holistically about the rejuvenation of districts surrounding those private investments. These days, however,

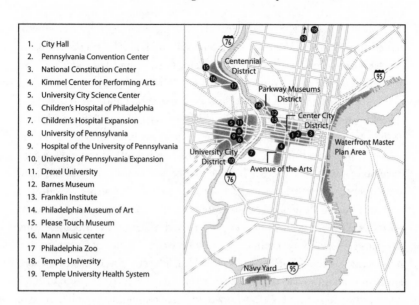

1. City Hall
2. Pennsylvania Convention Center
3. National Constitution Center
4. Kimmel Center for Performing Arts
5. University City Science Center
6. Children's Hospital of Philadelphia
7. Children's Hospital Expansion
8. University of Pennsylvania
9. Hospital of the University of Pennsylvania
10. University of Pennsylvania Expansion
11. Drexel University
12. Barnes Museum
13. Franklin Institute
14. Philadelphia Museum of Art
15. Please Touch Museum
16. Mann Music center
17 Philadelphia Zoo
18. Temple University
19. Temple University Health System

Figure 3. Major institutions and districts in central Philadelphia.

place making around major investments is led by nongovernmental organizations like the ones featured here. The pages that follow offer many examples of specific projects in order to demonstrate beyond a doubt how the Third Sector is strategically reshaping the city. My intention in providing this detailed tour of redevelopment is to display the number and variety of organizations leading the initiatives and the extent to which the Third Sector is in charge of planning the city's future.

The chief concern of Philadelphia's civic leaders in the 1950s was defending downtown against the suburbs that were already drawing population, jobs, and disposable income out of the city. Their response was to form a nonprofit organization, the Old Philadelphia Development Corporation (OPDC), to "aid and assist in the redevelopment, renewal, replanning, and general improvement" of downtown (Petshek 1973, 221). Despite the considerable corporate power represented by that group of company presidents and board chairs, OPDC stated its mission in modest terms: "to act primarily as a catalyst. . . . The OPDC is a nonprofit citizens' organization. . . . It has no public powers" (222). Notwithstanding that self-effacing description, it played a crucial role as a partner in urban renewal during the 1960s, and its successor organization today exerts a powerful influence on downtown.

More than many U.S. cities, Philadelphia placed a high priority on *residential* renewal downtown, focusing especially on rehabilitating the housing that had survived from the colonial era—albeit in a dilapidated condition—in an area near the city's commercial center. While other cities demolished old housing, Philadelphia favored historic preservation and rehabilitation of this old district, which came to be known as Society Hill. Planners chose it as their first target because they guessed that its historical and architectural value would appeal to developers. If housing rehabilitation could succeed anywhere, it would be there. That decision proved to have crucial long-term consequences because it created an anchor residential area that encouraged further housing development downtown. OPDC not only supported the Society Hill renovation in concept but played a key role in implementing the plan by serving as the intermediary between the city government and prospective buyers of housing in Society Hill. The city government exercised eminent domain to acquire properties and then conveyed them to OPDC, whose task was to find buyers who would agree to renovate the old homes to specific architectural standards. This early instance of nongovernmental responsibility for revitalizing an entire residential district led to adopting similar approaches in other development efforts.

Refurbishing Market Street East for Visitors, Commuters, and Shoppers

OPDC next turned its attention to revitalizing the city's main commercial corridor, Market Street, particularly the section stretching east from City Hall toward the Delaware River. Philadelphia's chief planner from 1949 to 1970, Edmund Bacon, projected a multiuse complex of transportation, shopping, and office space covering four blocks on Market Street. Bacon's plan called for building a tunnel to link the Reading and Penn Central railroad lines serving suburban commuters. OPDC lobbied hard for this commuter tunnel. Although it had to be financed by government, everyone understood that the accompanying retail revival of Market Street depended on attracting private investors. That was difficult, given the street's seedy collection of pinball parlors, drug stores, and other low-end retailers. The environment was perceived as dirty and unsafe. To spur private investment, the public spaces on Market Street needed to be upgraded, but the municipal services seemed inadequate to that task. So some of the larger retailers on Market Street East hired and trained their own small force of workers to remove litter and maintain a reassuring street presence. That small force was the predecessor to what would eventually become the Center City District.

Businesses joined together to create a special services district because they needed a reliable, ongoing source of funds to upgrade the quality of public spaces. In 1990 the City Council created the Center City District to collect fees from downtown property owners to improve the streets and public spaces. The new district shared a common staff and offices with OPDC, which by this time had renamed itself the Central Philadelphia Development Corporation. The two organizations maintain a sister relationship to the present day. While the CCD started as an organization promoting a clean and safe downtown, it quickly began investing in small-scale, scattered capital projects. It borrowed money, using the annual assessment paid by property owners to assure repayment, and employed the funds for lighting, signs, benches, trees, and other streetscape improvements (Kromer 2010, chapter 2).

Over time the CCD's ambitions grew beyond street cleaning and safety. By 2009 it had invested a total of $55 million in projects on the Parkway and other parts of downtown. That total included almost $20 million from federal, state, and local government sources, along with $7.2 million from foundations (CCD 2010, 60). Nothing illustrates that ambition better than the CCD's initiative to redevelop a derelict public space adjoining City Hall. Those few acres had deteriorated into a rundown, litter-strewn plaza mainly used as a passageway leading from the street via a barren, cracked-concrete stairway to subway and train lines that converge underneath City Hall. The redesign includes green space, shaded sitting areas, a fountain, public art, and an outdoor café, plus enough space to accommodate concerts and other events. This one project alone cost $55 million, as much as the CCD had previously invested over its entire history. Of that total, over $35 million came from federal, state, and local governments. Another $2 million was contributed by foundations and corporations. There is more than a little irony in the fact that this initiative to refurbish the site of Philadelphia's seat of government, with the majority of the cost covered by government funds, was designed and executed by a nongovernmental organization.

Convention Center

In reviving Market Street East a critical step was the decision in the 1980s to attach a massive new convention center to the Reading Railroad station fronting on Market Street. To build and operate that facility, the state and city jointly created the Pennsylvania Convention Center Authority. The construction took ten years of start-and-stop planning and political infighting before the center finally opened in 1993. The city government bore the largest portion of its cost, $338 million, while the state contributed another $185 million, bringing the total to more than a half-billion dollars.

Philadelphia's mayor Ed Rendell, who took office in 1992, used the convention center opening as a launch point for his two-term campaign to boost the city's visitor economy. Although earlier champions had initiated the project, Rendell made it the linchpin of his strategy to boost the city's image and its economy. He drove the planning and funding of three high-profile cultural projects and supported countless others that would appeal to visitors from out of town. Rendell's dedication to that mission is documented in one of the most interesting books written in the 1990s about Philadelphia, Buzz Bissinger's *A Prayer for the City* (1997). Bissinger shadowed the ebullient Rendell during his first term in office and offered this analysis of the mayor's determination to build the visitor economy: "He seized on the opening of the convention center with full force, and he transformed it from just an opening into an event of enormous psychic significance, as pivotal in its own way as the era of growth that had been ushered in by the Centennial Exhibition. He believed in tourism not necessarily because it was the best answer but because it was quite literally the only one" (223).

Rendell did not delude himself that bringing visitors would solve all the city's problems. Indeed it was reported that at one planning session for the eleven-day festivities marking the convention center opening he ruminated, "I feel like the Roman emperor. . . . I can't give decent city services, I want to close health centers, and I want to cut back on library hours, and here I am giving bread and circuses to the people" (Bissinger 1997, 202). Although a previous mayor had initiated the convention center, Rendell became the mayor who dramatically raised the city's profile as a convention and visitor destination.

Opened in 1993, the convention center almost immediately confronted labor problems. The governing board of this quasi-public authority seemed unable to resolve constant complaints from exhibitors concerning high labor costs and disagreements among unions over whose workers were entitled to perform which job on the exhibit floor. In 2002 a performance report documented that labor and management problems had become so acute that only 17 percent of the groups that had used the facility during the previous year said they would return. Frustrated state officials moved to exert greater control over the Pennsylvania Convention Center Authority by expanding the size of its governing board from nine to fifteen members and declaring that new members would be appointed from outside the city. That move intentionally diluted the city's voting power, giving the majority of seats to outsiders. The legislature was empowered to exert control over the Philadelphia facility because it had been originally constituted as a state-created authority, and they clearly recognized they had a stake in its success.

Once in control of the board, state appointees pursued a plan to expand the convention center by stretching the building across an additional city block. They feared that Philadelphia was already losing its competitive position to other cities with bigger convention centers. An expansion would allow Philadelphia to move ahead of the Washington Convention Center, to equal the Boston Convention Center, and to come closer to New York's Jacob K. Javits Convention Center. And so in summer 2004 the state legislature passed a first authorization of funds, totaling $400 million, a sum the state would eventually increase to $786 million. In the end the expansion became the largest building project ever funded by the state of Pennsylvania. The state's willingness to pay the entire cost of the expansion signaled state officials' recognition that Philadelphia's visitor economy benefits the entire state. Unfortunately that enormous investment in bricks and mortar did not resolve the operating problems that have dogged the Convention Center to the present day.

National Constitution Center

To advance his tourism agenda, Mayor Rendell helped to bring a major new museum to the historic district. As early as 1988 the U.S. Congress had authorized the construction of such a museum to honor and explain the U.S. Constitution to the American public. But the project languished for almost a decade because backers were unable to raise sufficient money. Planners eked out just enough funds to hire a museum designer whose early sketches appealed so much to Rendell that the mayor took over as chair of the project in 1997 and set about securing additional federal funds, working with Pennsylvania's senior senator Arlen Specter. Appropriately the site was located near the Liberty Bell and Independence Hall. But rather than belonging to the National Park Service, the impressive new facility was to be constructed and operated by a nonprofit organization created for this specific purpose.

The new attraction broke ground in fall 2000 and was completed in 2003. By that time the project had captured $100 million from government sources—more than half of its total cost of $185 million. The taxpayer funds had come mainly from federal agencies ($63.5 million), the state of Pennsylvania ($30 million), and the City of Philadelphia. The Delaware River Port Authority chipped in $7.5 million from its economic development funds (discussed in chapter 1). The city's major foundations, including the Pew Charitable Trusts and the William Penn Foundation, provided early gifts, as did Comcast, Wachovia, Lincoln Financial, Mellon, and other major companies in the region. As a national museum, the project attracted substantial support from wealthy citizens around the country, for example, a contribution in 2002 of $10 million from the Michigan-based founder of Amway Corporation. Closer to home, philanthropists Walter Annenberg and Sidney Kimmel together provided another $15 million. By 2004 John C. Bogle, the chairman of National Constitution Center, was able to announce proudly that the new museum had reached its capital campaign goal of $185 million, more than half from government sources.

Transforming the Waterfront

The banks of the Delaware River have presented an especially difficult development challenge to the Third Sector. That stretch of waterfront has been the target of one plan after another, all of them ultimately failing to materialize. As early as 1970 the quasi-public Penn's Landing Corporation was created to improve the waterfront district, yet decade after decade it failed to execute a unified plan for one of the city's most valuable districts. While other U.S. cities had successfully revived their waterfront, the Penn's Landing Corporation tried to lure one megadeveloper after another, each time expecting the developer to supply a master vision for the district. Five successive mayors promised and failed to transform the waterfront (Mc-Govern 2008).

How would Philadelphia break this string of failed megadeals? Equally important, how would the city overcome the unsavory reputation that Penn's Landing Corporation had acquired for operating in secrecy and tolerating corruption? The head of an important civic watchdog organization had complained that Penn's Landing Corporation "might not necessarily be doing anything wrong. . . . But at the very least, we can't have any confidence in it because it all seems to be happening in the dark" (Zack Stahlberg quoted in Gelbart & Sullivan 2005). The answer was not to put the project into the hands of a government agency, making it directly accountable to the public. Instead the city simply shifted responsibility within the Third Sector. The William Penn Foundation provided $1.6 million to assemble civic and community leaders along with planners from the University of Pennsylvania to seek broad input from citizens and community organizations. Their work resulted in a new master plan for the waterfront and a new nonprofit organization to implement that plan, the Delaware River Waterfront Corporation (DRWC).

Announcing the dissolution of the Penn's Landing Corporation and its replacement by the DRWC, Mayor Michael Nutter expressed confidence in handing over responsibility to this independent body: "Leading this new nonprofit will be a diverse group of dedicated volunteers with a broad base of experience and the skill to undertake the critical task of renewing our waterfront" (quoted in Brennan 2009). The head of the Center City District opined that the reason city government needed to establish the DRWC to create and implement a vision for waterfront development (rather than relying on government planners) was simply that "no one in City Hall will ever be capable of crafting a long-term vision for the 18-mile expanse of the Delaware because riverfront development plays out over decades, beyond the normal span of elected office" (Paul Levy quoted in Saffron 2006).

Instead of large-scale real estate development, including ranks of towering skyscrapers that had failed in earlier versions, the new plan emphasized public access to the waterfront. Rather than the gated communities, vast entertainment complexes, and big box stores that had dominated earlier development plans, this twenty-first-century approach combined high-density housing with street-level retail and a string of recreational trails punctuated by small waterfront parks and restored wetlands. The plan anticipated that development would occur piecemeal over thirty years, requiring only modest government subsidies (DRWC 2011). A good example is Race Street Pier, the first component of the plan to be realized. Sitting on the water's edge, the new park turned a vacant, one-acre pier into a welcoming public space with trees, a promenade, a lawn, and a terrace. The cost of the makeover was about $6 million, with the largest contributions coming from the city government ($2 million), the state ($2 million), and the William Penn Foundation ($1 million). This was only the first of a string of parks foreseen in the master plan, spaced about a half-mile apart and connected by a continuous recreational trail. Rather than realizing economic benefits through high-density real estate development, the plan hoped that a publicly accessible waterfront would improve the city's appeal to residents and thereby its appeal to businesses.

Performing Arts Corridor South of City Hall

Philadelphians have a hard time recalling how Broad Street below City Hall looked twenty-five years ago: "Office buildings stood empty, prostitutes strutted near the corner of Lombard Street, and the gloomy husk of the Ridgeway Library served as the face of the city's decline" (Saffron 2013). Since that time the library has become the Creative and Performing Arts High School, and cultural venues have multiplied to create a new brand for that once-forlorn street.

Avenue of the Arts

In 1990 the Central Philadelphia Development Corporation turned its sights on the city's second major commercial corridor, Broad Street, particularly the stretch of obsolete commercial buildings south of City Hall. Those older office buildings had lost prime tenants as commerce shifted into more modern office buildings. CPDC issued a report titled "South Broad Street—A Vision for the 1990s" (1990), which laid out a blueprint for creating a sense of place and establishing an arts and entertainment district along the street. Mayor Rendell took up the report when he entered office and quickly pushed to establish a new Third-Sector organization, the Avenue of the Arts, Inc., to oversee the redevelopment of South Broad Street as an arts corridor. It became the nonprofit fund-raising and operating arm of the project to transform South Broad Street.

That transformation started with a series of small arts venues seeded by grants from the William Penn Foundation. Between 1990 and 1995 the foundation invested about $13 million in capital projects that included gallery spaces, printmaking facilities, a jazz center, and streetscape improvements (Fairmount Ventures, Inc. 1998). New theaters opened, and the city expanded an existing structure to house the High School for the Creative and Performing Arts. Without question, however, the centerpiece of the Avenue of the Arts project was the Regional Center for the Performing Arts.

Regional Center for the Performing Arts

The Philadelphia Orchestra had long wanted to replace the historic Academy of Music, built in 1857 as an opera house, but seemed unable to raise sufficient funds to achieve that goal. By 1996 the Orchestra decided to merge its faltering campaign for a new concert hall with Mayor Rendell's proposal for a new performing arts center that would serve local arts companies performing many types of music and dance, as well as touring companies. The two plans were merged under the supervision and management of a new nonprofit entity that would ultimately be known as the Kimmel Center for the Performing Arts. That institution would control the design and construction of the massive new cultural complex to anchor the Avenue of the Arts (Bounds 2007).

To chair the ambitious building project, the nonprofit Center's board recruited the same Philadelphia developer who had guided the construction of the convention center when he chaired that authority board: Willard G. Rouse III. Although Rouse had been criticized for planning the convention center in secrecy, he held firmly to the view that opening up the process to continuous public scrutiny and input would slow down the construction. Rouse managed the planning of the Regional Performing Arts Center the same way, holding information tightly in order to maintain a brisk pace. Asked to justify that lack of openness, Rouse argued that he was leading a private nonprofit organization, and the construction was therefore not a public project that required open meetings and open books (Dobrin 1998).

Rouse was technically correct, even though many people saw it as a public project because the state of Pennsylvania had furnished $63 million and Mayor Rendell had committed $32 million from the city's budget. Another $2.5 million had come from the Delaware Regional Port Authority's economic development funds. In the end, however, the largest share of the funding came from private individuals, foundations, and corporations. In recognition of philanthropist Sidney Kimmel's lead gift of $35 million, the center bore his name. Together the Pew Charitable Trusts, the William Penn Foundation, and the Annenberg Foundation gave the project $37 million. Dozens of other families and individuals made multimillion-dollar contributions. Opened in December 2001 at a cost of $265 million, the Kimmel Center was governed by the same board that operated the historic Academy of Music. Together these two venues compose one of the largest performing arts complexes in the country.

Repurposing the Navy Yard

Three miles south of downtown on Broad Street sits another major development project launched in the 1990s. This one converted what was once a military base to new purposes. In 1991 Philadelphians learned that the U.S. military would pull out of a thousand-acre installation at the southern tip of the city where the Navy had built ships for more than a century. The announcement left the city in a quandary about how to repurpose an area as large as downtown Philadelphia, a challenge that preoccupied Rendell throughout his eight years as mayor.

The mayor assigned responsibility for the planning, operation, and redevelopment of the site to the Third Sector, specifically to the Philadelphia Industrial Development Corporation. PIDC is a quasi-public corporation established jointly by the city government and chamber of commerce in 1958. Its mission is to acquire underutilized land throughout the city and market the land to companies that would consider moving into the city or to existing companies that would expand. As with the OPDC (the quasi-public corporation tasked with redeveloping Society Hill), PIDC's business was to acquire parcels either through purchase or condemnation and find buyers who would put the parcels back into productive use. To compete with the suburbs, PIDC began selling unused parcels at subsidized prices and helped companies negotiate low-interest loans and grants from government. Its board comprised people appointed by both the city government and the chamber of commerce.

Over the years PIDC shepherded many development projects, but it had never attempted reconstruction on the massive scale required for the Navy Yard conversion. PIDC commissioned Robert A. M. Stern Architects to develop a master plan for the entire site. That plan, inspired by similar developments in Charlestown, Massachusetts, and the Mission Bay area of San Francisco, focused on converting the historic core of handsome hundred-year-old buildings for offices and apartments. Other areas were to be demolished and reshaped as a corporate center and research park. In addition shops, restaurants, services, and parks would be woven into walkable sections organized around Philadelphia's familiar grid pattern.

PIDC advertised the Navy Yard as a location that was just as convenient and accessible as suburban office parks, having direct access to I-95. PIDC also marketed the Yard's eligibility for government subsidies. When the state government declared the Navy Yard to be a Keystone Innovation Zone, it provided tax credits and other incentives to foster collaborations between research universities and start-up companies that commercialize academic discoveries. The additional designation as a Keystone Opportunity Improvement Zone meant that companies were exempted from many state and city business taxes for up to fifteen years. Moreover, since the Navy Yard is on the National Register of Historic Places, the federal government offered tax credits to private investors who renovated buildings in the historic core. Planners knew that the master plan would take years, possibly even decades to execute. In the first five years of implementation (2004–9) PIDC attracted Urban Outfitters, a soundstage for Paramount Pictures, a data center for the Philadelphia Stock Exchange, pharmaceutical laboratories, and a solar energy center. Somewhat later the pharmaceutical company GlaxoSmithKline moved its 1,300 employees from downtown Philadelphia to the Navy Yard. The Yard currently hosts 130 businesses with ten thousand employees, even more than had worked there when it was a defense installation. This burgeoning job center, easily accessible to suburban motorists via I-95, would be accessible to larger numbers of Philadelphia residents if the city's north-south subway line could be extended south to the Navy Yard. Sadly, as chapter 1 explained, there is little chance that SEPTA will have the capital to build that extension very soon.

Research and Innovation Hub

West of downtown, just across the Schuylkill River, sits University City, the region's most important concentration of universities, hospitals, and research and technology enterprises. While we think of these knowledge industries as emerging in the late twentieth century, University City was first conceived as an innovation district in the middle of the century, when a group of the city's leaders began promoting the area as a hub of research and technical innovation. Watching traditional manufacturing plants move to the suburbs or to southern states, the Philadelphia Industrial Development Corporation recognized the importance of developing an economic base in such emerging technologies as transistors, plastics, lasers, pharmaceuticals, and biomedical equipment. That agenda required forging links between university researchers and the business community. The obvious location to build an urban research park was West Philadelphia, with its already existing universities.

University City Science Center

In 1963 PIDC and several partners established a nonprofit corporation, the University City Science Center (UCSC), with a mission to foster R&D that would contribute to the city's economy. It was originally governed by eleven universities and medical institutions, later expanding to thirty-two partners. In its early years the UCSC sought federal research grants to undertake projects that, for either security or proprietary reasons, could not easily be conducted within the universities that were members of the UCSC. The science center also helped commercialize discoveries made by university researchers. These days an important part of the mission is to lure international business start-ups to Philadelphia by offering them investment and networking opportunities.

The first construction project in what would eventually become a seventeen-acre complex in West Philadelphia renovated a building that had previously housed a printing firm. Touting its location with the slogan "Come to Where the Knowledge Is," UCSC began adding new structures along Market Street. The cost of those ambitious building plans was not only monetary; they caused the dislocation during the 1960s of low-income residents and small store owners and generated angry opposition, including opposition from university students who supported the local residents. The protesters targeted the city government because it was responsible for condemning the property in order to make way for the Science Center's expansion (and probably also because protesters thought the city government would be more likely than a private nonprofit to negotiate with them). Ultimately it took five years of planning and public hearings to negotiate an accord with opponents and break ground for the complex in 1968 (Petshek 1973, 254).

Medical Research Facilities

As the new science complex was emerging, Children's Hospital of Philadelphia (CHOP) acquired five acres in University City so it could move from its cramped facility in South Philadelphia. CHOP's eminent surgeon in chief C. Everett Koop had built a nationally recognized staff covering an array of pediatric subspecialties. CHOP's move to University City in 1974 added not just a hospital but also a nationally recognized medical research staff to the emerging science district. CHOP welcomed the opportunity to expand in 1993, the year that the Pennsylvania Convention Center opened in the heart of downtown, replacing the Philadelphia Civic Center in West Philadelphia. CHOP and the University of Pennsylvania each acquired part of the disused civic center for demolition and redevelopment. CHOP raised $504 million to open the Translational Research Building in 2010 on its portion of the old civic center site, directly across from its main hospital and research facilities. On the rest of the site the University of Pennsylvania built its Perelman Center for Advanced Medicine. That $302 million structure (opened in 2008) was the largest capital project ever undertaken by the University of Pennsylvania Health System.

While CHOP and the University of Pennsylvania Health System were expanding clinical care and research, the University City Science Center was expanding its complex of offices and laboratories. Next to its original office building, UCSC built a ten-story building that rents laboratory and office space to companies in alternative energy, bioinformatics, radiopharmaceuticals, and other emerging technologies. On the same block UCSC broke ground on an eleven-story tower whose primary tenant is Penn Presbyterian Medical Center, part of the University of Pennsylvania Health System.

University City District

This growing collection of powerful and ambitious institutions faced a challenge similar to the one confronting Philadelphia's downtown employers: to assure a clean and safe public environment for the scientists, physicians, patients, students, and faculty members circulating through their buildings each day. They had built impressive structures to house leading-edge science, learning, and medical care, but they had not fostered equivalent improvements in the quality of street life and public spaces. During the 1980s and 1990s the streets of University City were seen as dangerous, particularly after a highly publicized stabbing of a university researcher occurred on a public street in 1996. That tragic incident galvanized a sustained effort led by the University of Pennsylvania to improve the environment surrounding its residential campus. According to one chronicler of this period, "More than any other event, the stabbing served as a major turning point in Penn's resolve to seek solutions to the 'West Philadelphia problem'" (Etienne 2012, 14).

In response the University of Pennsylvania led the formation in 1997 of a new nonprofit entity, the University City District (UCD). Although it operated like a special services district, UCD differed from the Center City District in its legal and financial structure. Rather than being created by the city government, it was established by a group of nonprofit institutions whose representatives sat on its governing board, along with community residents and small business owners. The large institutions, especially Penn and Drexel, pooled $4 million in financial support so that UCD could establish itself and hire a manager (Vicino 2010, 347). Like the Center City District, this new organization concentrated first on making public spaces clean and safe, augmenting the basic municipal services that the police and the streets department were supplying. Soon, however, UDC began to invest in streetscapes, lighting, landscapes, public art, and other infrastructure.

One of UDC's larger projects to date has transformed an area next to 30th Street Station (the nation's second-busiest train station) into an outdoor plaza with comfortable seating, tables, umbrellas, and plantings. UDC borrowed a model called "Lighter Quicker Cheaper" pioneered in New York to make modest investments in rehabilitating public spaces such as Herald and Greeley Squares, observing how pedestrians choose to use the space and adapting further investments to those patterns of use. Because of its location next to 30th Street Station, this new public space serves as a kind of gateway to University City for people crossing the Schuylkill River from downtown Philadelphia. UDC named this transformed half-acre The Porch, hoping it would serve as a comfortable space for people to sip coffee or soda and chat. It has hosted a weekly farmers' market as well as periodic activities like yoga and miniature golf. Not long after opening, The Porch secured a half-million-dollar grant from the William Penn Foundation for further improvements and programming.

University of Pennsylvania

In addition to supporting the UDC, universities in West Philadelphia have strengthened their individual campuses. In 2006 the University of Pennsylvania embarked on a plan to guide campus development for two decades. In only the first five years of implementation the university spent $1 billion to build or renovate over a million square feet of space on the campus. The second phase, 2011–15, is projected to cost over a billion more dollars (Loyd 2012a). Beyond these campus improvements, Penn simultaneously invested in transforming areas adjacent to campus. It expanded a long-standing program to subsidize the university's faculty and staff to buy homes in nearby neighborhoods. The university sponsored developments on commercial streets, introducing an upscale grocery store, a first-run movie theater, and a hotel and retail complex featuring high-end restaurants and shops. Penn also partnered with a neighborhood elementary school near campus to provide extra funding, support, and participation by the university's education faculty (Etienne 2012, chapter 3). Looking back on these investments, Penn's president Amy Gutmann did not try to cloak them in terms of public service: "This is not altruism or noblesse oblige; it's the right thing to do because it can make us stronger as well as [make] our community stronger" (quoted in Jan 2009).

Drexel University

Operating with a much smaller endowment, Drexel University has also undertaken ambitious building plans. In 2011 Drexel completed its five-story Integrated Sciences Building ($69 million), followed in 2013 by the eleven-story College of Business ($92 million). To limit the friction caused by its growing student body moving into nearby residential neighborhoods, Drexel decided to build three new residence halls within the existing footprint of its campus: two eight-story structures and a nineteen-story tower. The intention is to expand Drexel's footprint onto 3.5 acres purchased next to 30th Street Station, where it will build an "innovation neighborhood," combining academic classroom and research facilities with retail and residential space. Drexel's announced ambitions even extend to constructing an elevated platform across the massive rail yards outside 30th Street Station that are owned by Amtrak and SEPTA. (This idea was inspired by similar plans for developing rail yards behind Union Station in Washington, DC; Snyder 2012).

Pushing the Innovation District toward Downtown

Both CHOP and Penn have announced dramatic plans to enlarge their footprints by acquiring large parcels near downtown. In 2010 CHOP bought nine acres of land on the opposite side of the Schuylkill River from its current home. The site lies directly across the South Street Bridge, connecting West Philadelphia to Center City. It had been vacated years earlier by a factory, which CHOP proposed to replace with three research towers, a 1,600-car parking garage, and new restaurant and retail establishments. In that same year the University of Pennsylvania also reached across the Schuylkill River, to buy a twenty-three-acre parcel of land south of downtown. That property, which had been used by the DuPont Company for laboratories, would now house a data center for the university and health system (Loyd 2012a). With these two purchases University City began to merge with Center City Philadelphia—interestingly, not by the outward expansion of downtown but because the West Philadelphia innovation district that some have come to regard as Philadelphia's "second downtown" was pushing inward toward the historic core.

Temple Town in North Philadelphia

A mile and a half north of City Hall, Temple University began in the 1980s to develop its campus and surrounding area using the brand "Temple

Town." The university wanted to shift from being a commuter institution with only a small minority of its students living in dormitories to a residential campus for a much larger proportion of its student body. The goal was to make the campus "a bustling community—as active by night as it is by day—enlivened by residents, restaurants, shops and other businesses" (Hilty 2010, 192). With a fifteen-year building campaign that included new dormitories, a sports arena, a fitness center, state-of-the-art classrooms, campus walkways and greening, a new hospital, a children's medical center, and a medical education center, university officials dramatically improved the physical environment of both the Main Campus and the Temple University Health System, located a mile and a half north of the Main Campus. By recruiting students from outside Philadelphia who would live on campus, Temple built its residential student population from only a few thousand to more than ten thousand (out of a total student body well over thirty thousand). The area witnessed a flurry of construction and rehabilitation of housing near campus, as hundreds of developers moved in to provide rental housing for the university's expanding student body. Yet the university has been unable to draw to Temple Town a collection of ancillary activities comparable to the cluster of scientific, technical, and cultural enterprises in University City. That was not for want of trying.

As early as the mid-1980s the university tried to attract high-tech companies to the campus environs. One such effort succeeded initially, when Bell Atlantic agreed to construct a building on the North Philadelphia campus. The $25 million building opened in 1987, housing a computer center to process customer billing information, deal with service orders for installation and repairs, and handle advertising in the *Yellow Pages*. Both Temple and Bell hoped to train and employ low-income residents of the surrounding neighborhoods, but ultimately the job qualifications proved impossible for all but a few neighborhood applicants to meet (Bear 1990, 96). Encouraged by Bell's willingness to locate on the North Philadelphia campus, Temple launched an unsuccessful campaign to convince the city and state governments to fund the conversion of decaying industrial buildings to create a "science and technology campus" that would focus on commercializing university research, incubating small businesses, and providing job training for dislocated and disadvantaged workers. The university created a glossy booklet to promote the concept (Liacouras 1987) but never managed to sell the idea to government or private investors. By 1997 Bell had moved out of the computer center and sold the building to the university. These days Temple University rents space in the University City Science Center, at a considerable distance from its own campus, to bring its scientists into contact with venture capitalists who can help them commercialize their discoveries.

Several Temple presidents tried to foster an arts and culture cluster in this section of North Philadelphia. The university's campus renovations included creating two performing arts venues on Broad Street in the hope of spurring additional cultural investments near campus. At first glance North Broad Street makes sense as a cultural corridor. After all, it was originally developed as a boulevard for wealthy Gilded Age industrialists whose factories and mills were located in North Philadelphia. A number of major arts venues had historically located there, the largest being the Metropolitan Opera House a mile north of City Hall. When built in 1908 it was the largest opera house in the nation. That massive structure is now decaying. A few blocks farther north sits Freedom Theater, thought to be the oldest African American theater company in the country. It has struggled for decades to attain financial stability. Still farther north the Art Deco Uptown Theater, built in 1929, has been a movie theater, a vaudeville house, and a mecca of rhythm-and-blues that welcomed African American audiences to hear James Brown, the Supremes, the Marvelettes, Smokey Robinson, and other artists. In 2002 the Avenue of the Arts, Inc. (which had championed the cultural development of South Broad Street) began working with businesses, institutions, and developers to promote North Broad Street. That project has so far produced limited results beyond lighting and streetscape plantings.

What accounts for the slower pace of development surrounding Temple Town compared with the robust development of University City in West Philadelphia? First, Temple University and its health system stand virtually alone as major institutional investors there. As a publicly funded university, Temple has an endowment that is nowhere near that of the University of Pennsylvania, the largest institutional investor in West Philadelphia. Penn's endowment is about twenty-five times larger than Temple's. A second explanation is geography. Temple is located in a poverty-stricken, high-crime area of the city. But that alone would not necessarily deter development, as trends in University City demonstrate. Crime and poverty in surrounding neighborhoods challenged the institutions located in West Philadelphia, yet development proceeded even in the face of those challenges. A critically important locational difference is that University City sits next to the Schuylkill

Expressway, a distinct advantage for research labs, start-up companies, cultural venues, hospitals, and other enterprises located there. Temple University, by contrast, is miles from limited-access expressways in every direction, making it a less convenient destination for suburban hospital patients, arts audiences, business owners, or researchers to make daily trips to the campus. Unquestionably the university has succeeded in attracting residential students and the retailers that serve them, but without easy highway access North Philadelphia has more difficulty attracting large numbers of daily visitors. Figure 3 shows that the other development districts share the advantage of accessibility to I-95, I-76, or the Vine Street Expressway and therefore stand a greater chance of attracting visitors from beyond the city limits.

Museum District

Built during the City Beautiful Movement, the Benjamin Franklin Parkway is a grand diagonal boulevard that extends northwest of downtown for about a mile, connecting the office district to the massive green spaces of Fairmount Park. This majestic thoroughfare is home to the city's most important cultural institutions, from the Philadelphia Museum of Art and Rodin Museum to the Franklin Institute and the Academy of Natural Sciences. Yet it is not an inviting, walkable public space because it also functions as an eight-lane roadway where cars travel at speeds that discourage pedestrian traffic.

As it had done for the Avenue of the Arts a decade earlier, the Central Philadelphia Development Corporation took the lead in 2002 to promote coordinated planning and investment that could improve the Parkway as public space. The William Penn Foundation paid CPDC to begin this planning work, which initially proposed dramatic changes that included reconfiguring a major traffic circle to become a square and burying a second traffic circle underground. Those plans were never implemented because they would have inconvenienced thousands of motorists accustomed to commuting in and out of downtown Philadelphia by this route. Undaunted, the CPDC began taking a series of more modest steps to improve the Parkway for pedestrians: installing new lighting to illuminate walkways, monuments, sculptures, and building façades; installing new crosswalks and bike lanes; landscaping open spaces; and building an outdoor café.

Parkway Museums District

To manage and promote improvements along the Parkway, the museums
and businesses in the district created a new nonprofit organization in 2003
called the Parkway Council Foundation. It began raising money for planning, marketing, and special events, all in the service of its mission: "creating a distinctive, vibrant, and welcoming place for local residents, visitors,
and the institutions and businesses that share the Parkway" (Parkway
Council Foundation 2014). One of its continuing priorities is improving
transportation options, with a shuttle service and possibly a light rail line
running its length. It clearly focuses on the quality of the environment for
visitors and affluent residents who live nearby, a mission that has brought it
into conflict with low-income residents. Together with CPDC, the Parkway
Council has lobbied the city government to limit outdoor meals for homeless people provided by social service organizations in open areas adjoining
the Parkway. That effort illustrates a common goal of urban arts districts to
create a kind of "tourist bubble" where visitors are spared from witnessing
poverty, disorder, or unpleasant aspects of urban life (Judd 1999).

Barnes Foundation

Yet another cultural project fostered by Mayor Rendell was the proposal to
move a world-class collection of paintings from the Philadelphia suburbs
into Center City. The museum operated by the Barnes Foundation had initially been constructed in 1922 in a Philadelphia suburb by a wealthy art
collector, Albert Barnes, who assembled sixty Matisses, forty-four Picassos,
181 Renoirs, and many other important works. Barnes housed his astonishing collection in a quiet suburb near Philadelphia. When he died in 1951,
his will imposed tight limitations on attendance at the museum and on its
ability to raise revenue in ways that museums typically do: by lending art-
works, selling pieces in the collection, selling reproduction rights, and hosting events. The institution was increasingly asset-rich and cash-poor. The
trustees' struggle against the restrictive conditions in Barnes's indenture
played out publicly in a drama that fascinated the region's cultural community for several years. That drama was chronicled in books (Anderson 2003;
Rudenstein 2012) and a documentary film (Argott 2009).

In 2002 the five trustees petitioned the courts to allow them to move the collection to central Philadelphia. Three foundations, the Pew Charitable Trusts and the Annenberg and the Lenfest foundations, offered to raise $150 million to support the move if the Barnes would add ten new seats to the governing board for the purpose of expanding fund-raising opportunities. Albert Barnes's instructions had specified that the composition of the board of trustees was to be determined by Lincoln University in the Philadelphia suburbs. That university initially objected to the dilution of its control but ultimately relented, and in 2004 a state court ruled that the foundation could move to the Benjamin Franklin Parkway to complement the other arts and cultural institutions located there.

The project confidently broke ground in late 2009, well before completing the capital campaign to fund the project. By June 2011 the board was able to announce that it had achieved its campaign goal of $200 million. The state government had contributed over $47 million. The DRPA had provided another $500,000 from its economic development funds, and the city of Philadelphia had contributed the land, which it owned. The rest came from private foundations and individuals: $30 million from the Annenberg Foundation, $20 million from the Pew Charitable Trusts, $15 million from the Lenfest Foundation, $10 million from the William Penn Foundation, and $10 million from the Neubauer Family Foundation. The Barnes opened its museum on the Parkway in May 2012, hosting more people in its first two months than it had admitted during an entire year in its former suburban location (Salisbury 2012). Its paying membership now exceeds twenty-two thousand, compared to four hundred members before the move to the Parkway.

Franklin Institute

As the Barnes Foundation was building a home on the Parkway for its collection, other nationally recognized institutions were making major investments to add vitality to the museum district. The Franklin Institute pursued back-to-back capital campaigns to reinforce the southern end of the Parkway around Logan Circle. That venerable museum of science traced its founding to 1824, moving into its massive structure on the Parkway in 1933. Like the Chicago Museum of Science and Industry, it was one of the nation's first hands-on science museums. In the late 1990s the Franklin launched a fund-raising campaign that raised $61 million to renovate fully half of its interior space, with a goal to make the exhibits more engaging and entertaining for visitors, for example, using sports to teach science. Immediately upon concluding that campaign, the trustees set out in 2006 to raise $42 million more to construct a 53,000-square-foot addition housing a new exhibit on neuroscience, along with a conference center, classroom space, and additional room for traveling exhibitions, to open in June 2014. The Franklin's leaders made clear their national ambitions when they boasted in 2008 that their "new ongoing exhibits and live presentations have put the Institute on the radar screens of *Travel and Leisure, Parents Magazine, Zagat,* the *Today Show* and others, helping build attendance and the level of national and international recognition" (Franklin Institute 2008, 2).

Philadelphia Museum of Art

At the northern end of the Parkway, where the boulevard enters Fairmount Park, the Philadelphia Museum of Art made similarly aggressive moves at the turn of the twenty-first century. Its trustees expanded the museum's footprint for the first time since 1928, when the museum moved into the neoclassical palace dubbed "the Parthenon on the Parkway" by locals. By 2000 that enormous structure had become crowded, so the museum bought a landmark Art Deco building across the street that was built in 1926 by an insurance company. Another dramatic move came in 2006, when the museum hired architect Frank Gehry to design renovations that would substantially expand its capacity without affecting its classic exterior. Gehry designed an underground addition built into a hillside that camouflages utilitarian features like loading docks, service yards, and a parking garage—an $81 million project completed in 2012. That was only one step in the museum's ten-year master plan to create new entrances to the museum and major new galleries. Ultimately the price tag was estimated at $500 million. This massive expansion of museum space helps build the Parkway's national prominence by creating "extraordinary, state-of-the-art buildings that will serve as a magnet for new generations of visitors from the city, the region, the country, and around the world" (Anne d'Harnoncourt, director of the Philadelphia Museum of Art, in press release of October 19, 2006).

Family Entertainment District in Fairmount Park

Farther northwest in Fairmount Park, a regionally focused cultural district has emerged to provide family-friendly entertainment for suburban and city audiences. That development focuses on a seven-hundred-acre section of Fairmount Park, whose vast area stretches across 9,200 acres in total. There a Third-Sector organization known as the Fairmount Park Conservancy saw a special opportunity to coordinate and promote a cluster of family-friendly attractions in the portion of the park that had served as the historic site of Philadelphia's Centennial Exhibition in 1876. The 1876 Exhibition celebrated the nation's hundredth birthday with displays from around the country and the globe, attracting nearly 10 million visitors to two hundred buildings built on the fairgrounds in Philadelphia's central park. Like most such fairs, it was a temporary construction, almost entirely dismantled by 1877. One particular building, Memorial Hall, survived to house the Philadelphia Museum of Art until 1927, when the collection moved to its permanent home downtown. Afterward the elegant Beaux-Arts building in the park served a variety of temporary purposes: recreation center, police station, and recording studio. But many decades of neglect and deterioration finally led the city to close it in 2000.

Its plight came to the attention of the Fairmount Park Conservancy, a nonprofit organization that began raising money shortly after 2000 to strengthen all parts of Fairmount Park. The Centennial District is the brain-child of that organization, which secured funds from the William Penn and Lenfest foundations to coordinate the initiatives being undertaken separately by several family-focused attractions located near each other. In 2005 the Fairmount Park Conservancy commissioned a private firm to create the Centennial District Master Plan (MGA Partners 2005). When completed, the plan urged coordinated development of the zoo, the children's museum, and an outdoor music venue, all located near each other, as well as improved transportation, signage, and community development in neighborhoods near these attractions. In addition to the three anchor institutions the plan proposed eventually adding a children's theater, a Ferris wheel, and other attractions. The Negro League Memorial Park was taking shape near the outdoor music center, and the High School of the Future was opened near the zoo. The combination of those individual projects added up to a new center of gravity in the city, devoted to family-friendly attractions.

Children's Museum

The centerpiece was to reclaim Memorial Hall as a children's museum. In 2005 the Please Touch Museum secured an eighty-year lease on Memorial Hall and broke ground on an ambitious renovation that promised three times more exhibit space than its cramped downtown location. In fall 2008 the museum moved into its massive new home in the park. By opening day it had raised over $60 million to pay for the restoration, including more than $20 million from the state of Pennsylvania. But the project required $88 million. To open on time the museum had taken a leap of faith and borrowed tens of millions, hoping to pay off the debt using future contributions. Unfortunately the capital campaign stalled after the ribbon cutting. Fund-raising became particularly challenging because the timing coincided with the start of the recession. The board of this beautifully restored civic monument found itself asset-rich while struggling to pay its debts (Dobrin 2011). By 2013 the museum had defaulted on those debts, laid off staff members, and postponed the mounting of new exhibits. One consequence of this financial stress is that ticket prices at the museum were set beyond the reach of many neighborhood residents, and the museum became a resource for families from other parts of the city and region rather than for those living in the Parkside community.

Mann Music Center

At the western end of the Centennial District sits the Mann Music Center, built in the 1970s by a group of Philadelphians led by philanthropist Frederic Mann. They raised the money to build a pavilion with covered seating on the grounds of the Centennial Exhibition and opened it in 1976 as part of Philadelphia's bicentennial celebration. Like the Please Touch Museum, it is a city-owned facility operated independently by a nonprofit institution. In the face of increasing competition from other music venues, in 2002 the Center commissioned a new master plan that could be accomplished in stages, as fund-raising permitted. An initial capital campaign raised $15 million to execute the first phase of that plan, expanding facilities to include an education center and improving access to cars and parking. Then the Mann embarked on a fund drive to support another phase of development, annexing additional acres of parkland to create the Skyline Stage for popular acts and improving lawn seating and facilities for families and other patrons who want an inexpensive concert experience. With a target of $16 million, the campaign secured significant government funds ($3 million from the city and $2.5 million from the state), along with $1.75 million from the William Penn Foundation and a gift of $2 million from H. F. Lenfest. The Skyline Stage began presenting music acts in a general admission standing-room format in summer 2012, while the larger amphitheater showcased the Philadelphia Orchestra, interspersed with Broadway music, jazz, and pop music likely to appeal to a broad general audience.

Philadelphia Zoo

The third major institutional partner in the Centennial District is the Philadelphia Zoo, which actually predated the Centennial Exhibition by two years, opening on thirty-three acres of parkland in 1874. It entertained about 680,000 visitors who attended the Centennial Exhibition in 1876 (Toll and Gillam 1995, 819) and has remained continuously open since then. At times during that history, government funds have helped, for example, when the Zoo received substantial help from the federal Public Works Administration during the 1930s and when the city government funded the construction of a building for education and administration in 1972. But from the beginning the Zoo has operated as a nonprofit organization relying mainly on private contributions and gate receipts.

After a fire in 1995 took the lives of twenty-three primates, the Zoo moved quickly to rebuild its popular primate exhibit. That $24 million effort drew substantial government help; the city gave $7.9 million, and the state provided $3.9 million. Twelve foundations chipped in, and PECO Electric Co. gave a large enough gift to claim naming rights. In July 1999 the Zoo opened its PECO Primate Reserve of 2.5 acres. That major reconstruction was followed by several more large building projects: Big Cat Falls was built at a cost of $20 million (2006); a new Avian Center cost $18 million (2009); and a new Family Children's Zoo and Education Center (2013) was funded by a $32 million campaign. The Zoo's business plan calls for using all philanthropic dollars it raises to support capital projects, while covering its entire operating budget from ticket sales and other earned revenues. That means working constantly on audience development.

Transportation is key to the successful development of all the attractions in the Centennial District. That is the impetus behind a four-story, $24 million parking garage opened in 2013. The Zoo was able to secure major government funding for the project ($7.2 million from federal sources, $8.25 million from the state, and $700,000 from the city) and to work with the state Department of Transportation and the city to reengineer traffic patterns. Over the long term the goal is to reduce auto congestion by encouraging visitors to use public transportation by reestablishing a train station that had historically served that area of Philadelphia. It remains to be seen whether the Zoo's many suburban patrons might be persuaded to trade their cars for a rail ride.

The Nexus between Government and the Third Sector

Readers will no doubt have noticed how often the figure of Mayor Rendell has appeared in the pages of this chapter, launching new organizations and raising funds to construct facilities. He focused his eight years in office (1992–2000) on reinventing downtown as a world-class destination. As a government official, Rendell clearly favored Third-Sector vehicles to spearhead the civic projects he supported. The fact that the mayor worked tirelessly on their behalf, however, does not mean those projects function as agents of government. In fact one of the main themes of this book is how limited is their accountability to government and, through government, to the citizenry (a topic I will revisit in chapter 5). It is particularly remarkable how little control government exerts over Third-Sector entities, given the extent of government support for them.

As I observed in the introduction, government subsidies for nonprofit and quasi-governmental institutions in the United States come in many forms. Federal policy makers confer generous tax concessions on donors who give tax-deductible gifts to nonprofits. Governments at all levels exempt the Third Sector from taxation, a distinct advantage for nonprofits that operate large facilities such as hospitals, universities, museums, and performing arts centers; they pay no property taxes on these venues. Another form of subsidy is granting nonprofit organizations the ability to borrow money at tax-exempt rates, which means they pay below-market interest rates when they borrow to build or renovate their facilities, and again, taxpayers end up subsidizing the borrowing transaction. To support quasi-public authorities, government often confers the legal right to impose fees on users. In the case of business improvement districts like the Center City District, government grants the right to impose compulsory assessments on property owners. In the case of some quasi-public authorities, like the Delaware River Port Authority, government grants the right to collect tolls or other charges and use the proceeds to run the organization.

One state-level form of government support has gained particular notoriety in Pennsylvania, becoming the subject of acrimonious debate in recent years. A Pennsylvania program called the Redevelopment Assistance Capital Program (RACP) has provided generous state subsidies for redevelopment projects sponsored by Third-Sector institutions. When the legislature created the RACP in 1986 state officials described it as "a Commonwealth grant program . . . for the acquisition and construction of regional economic, cultural, civic, and historical improvement projects" (Wagner 2012, 1). To fund RACP projects, the state began borrowing money through bond issues to be repaid out of regular tax collections. Support was available only to pay for capital investments, not operating expenses. In creating the RACP program the state explicitly included nonprofit institutions that could be shown to benefit the local economy: "A project is eligible for a RACP grant if it has a cultural, civic, historical, regional or multi-jurisdictional impact and generates substantial increases in employment, tax revenues or other measures of economic activity" (3). This state program has operated since 1986 by granting state dollars to local governments or quasi-governmental bodies at the local level, which in turn channel those dollars to building projects.

In describing the efforts to build out strategic districts surrounding downtown Philadelphia, this chapter has highlighted two dozen Third-Sector organizations acting as either district planning organizations or major institutional investors. Of those two dozen organizations, twenty-one have captured RACP grants over the past two decades, most of them securing multiple grants. Table 2 shows that, altogether, the state's investments in these twenty-one Philadelphia institutions have exceeded a billion dollars (adjusting values to 2013 dollar amounts).

Pennsylvania's Republican governor Tom Corbett campaigned vigorously against this program when he ran for office in 2010, promising to freeze all

Table 2. Redevelopment Assistance Capital Program funds authorized for projects sponsored by selected Philadelphia institutions, 1986–2013

Sponsoring institution	RACP dollars (adjusted to 2013 values)
Avenue of the Arts, Inc.	$ 6,538,372
Barnes Foundation	61,331,828
Center City District	16,740,271
Children's Hospital of Philadelphia	37,754,668
Delaware River Waterfront Corporation	2,132,773
Drexel University	31,960,498
Franklin Institute	47,091,950
Kimmel Center	111,763,993
Mann Music Center	10,439,070
National Constitution Center	37,929,737
Pennsylvania Convention Center	414,034,985
Philadelphia Industrial Development Corporation (for Navy Yard only)	12,921,131
Philadelphia Museum of Art	106,923,166
Philadelphia Zoo	35,362,996
Please Touch Museum	28,483,061
Temple University	2,810,158
Temple University Health System	12,065,585
University City District	4,212,068
University City Science Center	17,612,094
University of Pennsylvania	27,982,534
University of Penn Health System	18,104,905
Total	1,044,195,843

Source: Project Balance Report: RACP, http://www.portal.state.pa.us/portal/server.pt/community /redevelopment_assistance_capital_program.

projects in the pipeline. Once elected, however, he saw the value in making these grants. Within six months of taking office Corbett had approved $437 million in new RACP spending across the state, more than half of which ($249 million) went to metropolitan Philadelphia (DiStefano 2011). The fact that the governor was compelled to soften his opposition to these "giveaways" (as he called them during the campaign) reflects the importance that legislators, campaign contributors, and the media attach to the civic building projects they help to fund.

It is worth noting that RACP represents only one source of state dollars for these twenty-one institutions. As we saw, state funds from sources other than RACP covered the entire cost of expanding the downtown Convention Center, a total of $786 million. In addition to project-based grants, state dollars in other forms also contribute substantially to construction by higher education and health care institutions. For example, the state makes annual capital allocations to state-supported universities like Temple. Since 1997 the state has routinely sent Temple University about $20 million every year to replace and renovate campus structures as they age. When all of these sources are considered, it is clear that the state has furnished a substantial share of the money fueling the development agendas of these Third-Sector organizations. That alone is sufficient reason to ask how accountable they are to the public, as I do in chapter 5.

Who Leads and Who Follows in City Planning

Geographers have traditionally used the term *central business district* to describe downtown. That term connotes such activities as buying and selling goods and working in offices. But in the twenty-first-century economy, downtowns that succeed are much more than collections of stores and offices. Increasingly they must offer amenities to both residents and visitors, including entertainment, education, dining, and first-rate hotels. And they must provide housing options for the growing number of urban dwellers who prefer downtown living. All of this leads to expanding geographic boundaries for downtowns. Rather than replacing the office district, the institutions featured in this chapter have spread outward, developing territory abutting the office district in order to enjoy the advantages of locating in the center of the metropolis. As they have spread, they have repurposed land, much of it in formerly industrial areas. (Examples are the waterfront and Navy Yard and the parcels southwest of downtown purchased by the University of Pennsylvania and Children's Hospital of Philadelphia.) Some critics worry that concentrating investments in centrally located cultural districts may undermine cultural clusters in other parts of the city. They propose instead that public planners encourage smaller scale, dispersed cultural developments as a more equitable pattern (Stern & Seifert 2010; Markusen & Gadwa 2010). Those proposals assume that government officials can guide the geographic distribution of Third-Sector institutions, but in practice governments exercise only limited influence over institutional development plans.

This chapter shows how often in recent decades government officials have empowered nongovernmental and nonprofit organizations not just to build individual institutions in Philadelphia but to design and implement broader plans for entire development districts in the city. Third-Sector achievements in refurbishing downtown as a cultural and visitor economy and fostering other development were clearly reflected in *Philadelphia 2035*, the first comprehensive plan produced by city government since 1960 (PCPC 2011). In 2011 city officials fashioned their forward-looking plan for 2035 to feature the districts discussed in this chapter (as well as numerous residential sections not discussed here). The starting focus for the plan was the metropolitan center, defined in terms found in virtually all urban planning textbooks these days:

> Philadelphia Metropolitan Center is critical to our region. It includes the major employment, institutional, and residential hubs of Center City and University City. Many of the region's largest public and private employers are headquartered or have major operations in the Metropolitan Center. The Metropolitan Center is a hub for SEPTA and Amtrak, and is connected to freight, port, and air facilities that link Philadelphia's residents, workers, and goods to the Eastern Seaboard and the world. (PCPC 2011, 38)

Using the headline "Building on Our Strengths" the 2011 city plan defined the metropolitan center as an expanding downtown between the two rivers, with a northern boundary stretching into North Philadelphia up to Girard Avenue, and a southern boundary extending down to Washington Avenue. The planners also included University City in their definition of the metropolitan center. They identified important districts of opportunity already familiar to readers of this chapter. The Avenue of the Arts, the Ben Franklin Parkway, and the Centennial District were especially singled out as target areas to be supported (PCPC 2011, 88–89, 162–63). "Industrial Legacy" areas were slated for reclamation in North Philadelphia around Temple University, on the Delaware River waterfront at the eastern edge of downtown, at the Navy Yard on the southern tip of the city, and on the Lower Schuylkill River southwest of downtown, where the Children's Hospital of Pennsylvania and the University of Pennsylvania have acquired land to expand research and commercialization (56–57).

Rather than being an ambitious forward-looking plan like the 1960 Comprehensive Plan, this twenty-first-century version was a ratification of existing trends, with suggestions about how to take advantage of them. The plan proposed transportation improvement as the chief means of encouraging further development in these emerging districts, for example, a new transit line running from downtown along the Benjamin Franklin Parkway to the Centennial District to link cultural attractions, a light rail line built along the Delaware River front, and an extension of the Broad Street subway south from City Hall down to the Navy Yard (PCPC 2011, 109). The city's most prominent architectural critic compared *Philadelphia 2035* to the 1960 Comprehensive Plan this way: "The new Comprehensive Plan is pared down in ambition. . . . The 2035 report is a collection of little plans" (Saffron 2011). When the city released this new plan to the public, the chair of the Planning Commission defended its modesty as a compendium of dozens of practical improvements rather than dramatic departures: "These strategies all fit together. They are not grand wish lists featuring big ideas that appear innovative but are not doable" (Greenberger 2011). City officials could confidently assert that these plans were achievable in large part because so many of them were already being executed by nongovernmental and quasi-governmental institutions. City Hall seemed to be following, not leading, the development plans hatched by dozens of independent organizations.

Chapter 3

OUTSIDERS RESHAPE
THE EDUCATIONAL LANDSCAPE

A day before the Philadelphia School District was scheduled to vote on massive budget cuts for the 2013–14 school year, two prominent philanthropists called a news conference to urge state and city politicians to give the city the funds needed to avoid the draconian cuts. As residents of the suburbs, they worried about the city schools: "I live in Wayne [an affluent suburb], and I care deeply about what happens in Philadelphia because Philadelphia is the hub of the region. If we let the education of our young people go down the drain, we're in big, big trouble" (Carole Haas Gravagno quoted in Woodall 2013c). While not all suburban neighbors recognize it as clearly as these philanthropists, they all have a stake not only in the city's built environment but in its education system as well. That is true not only in the Philadelphia region but across the nation. The public, the media, and business organizations complain that public schools are failing to prepare American youth to participate in the labor market, in communities, and in civic life. The most scathing criticisms are aimed at inner-city school districts that serve many children from impoverished and/or immigrant homes. Those same districts where students face the most serious academic challenges also confront some of the nation's most difficult fiscal problems because their property tax bases cannot produce enough revenue to support schools. That unfortunate convergence of high academic need and weak local tax base created a downward spiral in the fortunes of urban school districts across the country during the 1970s and 1980s.

The Philadelphia School District reflects this unfortunate pattern. Table 3 shows that the average expenditure per pupil by the city schools falls well short of the average expenditure by the districts located in the four suburban counties. To appreciate the significance of that dollar disparity, consider that if Philadelphia could spend an additional $2,000 per pupil (bringing it closer to parity with the suburban counties), each classroom of thirty students would benefit from an extra $60,000 across the school year. To a lesser extent such disparities also distinguish the suburban districts from each other. Within Montgomery County, for example, some lower spending districts allocate around $14,000 per pupil, while one high-spending district on the Main Line (in Lower Merion Township) spends over $25,000 per pupil. That is almost *double* what the city schools are able to spend on each child. The inequities result in part from the fact that, compared to many other states, Pennsylvania places more of the burden for school funding on its local districts, with the state government providing less.

Under virtually all state constitutions, the state government shoulders ultimate responsibility for providing public education to all children, so the possibility has always existed that states might intervene to address problems

Table 3. Average spending per pupil by the school districts in Greater Philadelphia, 2011–12

Bucks County school districts	$15,736
Chester County school districts	15,544
Delaware County school districts	15,768
Montgomery County school districts	17,372
Philadelphia school district	13,167

Source: Pennsylvania Department of Education, Expenditure Data for School Districts, Career and Technology Centers, and Charter Schools. http://www.portal.state.pa.us.

in urban districts. However, for much of the twentieth century states allowed inner-city schools to decline in ways that were widely seen as inevitable. The sorry state of urban schools rose to the top of state political agendas only when heightened educational requirements for employment began to play a role in company location decisions. During the 1970s escalating interstate competition to attract jobs and investment virtually ensured that states would start to see public schooling as an economic development issue. At that point states became more activist. The result, according to historians of education, was state intervention: "The most striking change in U.S. education governance in the last forty years has been the growth of centralized state control" (Kirst 2004, 28).

By 2001 eighteen states had taken over their local school districts (Wong & Shen 2003, 89), including highly publicized takeovers in Newark (1995), Chicago (1995), Cleveland (1997), and Baltimore (1997). Other states experimented with a model that removes control of individual school buildings that are failing from the local district and places those problem schools in a single "district" supervised directly by state officials. In 2003 Louisiana created a "recovery school district" to take over individual schools that had not met minimum academic standards for four consecutive years. After Hurricane Katrina devastated New Orleans in 2005, the state legislature transferred 107 of the city's low-performing schools to that state-run entity. In recent years Michigan created a similar education achievement system to remove the lowest performing 5 percent of schools across the state from local districts and place them under state control, starting with Detroit in the 2012–13 school year. State activism has increased at the same time that districts are relying more on nonprofit organizations and for-profit companies to operate publicly funded schools. Philadelphia serves as a good example.

Pennsylvania Takes Over Philadelphia Schools

In 1998 the Philadelphia School District presented the state legislature with one more in a long series of annual appeals to cover budgetary shortfalls by providing state funds beyond the normal state formula. The request in itself was unsurprising; such appeals were virtually an annual event. But 1998 was different in one respect: Philadelphia's determined superintendent of schools escalated the stakes by taking the risky step of threatening to close the city schools if the state failed to cover an $85 million deficit. That defiant stance so angered legislative leaders that they responded by passing legislation authorizing the state secretary of education to declare any district "distressed" if it failed to budget appropriately. Once labeled "distressed," that district could legally be taken over by the state. Although the legislation could be applied to *any* Pennsylvania school district, it was clearly aimed at persuading Philadelphia leaders to solve their own budgetary problem.

One might have expected that state legislators representing voters in Philadelphia would unanimously reject this assault on local control of their schools. But they did not. Among the city's delegation of thirty-two representatives and senators, eight actually *favored* the state takeover. Table 4 shows that even stronger support for the takeover came from Philadelphia suburbs. Suburban legislators badly wanted to see changes in the way the city was managing public schools. After the bill passed, state officials refrained from immediately invoking their new power to control the schools in the state's largest city. But the prospect of a takeover gave the governor leverage during several years of intense negotiation with Philadelphia's mayor about whether and how the school district's relationship to the state would change.

After several years of negotiation the state ultimately did take over the Philadelphia schools in 2001, placing authority to hire the superintendent and make school policy in the hands of a five-member School Reform Commission (SRC). State law gave the governor the power to nominate the majority of commissioners (three) and to name the commission chair. The mayor appointed two additional members. The SRC has managed the city schools ever since. As its first chair, the governor appointed a Republican investment advisor from Swarthmore, a Main Line suburb, to lead the SRC through its first half dozen years.

Table 4. Voting on 1998 legislation allowing the state government to take over Philadelphia schools

	Voting Yes	Voting No
Legislators from Philadelphia	8	24
Legislators from suburbs	39	6

Source: Pennsylvania General Assembly, House of Representatives. 1998. History of House Bills and Resolutions. Harrisburg, PA; Pennsylvania General Assembly, Senate. 1998. History of Senate Bills, Resolutions, and Executive Communications in the Senate. Harrisburg, PA.

What motivated the takeover? State politicians—both Democrats and Republicans, both city-based and suburban—saw the Philadelphia School District as incapable of managing resources competently. With a different approach to management, they hoped, the city would not need constant infusions of cash beyond what the state funding formula allowed. That clashed directly with the view of Philadelphia school advocates, who saw the constant budgetary shortfalls as the result of a funding formula that failed to account for the city's unusually high educational costs. In taking over the city schools, state officials aimed not merely to replace local control with state control; they wanted to transform school policies by changing school governance. As states have become more activist they have generally promoted a standardized curriculum along with testing and school choice (Kirst 2004). In Pennsylvania the agenda for Philadelphia included restructuring the delivery of education to emphasize competition and other market features that state leaders hoped would control costs. They sought to increase consumer choice, a basic principle of the Republican agenda.

In line with that Republican agenda, Philadelphia's newly created School Reform Commission moved swiftly to engage a large number of private school operators to administer individual school buildings. In spring 2002 the SRC announced that over forty of the worst performing schools would be handed over to educational management organizations (EMOs), some to profit-making operators and a number of others to nonprofit organizations. Those EMOs were given contracts to assume responsibility for all aspects of school operations, including administration, teacher training, and such noninstructional functions as building maintenance, food service, and clerical support. The EMOs ran their schools within the framework of the existing teacher contract and regulation by the central school office. In effect this represented an experiment with outsourcing the operation to several different kinds of school managers to test whether they could produce better educational results than the district had produced in neighborhood schools. Wary observers called it "the nation's largest experiment in the private management of public schools" (Gill et al. 2007, xi).

The experiment did not yield positive results. One evaluation after another concluded that the EMOs produced no greater academic gains for students than were being achieved by traditional district schools. Johns Hopkins University researchers found that "privatization has been an expensive experiment in Philadelphia. So far this experiment has not paid off by producing better math achievement in the privatized schools" (Lubienski and Lubienski 2005, 698). The RAND Corporation similarly reported that privately managed schools produced no higher test scores than district-managed schools (Gill et al. 2007). And an independent panel set up to track the progress of the Philadelphia experiment concluded in 2007 that there was little evidence that the EMOs running more than forty schools were making any greater progress than district schools, despite the fact that they disposed of more resources than the district schools (Snyder 2007). By 2011 the SRC had terminated EMO contracts for all but a few of the original forty-two demonstration schools.

Proliferating Charter Schools

At the same time that Philadelphia was gradually abandoning the practice of hiring educational managers for public school buildings, a different kind of educational experiment, the charter school movement, was spreading rapidly. Charters are independent schools that are authorized by government to provide education for students who choose them instead of enrolling in neighborhood schools. The "charter" received from government allows the independent schools to operate so long as they demonstrate that they are effectively educating the students they serve. Charter schools may be established by community groups or professional organizations who want to give families an alternative to sending their child to the designated neighborhood school.

The Pennsylvania legislature first opened the door to charter schools around the same time as the takeover of the Philadelphia schools, clearly motivated by the same frustration with the inability of Philadelphia and several other urban districts to deliver effective education with the resources available to them. Having lost confidence in superintendents to manage their districts effectively, state officials joined a national trend toward giving individual school buildings more autonomy to manage their own affairs. Unlike EMOs hired by central administrators to manage school buildings, independent charter schools would be allowed to choose their own locations, principals, and teachers and recruit their students from a wide area (as opposed to serving only the children living in a specific catchment area). In contrast to EMOs, all charter schools in Pennsylvania had to be governed as nonprofit corporations. It is worth noting, however, that quite a few nonprofit charter schools that were formed to pursue particular curricular or pedagogical innovations have signed contracts with for-profit EMOs to handle administrative functions. In that sense, profit-making businesses play a sizable role in those aspects of charter operations, but the ultimate responsibility for the charter school resides in its nonprofit board.

One of the most important reasons for the legislature to authorize nonprofit charters was that they represented a compromise when the Republican governor had to retreat from his preferred measure, which would have created school vouchers. During the 1990s Governor Tom Ridge had doggedly pursued vouchers. The governor's failed proposals would have sent taxpayer dollars to parents who chose to enroll their children in private schools, including religious schools, to defray the cost of tuition. Many critics opposed the use of public funding for parochial schools. Others disliked a provision allowing families to use the voucher to enroll their children in public schools outside their own district; that provision would have given Philadelphia families the option to use vouchers to enroll their children in nearby suburban districts, a prospect that alarmed suburban legislators. Suburban superintendents argued they did not have enough open seats to accommodate transfers and did not want to build more classrooms for nonresidents.

Although Governor Ridge did not succeed with his voucher proposal, he went back to the legislature for a bill enabling local districts to create charter schools. This time he got unexpected help from a pair of Democratic city legislators. Both were African American members representing sections of Philadelphia where public schools were failing their constituents. Both had expressed frustration with the city government, the district administration, and the teachers' union, and had put forward their own proposals to little effect. Representatives Dwight Evans and Anthony Hardy Williams saw the adoption of the charter bill as at least a step in the right direction, even though it delivered no new funding to the city. In exchange for a few concessions, the two agreed to lobby their fellow Philadelphia legislators to vote for the bill. In the end the two delivered positive votes from twenty of the twenty-two Democrats in the Philadelphia delegation, and the legislation passed (Eshleman 1997).

The Pennsylvania law gave local school districts the responsibility to review and approve (or deny) charters for applicants who wanted to operate independent nonprofit schools. Once chartered, each school's governing board has responsibility for the operation of the school, including budgeting, curriculum, operating procedures, and hiring and firing of employees. Charter schools must accept all students who apply, using a lottery if there are more applicants than available places. Since the school's charter is awarded only for a specified time period, its performance must be reviewed whenever the school wants its charter renewed. Despite those periodic reviews, the assumption undergirding the charter movement is that the most important check on school performance is the one exercised by the families who choose to enroll their children in the school, for parents can withdraw their children from unsatisfactory charter schools if they wish. The model assumes market accountability rather than accountability to the broader citizenry. Hence requirements for reporting to government (and thus to citizens and taxpayers) are looser for charter schools than for traditional public schools. (I will return to the issue of monitoring later in this chapter.)

As separate organizations outside the school district, charter schools are exempted from a number of regulations and requirements imposed on traditional public schools, even though they are financed with taxpayer dollars that come out of the school district's budget. For example, charters may hire some teachers who lack Pennsylvania certification, and charters need not honor the district teachers' union contract. Since charter schools must compete to attract enrollments, free market proponents assumed the competition from charters would force the regular district schools to improve themselves in order to keep enrollments from migrating to charter schools.

In the late 1990s few observers predicted how quickly charters would multiply. To the surprise of many critics of privatization, charter schools quickly gained popularity in urban districts, including among African American families who were deeply dissatisfied with the schools their children attended. As in other U.S. cities, many concerned parents preferred the role of educational consumer to that of constant petitioner for improvements from a district that seemed unwilling or incapable of responding (Pedroni 2007). One of Philadelphia's longtime political observers wrote in retrospect, "When the charter law passed in 1997, no one thought it would amount to much. The teachers' unions went along with the idea as less injurious to their monopoly than vouchers. That was a mistake" (Ferrick 2011).

Over the past fifteen years the School Reform Commission established by the state government has approved more applications each year from potential operators who want to establish new schools in Philadelphia. Many charters have been organized around a theme or special focus, for example, technology, architecture, literacy, math, science, or international affairs, or a multicultural or Afrocentric curriculum. From the initial four charters approved in 1998, the number climbed to more than fifty charter schools in 2004. By 2013 eighty-six schools were operating in Philadelphia, serving over one-quarter of all children attending taxpayer-supported schools.

Building the Portfolio Model

In late 2011 Philadelphia launched a vehicle for school improvement called the Great Schools Compact, intended to guide the city toward a governance model that had already been adopted in a number of U.S. cities, among them New Orleans, Chicago, and New York. Less far along but still moving gradually in this direction were Baltimore, Cleveland, Los Angeles, and Oakland. This so-called portfolio model is aimed at continuous improvement in operating urban school districts by expanding the options of different school types and allowing schools more autonomy than traditional school districts are allowed. Portfolio districts promote competition and choice as key elements of schooling; in effect they create an educational marketplace. They focus their efforts on investing in high-performance schools, whether public, charter, or private.

Since increasing numbers of schools operate independently, one might wonder what role the portfolio model assigns to the superintendent and the district office. Superintendents manage the decentralized portfolio with a smaller management team than traditionally employed by the school districts. They oversee the contracts that pay different school providers to run their buildings. Their main responsibility is to assess the relative performance levels being achieved by the different schools and to constantly redirect resources from low-achieving or underenrolled schools to successful or improving schools. In this model it is assumed that low-achieving schools should be closed. District leaders become the equivalent of managers tracking a financial portfolio who work continuously to eliminate "underperforming assets," releasing money to invest in higher performing assets. Portfolio districts seek continuous improvement via "expansion and imitation of the highest-performing schools, closure and replacement of the lowest-performing schools, and constant search for new ideas" (Hill et al. 2012, 11).

Needless to say, this approach to governing schools requires the application of common performance standards, reinforcing the regime of universal standards and testing that has pervaded public education since Congress introduced the No Child Left Behind Act.

Philadelphia's adoption of the portfolio model became official with the signing in late 2011 of the Great Schools Compact. It brought together the state Department of Education, the city school district, the mayor, and two coalitions of charter school operators. Their shared goal was to replace the poorest performing quartile of schools (including both traditional neighborhoods schools and charter schools) with high-quality alternatives by 2016–17. They estimated that this would require eliminating about fifty thousand existing seats and replacing them with the same number of new seats in higher quality schools. The mayor publicly acknowledged the state's influence on this move, hailing it as a sign of improving relations with the state government: "We want our partners in Harrisburg to know that we are doing everything we possibly can on the ground and in partnership with the state to improve the quality of education here" (Mayor Michael Nutter quoted in Snyder 2011). The compact was a bold enough initiative to win a $100,000 planning grant from the Bill and Melinda Gates Foundation, mainly because the compact expressed the signers' intention to "work together, not against one another, to expand the availability and types of high-quality options" (PGSC 2011, 1).

The Great Schools Compact even includes Catholic schools. The archdiocese of Philadelphia, not an original signer of the pact, decided in spring 2012 to join. That made sense to planners because it had become clear that children frequently migrate across the boundaries between Catholic and public schools. Recognizing that families often consider both public and parochial options, the Compact promotes a single application form that families can use to apply to Catholic or district high schools other than their neighborhood high school, as well as charter high schools. This requires all the participating high schools to adopt the same application deadline date. Changes like these deliberately communicate to parents and other public audiences the blurring of boundary lines between the different school sectors.

In other large cities the shift to a portfolio model has been accompanied by a substantial infusion of new money (Research for Action 2012). Given the Philadelphia district's constant budget deficits, observers wondered where the new money would come from to bankroll this venture. They soon learned that, as in many parts of the United States, wealthy donors had entered the picture to raise money to support their vision of a stronger school system. In 2010 a group of businessmen formed a nonprofit organization called the Philadelphia School Partnership (PSP) to raise private funds to improve the city's schools. The suburban businessman chairing the new venture said he and the other founders wanted "more students graduating from high school and college, a stronger economy, and a more vibrant future for Philadelphia" (Michael O'Neill quoted in Woodall 2010a). They planned to use the money they raised to donate to all types of schools—including parochial and other private schools, charters, and public schools—based on the schools' intention to adopt what they viewed as promising practices. They regarded their role as investors, deciding on grants through their investment committee. PSP's executive director explained to the city's business journal, "Our approach here is a lot like venture capital or private equity" (O'Donnell 2012).

The initiative was led by wealthy suburban activists. Among PSP's sixteen-member governing board, only three lived in Philadelphia, while the rest lived in the suburbs or beyond. Their initial goal was to raise $100 million to invest in the city's high-performing schools. Since 2010 they have secured over half that goal in donations, which they have used to grant over $30 million to a collection of charter schools, Catholic schools, and magnet public schools. Almost no support has reached traditional neighborhood schools. The money has come from a combination of sources, including several PSP board members and other wealthy individuals, corporations, and foundations. Some $10 million has come from donors in other parts of the nation, including the Walton Family Foundation (Arkansas), the Michael and Susan Dell Foundation (Texas), and the Bill and Melinda Gates Foundation (Washington). PSP's profile rose so quickly in the city that the signers committed to the Great Schools Compact chose PSP to act as the administrative office for their effort to build the portfolio model in Philadelphia. PSP became the fiscal agent for the Compact, submitting proposals for grant funding and carrying out the Compact's day-to-day business. In effect a nonprofit organization governed by a largely suburban board was taking responsibility for reshaping the educational landscape in Philadelphia.

Why do wealthy suburban businesspeople care this much about the future of schools in Philadelphia? To answer this, it is helpful to consider the national picture. Across the country corporate leaders and other powerful and wealthy individuals from both the Democratic and Republican parties have adopted the model of choice and competition as the most likely path to improve weak school systems around the country. Just two examples will illustrate that the commitment to school choice is spread across the political spectrum. A national political action committee called Democrats for Education Reform has contributed heavily to state campaigns around the country to elect governors and legislators who would be friendly to charters (Gabriel & Medina 2010). The committee is led by a board dominated by hedge fund managers. A more Republican-leaning group, the American Federation for Children, pursues an agenda that emphasizes a more extreme form of school choice. It calls itself the "Nation's Voice for School Choice," by which it means vouchers. The group describes its vision this way: "The American Federation for Children seeks the fundamental transformation of public education through parental choice. We believe public education must be defined as providing families, particularly low-income families, with the public funding they need to choose the education they determine is best for their children" (http://www.federationforchildren.org/mission). American Federation for Children has played an important role in voucher campaigns in Indiana, Pennsylvania, Florida, and elsewhere. They distribute model legislation to activists around the country who are lobbying for vouchers in their own states.

Observers of the portfolio model regard the linkage between local efforts and these national coalitions as almost inevitable. Portfolio models tend to expand the geographic focus of local school leaders because locals find themselves soliciting support from many outsiders beyond their traditional local political allies. In that way they become attached to a widespread network of education-oriented associations, think tanks, business interests, and venture philanthropists. An important advantage to local activists of connecting to those state and national networks is "to buttress their efforts and portray local opponents as parochial and out-of-date" (Henig 2010, 50).

The political arena now contains more than a dozen national organizations promoting various forms of government-supported school choice. They seek a new way of financing independently operated schools that is unlike the traditional private school sector in the United States. For more than a hundred years private schools have been funded by religious denominations, wealthy donors, and tuition-paying families to provide an alternative to publicly funded schools. The twenty-first-century brand of privatization differs from that older model in that it focuses on how communities spend *government* dollars on schooling. While wealthy donors are investing significant private money to build educational markets that offer choice, they expect the resources needed subsequently to operate the educational marketplace to come from taxpayers.

That ambition to channel tax dollars into independently operated schools has drawn both exuberant praise and fierce condemnation from education commentators. Journalist Steven Brill (2011) has written admiringly about the coalition of foundations, wealthy financiers, and President Barack Obama's Department of Education driving the "education reform movement" to promote school choice and competition. On the opposite side, Diane Ravitch (2010, chapter 10), a research professor at New York University and former assistant secretary for education under President George H. W. Bush, has roundly condemned the growing influence of money invested in education politics by what she labels the "Billionaires Boys Club." Both commentators emphasize the disproportionate role played by wealthy businessmen employed by financial firms, especially hedge funds, who are bankrolling the shift toward school choice. What motivates them? They are keenly aware of the value of education in fueling economic growth. School choice offers an opportunity to address a major social problem by applying a market-style approach: reduce regulation, provide customers with choices, and weaken unions. (The vast majority of charter, private, and parochial schools are not unionized.) In short, many of these wealthy financiers support changes in schooling that are consistent with their business experience in the marketplace (Scott 2009).

A prominent group of financial managers in the Philadelphia suburbs shares these values and works to propagate them, both nationally and in Pennsylvania. Susquehanna International Group (SIG) is a privately held global investment, trading, and technology firm headquartered in Bala Cynwyd, a western suburb just beyond the city border. SIG was founded in 1987 by six partners, three of whom have become prominent activists in conservative causes. Joel Greenberg and two of his fellow partners in SIG, Jeffrey Yass and Arthur Dantchik, also established their own political action committee, called Students First. Together the three financial managers contributed $5 million to bankroll a candidate supporting vouchers who ran for Pennsylvania governor in 2010 (unsuccessfully). They also contributed to the campaigns of legislative candidates who supported vouchers. Greenberg and his partners furnished the entire financial support for a political action committee called Fighting Chance PA, a Catholic coalition that supports vouchers as a way to save the financially distressed network of parochial schools in Philadelphia and elsewhere in Pennsylvania. That committee supports state lawmakers who are pro-voucher. The three suburban founders of SIG and their families are active not only in state politics but at the national level as well. Greenberg is one of the five board members of American Federation for Children who govern the national organization promoting vouchers, mentioned earlier. Dantchik helped found the Institute for Justice, a libertarian legal group that supports vouchers. Yass serves on the board of the Cato Institute, a conservative think tank supporting school choice. His wife, Janine Yass, is a board member and officer of the national Center for Educational Reform in Washington, a group that lobbies legislatures around the country on behalf of school choice.

This suburban group has staunchly supported school choice for the city of Philadelphia. Janine Yass is a board member and financial contributor to the Philadelphia School Partnership, the nonprofit that is administering the Great Schools Compact and building the portfolio model. Students First has distributed campaign contributions to four members of the Philadelphia City Council, giving each politician the maximum allowable by law. Those contributions prompted a political columnist to predict, "Those big 2011 Students First contributions could foreshadow a bigger role for the PAC in upcoming city elections. . . . Philadelphia is fast becoming ground-zero for the national school reform debate, a debate where Students First has a powerful voice" (Kerkstra 2012).

The Role Played by Foundations

Another important influence on the future of Philadelphia schools is the foundation community. The current reform thrust toward school choice and portfolio models is not the first wave of school reform to be promoted by foundations. In the mid-1990s the Annenberg Foundation offered to donate $50 million to support school reforms in Philadelphia if the region's major business coalition would contribute $100 million. The foundation wanted to support the superintendent's proposal to divide the massive school system into twenty-two clusters—small groups that include one high school along with its feeder elementary and middle schools. The goal was to provide continuity for children from kindergarten through twelfth grade. A key to the new structure was small learning communities at all grade levels.

Private donors to that effort were wary of handing the money directly to the school district. An example is Philadelphia's largest foundation, the Pew Charitable Trusts, which offered $9 million toward the initiative. Pew had been frustrated when making previous grants to the schools because the district had no real system to assess what children were learning. So the foundation made its gift to a private nonprofit, the Philadelphia Education Fund, relying on that independent organization to develop standards for assessing student performance. The school district had to agree to adopt these standards written by outsiders in order to secure the foundation's contribution. A political columnist labeled the arrangement "checkbook democracy" because it transferred the power to create learning standards from government to a nonprofit organization (Byers 1996). That kind of purposeful, strategic approach to foundation grants has become more common since the mid-1990s. Increasingly funders have adopted their own strategic objectives as opposed to responding to the objectives of grantees. Reforming public education is a widely shared goal of both national and local foundations. To pursue that goal, foundations have preferred to channel funds through nonprofit intermediaries instead of giving money directly to school districts (Reckhow 2010, 287). A poll taken in 2011 by Delaware Valley Grantmakers found that the sixteen regional funders who give money for education in Philadelphia preferred investing in education through nonprofits instead of making direct grants to the school district. Among the most supported grantees have been nonprofits working in schools, intermediary organizations, and charter schools. Among the least supported were the school district and the city government's office of education (DVG 2011).

The nonprofit Philadelphia School Partnership, described earlier, has tried to capitalize on funders' preference for intermediaries. PSP applied for and was granted $2.5 million by the Gates Foundation to support coordinated efforts among neighborhood schools, charter schools, and parochial schools. That effort was rewarded when Philadelphia was selected in 2012 for a further grant as one of seven cities that split a total of $25 million from Gates. To qualify for the money all seven cities signed district-charter collaboration compacts. The Philadelphia grant supported training for principals and teachers in all types of schools and the creation of tests aligned with the new Common Core standards adopted by schools around the country.

Those Common Core standards had themselves been developed nationally with heavy financial support from the Gates Foundation (Greenblatt 2011), so in effect Gates was using its 2012 grant to incorporate Philadelphia and six other cities into its national agenda. One feature that probably helped Philadelphia's application was that its district is run by a mostly state-appointed group of commissioners rather than an elected school board. National foundations like Gates tend to favor districts that are run by state entities like Philadelphia's School Reform Commission because state officials are not as susceptible to local interest group pressures that might stall efforts to overhaul schools (Reckhow 2010, 278–79).

Regional foundations have also supported the Philadelphia School Partnership. The William Penn Foundation contributed $15 million, the largest single gift received by PSP. Although the high dollar amount caused considerable comment among school activists, it was hardly surprising that this regional foundation would support the portfolio model since its president had long championed charter schools, having spent seven years chairing the nonprofit board of Mastery Charter Schools.

Emptying Out the Neighborhood Schools

Most evaluation concerning state takeovers and school privatization has focused on the academic performance of charter schools compared with traditional neighborhood schools. While that is surely a critical question, it is not the central question of this chapter. Instead my focus is on the role that actors outside the city have played in changing the governance structure, fostering school choice, and shifting responsibility to independent schools. In particular I focus on a little-discussed consequence of these trends: the land-use impacts of shifting to a market model of urban schooling.

State officials were intent on creating a market-driven solution to the education problems faced by Philadelphia and other distressed districts in the state. The system they designed did not guarantee any enrollments to charter schools but rather called upon charter operators to compete for enrollments and therefore (they reasoned) to offer families the highest quality services they could produce with the available resources. The goal was to create an open market in education—so open that the state decreed that charter schools in Philadelphia could recruit and accept enrollees from suburban districts if spaces were available after giving first preference to Philadelphia students.

Charter schools have competed more successfully than even their creators expected. Among the nation's big cities, by 2013 Philadelphia ranked third (behind only Los Angeles and New York) in the total number of students enrolled in charter schools, and ranked eighth in the percentage of all district students being served by charters (NAPCS 2013). In only fifteen years Philadelphia's charter schools had built a student enrollment that exceeded forty thousand; in 2012 an additional ten thousand students were enrolled in district buildings managed by charter operators under contract with the district. Adding those numbers together, we see that charter operators had gained responsibility for over a quarter of all taxpayer-supported enrollments in the city.

How can we explain the exponential growth of charter schools? School watchers disagree on whether families choose them because they think charters will yield better academic results for their children. As in other parts of the country, research in Philadelphia has *not* shown that charters on the whole achieve better academic results than traditional neighborhood schools (CREDO 2011; Zimmer et al. 2008; Zimmer et al. 2012). But we know that families also take other factors into account, such as school safety and discipline, the longer school day and year in some charters, the contact that schools maintain with families, and the schools' responsiveness to parent inquiries and concerns. In a portfolio school model like the one Philadelphia is building, parents face an increasing burden in collecting information about all their choices. Since it is difficult for researchers to know just how much information parents possess about schools, it is also hard to isolate the specific reasons for parental choice. Yet there is no doubt about the result. Figure 4 displays the constant upward trend in charter enrollments during the most recent decade, even as enrollments in both the district's neighborhood schools and the Catholic schools declined.

As figure 4 shows, the city's neighborhood schools lost about fifty thousand enrollments in the space of a decade. While that loss is partly attributable to declines in school-age population in many parts of the city, it is also due to the exodus of children who left neighborhood schools in what one local report called a "slow-motion stampede" (Ferrick & Horwitz 2010, 8). A 2011 district-commissioned study analyzed demographic and enrollment trends and the utilization of school buildings and estimated the excess

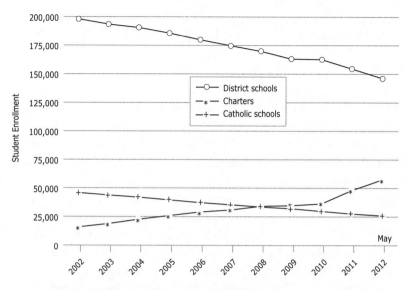

Figure 4. Trend in enrollment in Philadelphia district, charter, and Catholic schools, 2002–12.
Source: Philadelphia Research Initiative, "Philadelphia: The State of the City—2012 Update" (Philadelphia: Pew Charitable Trusts, March 31, 2012), 11.

capacity at about seventy thousand seats (URS Corporation 2011). The study predicted that enrollments in traditional district schools would continue declining, while charters would keep growing, leading inevitably to the conclusion that the district must close down some of its schools.

That was a politically difficult step to take in a district that had not engaged in large-scale closures since the early 1980s. From 2000 to 2010 the number of school buildings had mushroomed from 281 to 355, as charter schools were added to the already existing inventory of buildings. For decades the district had been closing perhaps one school a year when buildings became obsolete. Faced with a much larger number of closures, the School Reform Commission approached its unpopular task in stages, closing only a half-dozen schools in summer 2012, but then forging ahead to close twenty-four more in summer 2013. The criteria used to select schools for closure included their academic performance, in keeping with the Great Schools Compact that committed the city to close seats in low-performing schools. The other main criteria used to make the difficult choices were the number of vacant seats, the cost per student to operate the school, and the building's physical condition. As contentious as they were, these unpopular closings boosted the district's overall rate of building utilization to only about 75 percent. Fully 25 percent of seats remained unoccupied.

The city's Catholic schools suffered similar enrollment declines in recent decades. The regional network of schools operated by the archdiocese of Philadelphia has shrunk from 261 to 173 in the past twenty years. Despite eliminating all those schools, by 2012 it was clear that even more closures were inevitable, given that enrollments in parochial schools had dropped 40 percent just since 2000 (recall figure 4). The Church formed a commission to study enrollment patterns throughout the archdiocese, whose scope extends well into the suburbs surrounding Philadelphia. Parochial schools had lost enrollment not only because Catholic families had moved out of the city but also because charter schools offered another option to families looking for an alternative to neighborhood public schools. And charter schools charged no tuition, a distinct advantage over parochial schools.

The Blue Ribbon Commission (2012) that planned the fate of the entire network of diocesan schools, both urban and suburban, contained only one Philadelphian out of sixteen regional members. It recommended closing thirty-six schools in Philadelphia and thirteen in the suburbs. But public reaction was so strong and so emotional that the archbishop sought a way to preserve some of those targeted schools. He was helped by a group of businesspeople who had already taken over the operation of one inner-city school serving low-income children. That group (consisting of two Philadelphians and ten suburban members) volunteered to adopt thirteen parish schools in Philadelphia, including some of those targeted for closure, into a new nonprofit organization called Independence Mission Schools. They pledged to try to save those city schools by "combining the best attributes of a Catholic education with lean, entrepreneurial business management practices and academic accountability" (Woodall 2013a). The Independent Mission Schools gained some financial support from another business-led organization called Business Leadership Organized for Catholic Schools (BLOCS). The largely suburban board of BLOCS (thirty-two out of thirty-six members were from the suburbs) had for a number of years raised over $3 million annually in scholarship funds for Catholic school students. That scholarship aid came mainly through a state program giving businesses state tax credits for contributing to charitable educational causes, a policy clearly intended to assist private and parochial schools. Seeing the distress of the city's schools,

BLOCS created the Urban Endowment Initiative to help more schools become independent so they need not rely on subsidies from the archdiocese. As the group's executive director explained, they were determined to preserve school choice for families trapped in failing neighborhood schools: "In many of these schools, the majority of their students are not Catholic, are living in poverty, and they're just looking for a good education" (Joseph Garecht quoted in Fiedler 2012). Even with this support, however, the archdiocese was ultimately forced to close a dozen Philadelphia schools, mostly in low-income communities.

Reshaping the Educational Landscape: Effects of the Closures

These massive enrollment shifts are changing not only school operations but also school locations. They are reshaping the education landscape by changing land-use patterns. While there is no reason to think this was the intention of state lawmakers pursuing school choice, geographers could certainly have told them that market structure invariably influences land-use patterns. When they established an educational marketplace featuring competition, lawmakers appeared unconcerned that charter school operators would make different location choices than the ones made by traditional school administrators.

Traditionally school buildings have been built where the school-age population lives, and yet we know that school populations can shrink dramatically in certain neighborhoods, particularly where poverty and crime drive families to seek other places to raise their children. Figure 5 shows the locations of the older schools being closed by the school district since 2012 (marked by circles). It shows that the communities of North Philadelphia sustained especially large losses. The combination of closures in summer 2012 and 2013 brought the total to ten schools, more than any other section of the city. Here, as in other large U.S. cities, school closures have disproportionately occurred in neighborhoods like North Philadelphia, where the population is predominantly Africa American and Latino. That led activists in Philadelphia, along with Detroit and Newark, to lodge a civil rights complaint with the U.S. Department of Education (Hurdle 2013), asserting that the pattern of closures is discriminatory. The Department of Education

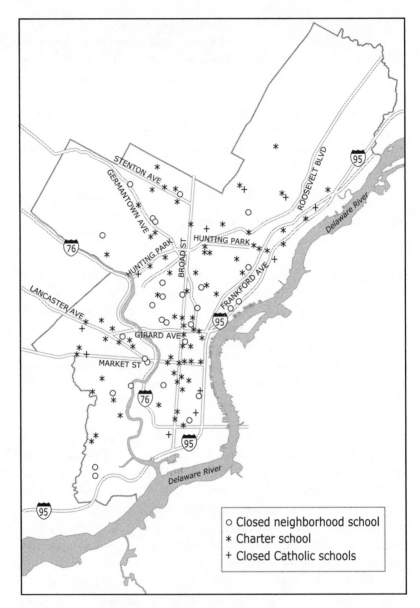

Figure 5. Locations of charter schools in relation to closures of district and Catholic schools, 2012–13. *Sources:* School District of Philadelphia, "School Reform Commission Approves Facilities Master Plan," March 7, 2013, https://webapps.philasd.org/news/display/articles/1458; Archdiocese of Philadelphia, "2012 School Report," June 30, 2012, http://www.catholicschools-phl.org/uploads/School-Report.pdf.

agreed to investigate the complaint but made clear that it has rarely halted locally determined school closings.

It is difficult for complainants to substantiate charges of racial discrimination because districts can point to objective criteria they have used to make decisions. In the case of North Philadelphia, the school district's most recent study of enrollment patterns across the city showed that fewer than half of the available seats were occupied in the schools in Lower North Philadelphia (SDP 2011). That is the lowest utilization rate found in any part of the city, partly because the neighborhoods of North Philadelphia lost substantial population in recent decades but also because so many families have decided not to enroll their children in neighborhood schools. Instead they have chosen district magnet schools, parochial schools, or, increasingly, charter schools.

Making independent choices about where to locate, charter operators are shifting enrollments out of residential neighborhoods and into buildings that are clustered in the center of the city and along the city's major commercial corridors. Figure 5 (which marks charter school locations with asterisks) shows that a disproportionate number of charter schools have chosen locations in Center City, probably because it serves as the city's main employment hub. Parents who work downtown find it convenient to enroll their children in a school close to their workplace. Beyond this cluster many charter schools have chosen locations along the city's main commercial corridors.

A number of factors account for this geographic pattern. First, charter operators benefit from choosing locations with good transportation access, which means parents can easily drop off children on their way to work and school buses can easily deliver children. Starting in seventh grade, students can conveniently take public transportation to these locations using subsidized transit passes that allow them to ride on subways and buses. Since they operate in a competitive marketplace, charter schools want to be accessible to the widest possible audience. Schools that enroll students from long distances gain an advantage by locating on major transportation routes.

Second, commercial corridors offer large, affordable spaces for lease or sale. Charter operators must find physical facilities on the open market. Typically they have difficulty securing mortgages to buy property because their operating charters are guaranteed for only five years, with a possibility, but not a certainty, of renewal. On commercial corridors they can rent large, empty, affordable buildings whose landlords are glad to have them as tenants.

Third, charter operators are aware of the importance that parents attach to the safety and security of their children, not only in the school buildings but in the immediate vicinity. Commercial corridors provide the advantage of heavy foot traffic and a constant presence of adults around school buildings.

Fourth, charter operators are less likely to encounter neighborhood opposition to opening a school on a commercial street than on a neighborhood block. Schools that attract students from long distances may generate significant traffic or increase the demand for parking—a prospect that may be opposed by neighbors in residential areas. Those same charter schools are unlikely to generate resistance if they move onto commercial corridors. In fact they may be welcomed as productive tenants for previously vacant properties.

In sum, the charter school locations in figure 5 make perfect sense from the market perspective of school operators who are competing for enrollments and therefore must take into account business concerns like transportation access and availability of affordable space. But those choices are changing the geographic distribution of education, as school buildings are closed in residential neighborhoods while charter schools multiply in market-dictated locations. That pattern of location choices weakens the historical links between public schools and their surrounding neighborhoods. This result should not surprise us. After all, the whole point of school choice is to release families from the need to send their child to the neighborhood school. According to a 2010 poll of Philadelphia school families, fully 36 percent of district parents reported that their children did not attend the closest public school (Ferrick & Horwitz 2010). That number has steadily risen with the shift to an educational marketplace.

The closure of a dozen of the city's Catholic schools in summer 2012 also removed important neighborhood anchors. Figure 5 marks the locations of Catholic school closures with a cross. According to urban historians, the presence of parish churches and schools in city neighborhoods during the twentieth century encouraged Catholic families to stay in areas they otherwise would have abandoned (Brinig & Garnett 2010; Gamm 2001). When closing school buildings, the archdiocese has asked affected families to switch to other Catholic schools, yet many have not done so. Nor have they automatically enrolled their child in the neighborhood public school. Since these families were accustomed to making choices for their children, many have sought a charter school option. The mayor's chief education officer has estimated that as many as a third of charter students in Philadelphia have come from outside of district schools, mainly from the Catholic system (Lori Shorr quoted in Jablow 2013).

Shuttering neighborhood schools not only removes an important educational and social institution; it imposes the additional burden of a blighting influence exerted by vacant and abandoned school buildings. The city controller conducted a spot audit in late 2011 of eight unused school buildings that had been vacated between 1998 and 2010 and found conditions ranging from unpleasant to dangerous: two had become drug havens, collecting empty syringes and piles of garbage; three were the sites of reported crimes such as robbery, theft, and assault; and three more had serious structural problems, including exposed rebar and broken and falling cement (Butkovitz 2011). If left untouched, the controller warned, these buildings would become greater threats to health, safety, and property values.

Both the school district and the archdiocese want to sell their vacant buildings. How difficult will that be? School districts across the country have found it a daunting task. In theory there are many conceivable reuses, including retirement housing, luxury condominiums, day care centers, art studios, and business incubators. Yet a recent study of reusing shuttered school buildings in twelve U.S. cities found that local districts could find buyers for fewer than half the vacant buildings they wanted to sell (Philadelphia Research Initiative 2013b). As with all real estate transactions, the key to repurposing old schools is location. Developers have shown considerable interest in a few of the properties in privileged locations. The district has already found a buyer for a complex of several buildings in the heart of University City. A joint venture formed by Drexel University and Wexford Science and Technology will purchase the complex to convert to a mixed-use development including educational laboratories and offices, residential, and retail spaces. But properties in many lower income neighborhoods are less attractive to developers, and therefore those already disadvantaged neighborhoods are further burdened by large, long-term vacant buildings.

One sales strategy considered by the school district was to sell the entire portfolio of vacant school buildings to a single buyer. Such an offer came unexpectedly in fall 2013 from a Washington real estate investment firm that bid $100 million for the entire vacant inventory. The advantage to the district was that bundling all the properties into a single transaction guaranteed the sale of the least attractive buildings, since the buyer would have to take them in order to get the choice properties. Yet the district declined the offer because it would have violated a district policy, that selling closed buildings requires citizen input before the properties can be repurposed (Graham & Graham 2013).

In some neighborhoods residents would like to see the shuttered buildings sold to charter school operators, yet few charters have purchased vacant schools. For one thing, the average age of the buildings for sale by the district in 2012 was ninety-one years, and those vacant buildings were likely to be in a state of serious disrepair. That is because one of the SRC's criteria for selecting schools to close was the relative expense of repairing them to reasonable standards after decades of neglect. Furthermore, as already noted, the charter schools' business model does not incline them to locate in the center of residential neighborhoods. Lamenting the difficulty of selling large old neighborhood schools, analysts observed that such buildings "would be better candidates for commercial or institutional conversion if they were on busy roads or commercial corridors" (Philadelphia Research Initiative 2013b, 7).

Although the state-dominated School Reform Commission has aggressively promoted charter growth since 2001, the dramatic drain of students and dollars away from the district has begun to cool the SRC's enthusiasm for charters. Every additional enrollment in a charter school legally compels the district to transfer about $8,000 from its budget to that charter school. Those losses, along with mounting evidence that many charters are performing poorly, have prompted the SRC to try to control their rapid growth. Pennsylvania's original charter legislation in 1997 prohibited a district from imposing enrollment caps on schools. But since 2008 state law has held that it is legal to cap enrollments if the limits are mutually acceptable by the district and the charter. The SRC began introducing such caps into renewal agreements in recent years, only to find that the charter operators, who appeared to have accepted the limitations during negotiations for renewal, subsequently violated those caps by adding more students than the negotiated agreements allowed. In such disputes between charter operators and schools districts, the state's procedures have favored charters, withholding money from the district in order to pay charters for their reported increases in enrollments. The SRC has sued for the return of that money, but charter operators have resisted, claiming that the limitations written into their charters were imposed on them rather than "negotiated" willingly. The SRC lost the first case when the state court ruled the district had illegally capped a charter's enrollments (Woodall 2012a) but is still fighting similar cases against other charters because the principle is so important to the school district. If the SRC can succeed in slowing charter expansion, that may help ease the burdens created for neighborhoods when enrollments shift away from their local schools to more distant charters.

Slowing charter expansion, however, may have the unintentional effect of hampering the district search to find alternative uses for the buildings it is closing. That became clear when the Philadelphia School Partnership offered to grant $1.6 million to the Knowledge Is Power Program (KIPP), a national charter school network operating several schools in Philadelphia. In offering the grant PSP made clear it was contingent on the school commission approving KIPP's application to expand its student body by nine hundred seats. The PSP director openly acknowledged that he was using the prospect of this investment to persuade the district to expand the number of charter seats (Herold 2013). When the school commission denied the request for additional seats, KIPP responded by withdrawing its offer to purchase a vacant school building in North Philadelphia.

Another strategy with the potential to salvage some neighborhood schools is an experimental hybrid that combines the advantages of neighborhood locations with charter school models. The SRC has contracted with successful charter operators to take over some traditional neighborhood schools in a new hybrid form dubbed Renaissance Charter Schools. The particular buildings chosen for this experiment are among the lowest performing in the district. The charter organizations chosen to take them over are operators who have already established a successful track record in Philadelphia. The Renaissance schools represent attempts to maintain schools in neighborhoods rather than closing them down as a response to low performance. Since 2010 twenty schools have been designated to be operated by charters. Some have begun to show academic gains, and they are experimenting with programs to engage the community. For example, Simon Gratz High School, a Renaissance high school serving a poor section of North Philadelphia, draws community residents in its doors with a GED program for adults, a free legal clinic, tax preparation services, and a free food pantry once each week (Westervelt 2013).

While optimists may see geographic changes in the education landscape as a brief upheaval that will eventually settle down, that is not the future scenario implied by the portfolio philosophy: "In a portfolio district, schools are not assumed to be permanent but contingent. . . . A portfolio district is built for *continuous* improvement via expansion and imitation of the highest-performing schools, closure and replacement of the lowest-performing, and constant search for new ideas" (Hill et al 2009, 1). That means no neighborhood is assured that its local school will remain in place. Even neighborhoods that currently possess successful neighborhood schools cannot count on their permanent presence as anchors of the community.

Transparency

When nonprofit institutions provide essential public services, their operations are typically less transparent than government's, even when they are spending government funds. The fact that nonprofits function as independent corporations outside government poses a distinct challenge to government's role as the "prime contractor" in the portfolio model. To work properly, that model of continuous improvement requires up-to-date, reliable data on school performance and enough staffing to monitor the information, identify problems, and recommend changes. However, the Philadelphia district does not devote sufficient resources to monitor charter schools because of its tight budget. Half a dozen employees in its Charter Schools Office have responsibility for overseeing eighty-six independently managed schools. The city controller found that this understaffed office neither receives complete information nor conducts thorough annual assessments, as it is mandated to do. He concluded that the office "is only providing minimal oversight of charter schools" (Butkovitz 2010, i).

In the worst cases inadequate financial monitoring has enabled criminal misconduct, as in 2008, when the president of the board and the CEO of Philadelphia Academy Charter School pled guilty to federal fraud charges (Bulkley et al. 2010). After spending several years investigating additional charter schools, a federal grand jury brought indictments in 2012 against a charter operator accused of defrauding three charter schools of over $6.5 million in government payments (Woodall 2012b). As of this writing, that case is still proceeding.

A more common result of inadequate monitoring is simply that charters are not held accountable for the quality of educational services they provide. In fewer than a dozen cases in fifteen years has the SRC exercised its right to deny renewal to schools, including schools with poor academic performance. The result of charters' insistence on autonomy, coupled with lax oversight, was described this way by a frustrated city controller: "Charter schools are an experiment in using private business models in the educational field, but this is not private money. Charter schools are spending tax dollars as if it's nobody's business—as if they were private fiefdoms" (Alan Butkovitz quoted in Woodall 2010b).

Even when nonprofits enter the educational field to spend *private* funds, citizens suspect that people with money are unduly influencing public institutions. For example, in 2011 the School Reform Commission chose to buy out the remaining years of the superintendent's contract at a total cost of $905,000. The Commission, in collaboration with the mayor, sought to relieve the cash-strapped district from having to pay that entire sum. They solicited $400,000 in donations from wealthy civic patrons, asking the donors to send checks to the Children's First Fund, a charitable nonprofit that collects private contributions to support the city school district. The donors demanded anonymity, which the SRC was able to promise them because the money was being channeled through a private nonprofit organization. However, when the deal became public, education advocates protested loudly and demanded the release of the donors' names. At a raucous public meeting one speaker captured the crowd's general reaction: "We want to know their intent and their motive. . . . Corporations don't do favors for nothing." At the same time, a prominent government watchdog, the Committee of Seventy, formally demanded the names of donors, warning that "the inescapable message sent by this lack of transparency is that there is something to hide" (Graham 2011). The deal collapsed when the donors withdrew, leaving taxpayers to pay for the entire severance package.

Similar public suspicion was aroused by an episode that involved hiring an outside consulting firm to plan the district's future. The William Penn Foundation provoked stiff public opposition when it gave $1.5 million of its own money and raised an additional $1.2 million from other private sources to pay a Boston consulting company to write a plan to restructure the Philadelphia district. That plan recommended closing sixty neighborhood schools, expanding charter schools, massively downsizing the central administrative offices, and outsourcing significant services like custodial and transportation services (BCG 2012). When the report was published in 2012, education activists were outraged by both its recommendations and the process by which a foundation—rather than the school district itself—had commissioned a plan to determine the future of the city schools. School parents and others were dismayed that the unelected School Reform Commission had colluded in this privatization of school planning. They especially complained that the consulting contract was financed through private channels without public review: "Had BCG (the Boston Consulting Group) gone through public channels, the SRC would be required to make BCG's contract public. BCG's specific findings and recommendations, which have never been released, would have been subject to public review. Questions could have been asked about the bidding process, criteria, and scope of work" (Gym 2012). Instead the report was commissioned by a private foundation governed by a ten-member board that included only two city residents; the rest lived in the suburbs or farther away from the city, which fueled a widespread perception that outsiders were shaping the city schools. An observer unhappy about the foundation's role in reshaping the school district complained, "It is a shadow school district that's being bankrolled by people who don't even live in the city" (Denvir 2012).

Working at Cross-Purposes

This chapter has shown that a combination of state policy intervention along with activism by philanthropists created a tidal wave of change in Philadelphia school governance during the past fifteen years. Those changes dramatically elevated the role of Third-Sector organizations, both at the system level (e.g., the Philadelphia School Partnership that is leading the transition to a portfolio model) and at the school level, where charters have multiplied at the same time that dozens of traditional neighborhood schools have closed. Wealthy suburban activists have brought resources into Philadelphia via the nonprofit Philadelphia School Partnership to construct the portfolio model and to attract additional funds from foundations and venture philanthropists who want to foster an educational marketplace. Affluent suburban Catholics who support parochial education have realized that their interests coincide with school choice advocates who want to channel taxpayer dollars to help families opt for either charters or private schools. And they have stepped up to establish a new nonprofit organization, Independent Mission Schools, to try to salvage more than a dozen inner-city Catholic schools that can no longer be assured of subsidies from the archdiocese.

In reshaping the governance structure of public education to emphasize market models, Third-Sector actors have also been reshaping land-use patterns. Charters have loosened the link between residence and school attendance, giving families choices beyond the neighborhood, and large numbers of families have exercised those options. If this pattern continues, it will become less and less possible for public schools to serve as anchors in city neighborhoods. School buildings can make crucial contributions to neighborhood vitality by providing meeting spaces for community clubs and associations, adult education, job training, athletic leagues, drama clubs, and other recreational and cultural programs, as well as health and social services. Demonstrations undertaken by the Annie E. Casey Foundation (2008) have suggested that these activities can increase parent participation and contribute to community safety. Based on work for the Ford Foundation, Harvard researcher Mark Warren and his collaborator Karen Mapp have argued that if urban school reform is to be successful, it must be linked to revitalization of the communities surrounding schools (Warren & Mapp 2011). Their book uses case studies in Chicago, New York City, Los Angeles, Denver, and other communities to show how community organizers created beneficial collaborations between educators and community residents. Unfortunately Philadelphia charter schools are distributed in a geographic pattern that makes it unlikely they will provide that kind of community-school link. Since most charters cater to larger market areas than neighborhood schools, they have less incentive than neighborhood schools to serve as anchors.

This means that the shift to charter schools is working at cross-purposes with many of the efforts expended by community groups. As charter schools shift enrollments out of neighborhoods, they undermine the efforts of community-based organizations to help those same places recover from the effects of job and population losses. The next chapter will show that nonprofit community corporations are mobilizing substantial outside funding—including significant government support—to preserve and rebuild disadvantaged neighborhoods, even as the charter school movement in many parts of Philadelphia has undermined the very neighborhoods that community development corporations are struggling to rebuild. One group of Third-Sector organizations ends up working in opposition to others in a complicated organizational field where the proliferation of nonprofits has made coordination difficult.

Chapter 4

Neighborhood Nonprofits Tap Outside Resources for Development

At first glance one might be tempted to dismiss the influence of outside actors in redeveloping the city's disadvantaged neighborhoods. The challenges of blight, crime, and economic disadvantage are being addressed mainly by the city government and by community nonprofit organizations, often working in tandem. And yet actors and institutions situated beyond the city limits do play an important supporting role in the redevelopment work undertaken by community-based nonprofits. They do not exercise influence by joining the boards of neighborhood organizations. In fact it is rare to find outsiders on neighborhood boards. But outsiders exert influence through the web of institutions that compose the community development financing system. As we will see, the process of rebuilding neighborhoods calls heavily on resources controlled by that system.

For-profit real estate developers prefer to invest their money in sites adjacent to downtown, near anchor institutions like the ones featured in chapter 2, or near parks and rivers. Particularly attractive are neighborhoods with architectural value for historic preservation. Where such neighborhoods exist in Philadelphia, they have drawn hordes of real estate developers, pushing southward beyond Society Hill on the east side of downtown and also into the southwest quadrant of downtown. Developers have also targeted sections of West Philadelphia, as well as neighborhoods north of downtown like Fairmount, Spring Garden, and Northern Liberties.

Yet large areas that were once industrial zones lack those attributes that developers seek. In many nineteenth-century landscapes, abandoned factories are surrounded by block after square block of modest row homes built for factory workers whose lives revolved around local churches, corner stores, and bars. During the second half of the twentieth century both the factories and the people who worked there fled in huge numbers, leaving only 1.5 million residents in 2000 to occupy housing and community facilities built to accommodate a population of 2 million at its peak in 1950. Dramatic losses in jobs and population undermined property values in older neighborhoods and led to abandonment and tax delinquency. By 2010 over forty thousand abandoned properties were spreading blight in declining Philadelphia neighborhoods. While we think of this as an inner-city scourge, it is worth noting that outsiders have contributed significantly to the problem in Philadelphia neighborhoods. A 2013 analysis of Philadelphia's tax-delinquent properties found that at least eleven thousand of them belonged to people living outside the city. The author of that study offered this wry observation about those absentee-owned properties: "Cumulatively, suburban-based property owners are 44,500 years in arrears on their city real estate taxes" (Kerkstra 2013).

Nonprofit community groups have worked against the overwhelming tide of losses in population and property value to shore up these disadvantaged areas. Their investments in the city's low-income neighborhoods have been sizable, as documented in a 2012 report on the economic impacts of the work done by the city's most active community development corporations (CDCs). That study (Econsult Corporation 2012) established that since 1992, forty-four leading nonprofits had completed 1,500 construction projects in their neighborhoods, resulting in nine thousand new and rehabilitated housing units (3), as well as many additional improvements in the form of stores, streetscapes, and greening vacant lots. The researchers estimated the total value of those investments at $2.2 billion in direct expenditures, which generated an additional $1 billion of indirect expenditures within the city (8). Those dollars flowed mostly to the construction industry but also bought professional services, manufactured products, and other goods and services. In sum, the report documented an impressive aggregate contribution by these nonprofits to the city economy.

How Neighborhood Redevelopment Became a Nonprofit Responsibility

In cities across the United States the nonprofit community development sector was born out of a conviction that government should *not* tightly control neighborhood revitalization. The launching pad for CDCs, according to most historians of the community development movement, was in Brooklyn's Bedford Stuyvesant neighborhood through a joint project of Senator Robert Kennedy and the Ford Foundation. In the 1960s Bedford Stuyvesant was a neighborhood whose majority African American population suffered rates of infant mortality, unemployment, crime, and delinquency far above city averages. Many of the neighborhood's brownstones were decaying. In late 1965 Kennedy visited Bedford Stuyvesant, an experience that led him to champion federal legislation giving nonprofit neighborhood development corporations the responsibility for the physical redevelopment of inner cities, using federal and foundation funds. The designers intended to separate community development from state and local governments, which had historically neglected the needs of disadvantaged neighborhoods. They suspected local and state governments of discriminating against poor and minority communities in allocating federal resources and did not want antipoverty funds from the federal government to be siphoned off in the same way. To disrupt the political status quo in local politics, federal funders would send money directly to nonprofits.

Antipoverty advocates supported nonprofit community organizations because they could offer neighborhood residents higher levels of participation than traditional political institutions. The oft-quoted slogan for these programs was "maximum feasible participation." Some of their staunchest supporters hoped they would serve as urban communities' defense against outsiders seeking to control their destiny. A second reason for relying on nonprofit corporations instead of local government was the sense that community corporations, run on a business model of efficiency, would be able to tap private capital to invest in community development in a way that government-run programs could never do (Johnson 2004, 111).

The Bedford-Stuyvesant Restoration Corporation was the first community development corporation funded under the federal Special Impact Program established with Kennedy's support. From its inception in 1967 it faced a dilemma that continues to challenge CDCs to the present day: how to balance accountability to community residents with accountability to funding sources. The policy historian Alice O'Connor (1999, 106–7) described the problem facing the Bedford-Stuyvesant CDC this way: "It established a parallel structure of corporations that dramatically, if unwittingly, replicated the very inequities the program was established to redress. One corporation was run by Blacks, community-based, and designated to run the 'inside' operations. The other was made up of prominent white business executives who signed on to generate private investment and deal with the 'outside' financial world." Part of the reason for this twin corporate structure was that the major foundations that had pledged to support the project (Ford and Astor) were unwilling to put all their funds in the hands of a community-run organization (Johnson 2004, 118). The challenge of juggling accountability to neighborhood residents and to outside funders continues to be a problem to the present day, as this chapter will show.

From the beginning of these federal efforts, mayors across the United States resisted the federal government's end run around city halls and pressured Congress to roll back the trend to direct grants from Washington to community-based groups. In Philadelphia the "post-reform" Democratic mayor James Tate exerted strong control over the war on poverty programs. One historian has flatly declared that Tate "ran the antipoverty agency as the Black patronage wing of the machine" (Countryman 2006, 297). Other mayors were not so able to manipulate the antipoverty program, which they came to regard as a federally funded rebellion against local government policies and operations.

In the early 1970s federal officials acceded to complaints from across the country in a way that dramatically reestablished the power of elected state and city officials as the guardians of federal community development funds. Under the Community Development Block Grant (CDBG) legislation of 1974, federal redevelopment dollars that had previously been allocated by federal program staffs were consolidated into block grants. CDBG funds were awarded to state governments and to all major cities according to a formula based on such factors as the poverty rate, population size, overcrowding, and age of housing stock. Almost as soon as the new block grants were introduced, critics expressed concern that without federal controls city and state politicians would divert the money to projects located outside the low-income neighborhoods it was intended to serve. A national advocacy coalition, the Working Group for Community Development Reform, complained that "funds have too frequently been diverted from low and moderate income persons who need them most" (Kettl 1988, 61). There were racial dimensions to this pattern, for example in Philadelphia in 1978, when compliance auditors from the U.S. Department of Housing and Urban Development (HUD) cited nineteen specific instances when Mayor Frank Rizzo's use of community development funds violated federal policies on nondiscrimination. HUD found that Rizzo's housing rehabilitation program gave only 30 percent of the funds to minority neighborhoods, even though minorities owned 60 percent of the homes in the eligible areas (Davidson 1978). During the 1990s it was widely suspected that Mayor Rendell's administration diverted CDBG funds to support downtown development initiatives. Complaints like these weakened support for the CDBG program even among urban liberals, allowing a gradual decline in CDBG allocations relative to the growing need for redevelopment in cities.

When Congress shifted control of CDBG downward to cities, national politicians declared they were reestablishing the role of city governments in directing neighborhood reinvestment. One might therefore assume that the most powerful influence guiding the investments by CDCs would be city government. After all, CDCs need to work with city government to accomplish land acquisition, a critical piece of the redevelopment process. But beyond site acquisition, how strong an influence does city government really exert on CDCs? Not as strong as one might suppose.

One reason is that the dollar amounts distributed by city government have shrunk dramatically, as table 5 shows. Since 1995 Philadelphia's annual allocation has lost almost two-thirds of its value in constant dollars. CDBG and the HOME Investment Partnerships Program (HOME), the largest federal block grant provided to cities exclusively for affordable housing, have been the main sources of local government funds for neighborhood investment, since there is little or no money spent from the city's regular operating budget or from its capital budget for neighborhood reinvestment. (Like CDBG, HOME funds are distributed by formula to state and local governments, with a percentage earmarked for local community housing development organizations.) Over several decades, however, those block grant funds shrank

Table 5. Total dollars assigned to Philadelphia by the federal
CDBG and HOME programs, 1995–2012 (values adjusted to 2012 $)

1995	$128,854,360
2000	111,683,750
2005	89,362,970
2010	75,568,620
2012	46,836,405

Source: U.S. Department of Housing and Urban Development, Community
Planning and Development Program Appropriations Budget 1995, 2000,
2005, 2010, 2012. http://portal.hud.gov/hudportal/HUD?src=/program
_offices/comm_planning/about/budget.

dramatically. Reductions in the federal block grants have reduced the city
government's centrality in community development.

Another reason is that block grants gave broad latitude to cities, enabling
them to spend federal dollars in a wider variety of neighborhoods rather
than restricting the use of federal money to a small number of urban renewal areas. Spreading the dollars became the common pattern, as opposed
to concentrating funds in a few neighborhoods in order to transform them.
A couple of notable exceptions to this pattern help to prove the rule. One
exception came early in the CDBG years of the 1970s, when the city's housing director proposed a triage approach to concentrate federal dollars in a
small number of neighborhood housing markets to shore them up against
imminent blight. He reasoned that the city could gain the maximum benefit from limited resources by directing its dollars to neighborhoods where
blight had not advanced beyond the point of no return. That meant ignoring both better-off areas and also the worst-off areas in order to focus exclusively where the available dollars could prevent further deterioration. He
encountered a political firestorm of complaints from the areas left out of the
plan. That episode demonstrated to subsequent administrations the political
risk of concentrating resources. In 1993 Mayor Rendell's housing director
chose to run that risk when he adopted a six-year plan to concentrate housing
investments in one section of Lower North Philadelphia. He demolished
blocks of deteriorated and abandoned buildings near the Temple University
campus and replaced them with over four hundred houses built at low den-
sities for sale and rental to low- and moderate-income households. While
the *New York Times* trumpeted the success of that transformation (Janofsky

1998), the reaction in the city was different. Opponents thought that dedicating so much money to a single neighborhood prevented the city government from addressing decline in more stable neighborhoods. They also disliked the low-density suburban style of the housing units, which did not fit with surrounding architecture. Even the city council member who represented the district where the development took place complained that other parts of his district remained untouched (Kromer 2010, 86).

The city's general aversion to concentrating investments geographically was evident in the widely publicized Neighborhood Transformation Initiative (NTI), launched by two-term mayor John Street (2000–2008). NTI relied on bond funds and was presented to the public as a strategic plan for blight removal. The NTI budget for acquiring blighted properties for rehabilitation was divided up among all ten councilmanic districts to garner political support in City Council for this $300 million initiative. That spread the dollars so widely that it limited their impact in any single section of the city (Kromer 2010, 131). Reflecting on NTI and other housing challenges, Philadelphia's one-time housing director explained his disheartening conclusion that Philadelphia's elected officials do not place a high priority on solving the problem of neighborhood disinvestment. The reason is not only the political risks inherent in concentrating investments in only a few places; it is also because neighborhood reinvestment is low on the list of issues that determine the outcome of city elections. Therefore neighborhood reinvestment does not call forth strong campaign promises from candidates or office holders (107).

How Do Community Organizations Get Investment Capital?

The political scientist Janice Bockmeyer (2003) coined the term *contest federalism* to describe the results of federal devolution of community redevelopment and increased reliance on private resources. Together those trends produced "increased competition between nonprofit organizations for public and private grants" (183). Once the federal government began sending block grants to cities during the 1970s, nonprofit community organizations competed against other neighborhood organizations for their respective shares of resources from the city government. Mainly that meant securing a share of the federal funds flowing through CDBG (and after 1990 the HOME program). Federal cutbacks are clear in table 5. Given the shrinking federal allocations, local government is not a major source of investment capital now.

Nor are foundations a ready source of investment capital. Foundations are more likely to provide grants for planning and capacity building than for bricks and mortar. Foundations were instrumental in fostering the community development movement, as Ford and others took an early lead. However, even very large foundations quickly realized that they did not have enough money to become the primary funders of bricks-and-mortar projects. Instead their efforts have gone mainly into planning, technical assistance, and working to develop the institutional capacities of community development organizations. Perhaps the most important contribution that foundations have made is helping to establish intermediary organizations known as community development financial institutions. Here again the Ford Foundation played a leading role.

Community Development Financial Institutions

At about the same time that Congress was reshaping federal community development funding, it also passed two crucial pieces of legislation that would have deep impacts on the financing structure of community organizations. The Home Mortgage Disclosure Act of 1975 and the Community Reinvestment Act of 1977 (CRA) created new regulations that increased the pressure on private banks to invest in community development. The legislation required banks to lend money in neighborhoods where they do business and to document their compliance. Although these regulations were put in place in 1977, the CRA became far more effective in the mid-1990s, when banks were obliged to make records on their lending activity widely available publicly and when federal regulators announced they would not approve bank mergers until the bank applying for the merger documented its compliance with CRA regulations. Those two factors prompted banks in Philadelphia, as in most U.S. cities, to commit increased funding to community development.

In 1979 the Ford Foundation, along with six private corporations, created the nonprofit Local Initiatives Support Corporation (LISC) with

$9.35 million contributed by the consortium's members. Its mission was to raise corporate and foundation funds and use the money to support community development projects. LISC has branch offices in several dozen city regions across the United States, including Philadelphia, where it works to identify worthy projects and connect those projects to working capital. As a national intermediary, LISC assembles funds from all over the country, giving local CDCs access to capital markets beyond their own region. That is particularly important for a city like Philadelphia that has lost corporate headquarters and experienced a spate of bank mergers, making it hard for CDCs to count on local corporations alone to furnish their capital.

Not only major institutions like LISC but hundreds of smaller community development financial institutions (CDFIs) now operate in the United States, and they have become indispensable to nonprofit developers. They perform the critical function of pooling capital for redevelopment projects in low-income neighborhoods. They make it possible to spread the risks inherent in individual projects among multiple investors. Often they provide early loans at low or no interest in order to cover the up-front costs of a project so that conventional lenders can subsequently take on the project with greater confidence in its success.

Local and regional CDFIs secure funds from regional bankers who want to meet their CRA obligations by making investments in the markets they serve. They also solicit funds from other corporations, philanthropists, churches, and individuals who prefer to channel dollars for community development through these intermediaries rather than providing funds directly to CDCs. The reason for that preference is simple: CDFI staffs specialize in assessing the viability of investments in low-income neighborhoods; they have deep knowledge of economic conditions in low-income areas of the cities where they work; and their job is to direct investments to finance affordable housing and small businesses where those projects can succeed. Many corporations and individuals with money to invest in community development choose to take advantage of that special expertise by giving their funds to a competent CDFI that makes investment judgments for them.

For much the same reason, foundations sometimes work through CDFIs. For example, the largest Philadelphia foundation with a local focus for its giving, the William Penn Foundation, has developed a strong working relationship with a regional CDFI known as The Reinvestment Fund. TRF began in 1985 as a small community development organization but has grown dramatically, making over $1 billion in community investments that have financed over 2,670 projects. TRF finances homes, community facilities, schools, commercial real estate, businesses, and sustainable energy projects using loans, equity, and other financing tools. In 2002 the William Penn Foundation took the unusual step of lending TRF the sum of $5 million as working capital for neighborhood development. In the decade since that award the foundation has continued to support TRF with grants exceeding $5 million, including $1.5 million to create a new affiliated development company that could assemble parcels of vacant land for resale to developers who would not otherwise invest in blighted areas (Horn 2005). The William Penn Foundation's pattern has been to make direct grants to CDCs mainly for capacity building, planning, and evaluation, while channeling funds to support bricks-and-mortar projects through other intermediaries like TRF.

Low-Income Housing Tax Credits

Another route for CDCs to gain access to private capital is through the state-level nonprofit corporation known as the Pennsylvania Housing Finance Agency. PHFA administers the tax credit regime that has become the most important federal subsidy program for affordable housing. Congress created substantial incentives for corporations to invest in community development by passing national legislation establishing Low-Income Housing Tax Credits (LIHTC) for affordable housing development in low-income neighborhoods. That shift away from direct subsidies, according to one observer, amounted to "a new approach for government as a sort of angel venture capitalist for third sector market interventions" (Pinsky 2001). It meant that now the largest federal contribution to equity comes through LIHTC, which brings private investment, usually in the form of corporate dollars, into community redevelopment. The federal contribution takes the form of tax forgiveness. The IRS grants investors a dollar-for-dollar reduction in the federal taxes they owe in exchange for investments they make in qualified affordable rental housing. This policy, which was introduced with the passage of the Tax Reform Act of 1986, is now virtually the only federal program subsidizing the construction and renovation of affordable rental housing. It has essentially replaced federal subsidies for public housing projects.

The federal government grants each state a dollar value of tax credits that can be assigned to affordable housing projects each year. PHFA administers a $20 million annual allocation for Pennsylvania from the federal government. When the agency assigns the credits, the winning development corporations typically "sell" those credits to investors and use the proceeds to cover the building costs. Banks, which are the main buyers of tax credits, are largely driven by the need to meet their CRA obligations. (Investment in LIHTC projects is encouraged under CRA regulations.) Besides banks, insurance companies are large purchasers of the credits. Typically banks and other corporations that decide to buy tax credits make their purchase through fund managers or "syndicators," whose job is to match investors with eligible development projects. Through this network corporate money helps to support development deals, usually in combination with grants and loans from banks, intermediaries, and foundations. These funding streams are packaged together in transactions that become extremely complicated to build.

New Market Tax Credits

New Market Tax Credit (NMTC) represents another form of federal tax credits that can help finance community reinvestment. These credits are designed to generate private-sector capital for commercial and business development (as distinct from housing) in low-income areas. The federal NMTC Program permits individual and corporate taxpayers to receive credit against their federal income taxes for making qualified investments in projects that finance community development, stimulate economic growth, and create jobs. Established by Congress in 2000, the NMTC Program has allocated over $33 billion in tax credit authority through a competitive application process. The program attracts investment capital by permitting individual and corporate investors to receive a tax credit against their federal income tax in exchange for making equity investments in financial institutions that use the money to finance development in low-income areas.

In Philadelphia two Third-Sector organizations have acted as the principal agents for allocating NMTCs: the Philadelphia Industrial Development Corporation, the quasi-public corporation that has had responsibility for attracting manufacturing and commercial investors to the Navy Yard (see chapter 2) as well as other underutilized sites, and The Reinvestment Fund, the major regional CDFI. In several rounds of distribution the U.S. Treasury has assigned over $110 million worth of tax credits to PIDC and over $400 million to TRF. These tax credits can assist building projects sponsored by both for-profit and nonprofit developers, and they have been used both ways in Philadelphia. PIDC and TRF have deployed some of their allocations to help build grocery stores and other retail businesses in low-income neighborhoods, but TRF's allocation has been aimed particularly at building nonprofit charter schools to serve low-income students.

This section has described a complicated financial network comprising multiple funding sources that must be patched together to finance neighborhood reinvestment. CDCs typically need a combination of loans and grants in order to build affordable housing for sale or rent to low-income residents who cannot afford to pay the full cost of producing the housing units. Community nonprofits that were once part of a grassroots movement now find themselves putting together complicated transactions that pull resources from a complex web of financial and governmental institutions and philanthropic organizations (Walker 2002; Frisch & Servon 2006). O'Connor (1999, 82) has described the world of CDC financing as "an interdependency and blurring of the lines between public and private, and a complicated system of public, private, local, state, and federal funding arrangements for communities in need. . . . [These arrangements] demand savvy grantsmanship—the entrepreneurial capacity to work the system—and flexibility."

Winning the Community Development Competition

The federal policy shift described earlier changed the mechanism for subsidizing neighborhood reinvestment from direct government support to indirect support via tax credits and changed the nature of the transaction from grants to investments. These shifts spurred new institutional arrangements that gave major roles to intermediaries and introduced a new calculus into decisions about which projects and which neighborhoods attract dollars. A self-reinforcing cycle has developed in which CDCs that have support from intermediaries can increase their organizational capacity and improve their ability to deliver services (Bockmeyer 2003, 183). In this way the strong CDCs become stronger, in part because the tax credit regime to fund community development produces conservative investment decisions. Private-sector funders who invest in projects to gain tax credits appear to be more risk-averse than city governments. The corporate investors who are seeking tax credits do not reap the full reward of purchasing the tax credits until ten years after the project's construction, and projects are allowed to fail if their financial condition falters. Knowing this, the state-level PHFA chooses to assign tax credits to high-performing CDCs whose track record and organizational capacity show they can complete and sustain projects. The quality of the transaction and the likelihood of the project's being built on schedule and on budget are the primary criteria for awarding resources. The winners in this contest are experienced, sophisticated CDCs that can put together a complex financial package of which tax credits are typically only one component. This pattern of a select group of high-capacity CDCs within the city producing a disproportionate share of affordable housing has been observed across the United States (Stoutland 1999; NCCED 2005; Silverman 2008).

The pattern is reflected in the data that HUD provides about the non-profit development projects that have won LIHTC awards in Philadelphia (available at http://lihtc.huduser.org). Since the program's inception in 1986 PHFA has assigned LIHTC tax credits to about 130 nonprofit housing projects in Philadelphia. Mostly small in size (fewer than fifty housing units), those projects were proposed by dozens of development organizations. Over the years only a half-dozen CDCs have won approval for as many as five projects. All of those organizations have annual operating budgets of $2.5 million or more (Econsult Corporation 2012, 15–16). The large number of nonprofit developers receiving one or two LIHTC awards shows that the funds are broadly accessible to nonprofit developers, yet only a small number of organizations depend on them as a steady source of investment capital. Putting together a successful proposal for syndicated tax credits requires skill, sophistication, and time—resources that may simply be out of reach for many community organizations. The man who served during the 1990s as Philadelphia's housing director was blunt in saying that the combination of strengths needed for this task is unlikely to be found in more than a handful of CDCs in any city: "Real estate development requires an operating budget and an internal organizational capacity that most CDCs don't have and can't get in the short term" (Kromer 1999, 129).

Like the PHFA, CDFIs also take into account the creditworthiness of the projects and transactions they fund. Since their work requires that they constantly draw investment capital from foundations, corporations, government, and even individuals, they must establish a reputation for deploying those funds wisely if they are to stay in business. That means CDFIs judge projects based on the same criterion as the state PHFA: the likelihood that the CDC can bring the project to fruition successfully. It also means that the same group of high-performing CDCs favored by PHFA tends to show up in the list of organizations funded by CDFIs.

Roles Played by Outsiders

The complex new funding pattern for CDC projects has reduced the control exerted by city government and enhanced the influence of other funding sources. Neighborhood groups that once marched on City Hall to demand reinvestment in their neighborhoods now must focus their appeals on corporations, foundations, CDFIs, and other institutional funders. In many cases, as the urban sociologist Randy Stoecker (1997) has persuasively argued, CDCs are more accountable to those who fund them than they are to those who live in the surrounding neighborhoods. Although born in an era of community organizing, CDCs moved away from a community organizing model, becoming less directly tied to a community base and more intent on development, which has made them more accountable to outside funding sources than to residents. Bockmeyer (2003, 185) has observed that "privatization and nonprofitization have moved a significant portion of policy making out of the public sector and into areas—CDC, foundation, intermediary and corporate board rooms—where few community residents have access." She concluded, counterintuitively, that when the federal government devolved community development to localities and nonprofits, the shift suppressed participation rather than enhancing it.

Surveying community development at the city level, as I do in this chapter (instead of the more common approach of studying individual community organizations), makes it clear that critical influences are exerted not only from outside the neighborhood but from outside the city altogether. The reality of the new funding arrangements is to privilege external actors even as the role played by city government has receded. For example, I have noted that since the Community Reinvestment Act, CDCs have relied significantly on banks for loans and grants that help those financial institutions fulfill their CRA obligation. Few banks are now headquartered in Philadelphia. Mergers in the last decades of the twentieth century placed much of Philadelphia banking under the control of owners outside of the city. From 1983 to 1998 seven of the eight largest locally based banks were taken over by outside corporations. National banks that accept deposits in Philadelphia can meet their CRA obligations in part by supporting local CDCs, but Philadelphia represents only one part of geographically broader compliance strategies. Under the tax credit system that provides a large share of private funds for community development, banks and corporations supply investment dollars in order to secure tax credits. Those decisions are as likely to be made by accounting departments of the corporations as by offices of community affairs or corporate foundations (Guthrie & McQuarrie 2008, 47). And the investment decisions follow a different logic than would be used to make philanthropic grants. Investors look for projects that promise strong returns, not necessarily those that meet urgent social needs or advance comprehensive land-use plans.

Consider also the outside influences exerted through the Low Income Housing Tax Credits, which now constitute the nation's leading financing program for affordable rental housing. LIHTC assigns the crucial decision-making role to the states. Each state has a housing finance agency that decides which housing projects and which housing developers will be awarded tax credits; in the case of Pennsylvania it is the PHFA. States have broad discretion in determining which projects will be awarded those credits, including the type of housing, the location, and other characteristics. States can take many factors into account when deciding which projects will get the benefit of tax credits, for example, the track record of the sponsoring development corporation, the type of residents that the housing will serve (older residents, persons with disabilities, families with children, etc.), and even building characteristics. State agencies review and rate the developers' applications, decide which ones best meet their established criteria, and award the tax credits.

The Housing Finance Agency's process is highly competitive; the number of applications exceeds the volume of available housing credits. Developers apply for the credits by proposing housing plans, but only about 25 percent of the proposals are funded each year in Pennsylvania. Operating as a nonprofit corporation at the state level, PHFA is controlled by decision makers from outside the city. The fourteen-member governing board includes only two Philadelphians. Of the other dozen members, three are residents of Philadelphia suburbs and nine live in other parts of the state.

The same is true of the large institutions that mobilize capital for neighborhood reinvestment by matching eligible nonprofit projects with willing investors. They tend to have a broad geographic scope rather than being focused on a single city. For example, Local Initiatives Support Corporation is a national CDFI with branch offices in thirty cities that help to identify worthy projects and then connect those projects to working capital. (One of LISC's branches operates in Philadelphia.) LISC's National Equity Fund conducts transactions all across the United States, as does Enterprise Community Partners, the other major national intermediary working with nonprofit community organizations. These national intermediaries perform the valuable service of linking neighborhood projects with national pools of capital, but at the cost of moving decision making away from the city.

As mentioned earlier, CDCs in Philadelphia have a strong regional intermediary that can help them find capital for their projects: The Reinvestment Fund. At the end of 2012 TRF had $672 million in capital under its management (TRF 2013). Yet even the decisions made by this Philadelphia CDFI are strongly influenced by outsiders. Although headquartered in the city, TRF makes loans and investments in multiple locations in the Mid-Atlantic region. Its market area extends across all of Pennsylvania and into the states of Delaware, Maryland, and New Jersey, and its governing structure reflects that regional scope.

That structure includes not only a board of directors but seven additional advisory boards to oversee different parts of the program. The elaborate governance structure involves almost seventy people who guide TRF's financing programs for community facilities, housing and commercial real estate, sustainable development, and more. As of late 2011 only ten of those people were Philadelphia residents. The rest were almost evenly divided between the Philadelphia suburbs and other locations in the Mid-Atlantic region. Having a group of prominent, highly credentialed people serving on TRF's board and on advisory committees builds investor confidence, which is critical to attracting a constant stream of revenues to support community projects. Jeremy Nowak (2001), the founder and longtime leader of TRF, clearly believed the intermediary should maintain a regional rather than a neighborhood perspective: "CDFIs are not committed to locality in the same way as neighborhood-based institutions.... A good deal of community development investment—particularly as defined by philanthropic initiatives—makes neighborhoods and neighborhood institutions the starting point for interventions. This can result in a reification of place and an under-appreciation of the connections between places, households and regional economic and social processes."

Tapping Outside Resources through Political Patronage

In addition to the state's power to distribute Low-Income Housing Tax Credits, Pennsylvania government has a long-standing tradition of distributing dollars to community nonprofits through its Department of Community and Economic Development. That money has been dispersed in response to requests sponsored by individual legislators. Such awards are known as WAMs in Pennsylvania politics, an acronym for "walking-around money." These grants have existed in one form or another for at least two decades. There have been no open hearings on these allocations nor any publicly available formula that determines how the money is distributed.

Legislators have used the funds to help nonprofit organizations carry out projects in their districts. WAMs were ruled unconstitutional in 1995, but the legislature simply renamed them Legislative Initiative Grants and reintroduced them into annual budgets to preserve this important perk. The dollars were inserted in the budget under program headings like "Urban Development," "Employment and Community Conservation," "Economic Growth and Development Assistance," and "Cultural Activities." In 2010 the Pennsylvania Budget and Policy Center, a nonpartisan think tank, estimated that the state's budget contained about $57 million in the categories designated as WAMs. Each year the legislature approved the total dollar amount in each program, and those totals were then distributed by the governor and legislative leaders to senators and representatives who applied for funding for district projects.

To bring such resources into their neighborhoods, some CDCs have forged direct political relationships with state politicians. Rather than openly competing for resources in public forums, neighborhood organizations sometimes link to individual politicians through personal connections, hoping to benefit from sponsorship by those patrons. As an example, consider the Community Revitalization Program, a long-standing source of WAMs for legislative districts. For decades the state Department of Community and Economic Development administered that program under broad guidelines. It was officially intended to promote community stability, increase tax bases, and improve the quality of life in communities. Nonprofit organizations and other community groups could apply for funds to support infrastructure, community revitalization, rehabilitation of buildings, and demolition of blighted structures, as well as for public safety and crime prevention. The award process over several decades was informal, to say the least. In the mid-1990s the state's auditor general complained that the applications submitted by community organizations were handled in a highly politicized fashion: "The decision to review certain applications is based entirely upon considerations external to the applications, such as contacts from the Governor's Office, legislators and local officials. . . . Only these selected applications are considered for funding. Moreover, there is nothing to support a competitive evaluation process, even among the selected applications" (Casey 1997). The dollars were doled out in amounts both large and small. A neighborhood association received $5,000 to support a Flag Day celebration, while the Kimmel Center in downtown Philadelphia received $500,000 to support its 2005–6 season of performances.

Interestingly the high-performance CDCs that have secured the most funds for their projects through tax credits and CDFIs are *not* heavily represented among the recipients of WAMs. Instead that list of beneficiaries (accessible online at http://www.dced.state.pa.us/investmenttracker/default.aspx) consists primarily of several hundred smaller, less professionalized organizations with smaller budgets, staffs, and projects. From 2000 to 2010 the state awarded over three thousand grants through this program in Philadelphia alone. Admittedly some of the city's high-profile CDCs have appeared on the list from time to time, but they have not dominated it. Instead those receiving the largest dollar amounts from this collection of state programs are nonprofits favored by those legislators who exert the strongest influence on the allocation, namely, those who hold leadership positions in the state legislature.

Why have WAMs persisted so long, even though courts have ruled them unconstitutional? WAMs are incredibly useful in a political climate where compromise on issues is hard to achieve. A richly detailed study of Pennsylvania legislative politics in 1999 emphasized how useful these "selective incentives" have been as tools to help leaders build party coalitions (McLaughlin 1999). WAMs have lubricated the legislative process in a state composed of dramatically different communities and even different political cultures. (When he worked for gubernatorial candidate Robert Casey in 1986, James Carvell described Pennsylvania as "Philadelphia in the east, Pittsburgh in the west, and Alabama in the middle.") Over the past decade leaders trying to form majorities to pass legislation have often dispensed WAMs for district-level projects in return for votes. This is a common practice in legislatures at all levels of government, particularly as party ideologies have hardened and made it increasingly difficult to forge any policy consensus across party lines. In many legislative bodies now, the *only* way to build a coalition is by promising tangible rewards to members' districts in return for votes.

Nicole Marwell (2007) has portrayed the positive side of patronage relationships that connect community nonprofits to state politicians. Her book about community organizing in Brooklyn describes a triad formed by a state legislator, a community organization, and voters in one legislative district. The nonprofit organization became an intermediary in transactions that exchanged government resources for electoral support from neighborhood voters (111–12). That model has become increasingly common as nonprofits have taken on more responsibilities in the privatized pattern of urban development and service provision. The benefit of this model, according to Marwell, is that it allows poor neighborhoods to turn their voting power into leverage. Focusing on State Assemblyman Vito Lopez, who represented one of the poorest districts in the nation, she observed, "Lopez has very limited access to campaign donations from his constituents. He concentrates instead on building and maintaining a reliable voting constituency. . . . By reliably delivering his constituency, Lopez gains increased access to government resources" (114). The Brooklyn community-based organization (CBO) mobilized clients and staff into a reliable voting bloc to support Assemblyman Lopez and in return received his patronage in securing state resources for them. Marwell regards this is an inevitable result of the CBO's position in the state funding system: "Decisions about awarding government contracts are almost always made outside of the neighborhoods where CBOs . . . operate. Thus, to the extent that CBOs are dependent upon government contracts to continue providing services and to survive as organizations, they have a built-in incentive to try to influence those bigger systems that decide how contracts are disbursed" (110).

Others disagree with Marwell's call for community organizations to act as political middle men, delivering votes in exchange for government largesse. Robert Mark Silverman (2009) argues that when organizations accept spoils from political machines, decision making and agenda setting are predominantly top-down processes that discourage dissent from the grassroots. Such arrangements lack any formal mandates for citizen participation, incentives for empowering the poor, or transparency in decision making (19). Silverman's reservations have been echoed in Philadelphia by critics of the way that several high-profile state politicians have used nonprofit CDCs to their advantage.

Legislative Patronage to Favored CDCs

Pennsylvania legislators in the best position to disburse WAMs are legislative leaders. The publicly available data on grants made to communities from these programs reveal that by far the largest dollar amounts have gone to nonprofits in the districts represented by legislators who held leadership positions. The three most powerful representatives to the state legislature from Philadelphia over the past two decades brought sums to their own districts far larger than the money allocated to other legislative districts. In fact the extreme disproportion of spoils going to their districts fueled criticism of WAMs from fellow legislators who watched their own districts being shortchanged.

The three legislators described below represent different types of Philadelphia neighborhoods. The first is a working-class brick row-house district in the lower northeast section of the city. Once entirely white, the area has attracted new African American and immigrant residents across the past decade. The Mayfair neighborhood, as it is known, first elected John Perzel to the state Assembly in 1978 and regularly reelected him as one of the few Republicans representing the city. Over decades Perzel steadily gained seniority, eventually becoming majority leader of the lower chamber in 1994. That made him arguably the Philadelphian with the most clout in the state capitol, yet Perzel preferred to maintain a low profile. Political reporters described him as "the consummate insider, not a public figure" (Infield 2001). As a legislative leader, Perzel distributed WAMs to fellow legislators to gain support for legislation. One of his arch rivals in the legislature complained about his constant reliance on side payments, "It is certainly not his agility or innovations that made him powerful. . . . It is raw cash on the barrelhead"

(Democratic House member Bill DeWeese quoted in Infield 2001). Although he represented a city district, Perzel did not necessarily garner support from his fellow legislators (mostly Democratic) from Philadelphia, nor did he help them. He actually encouraged anti-Philadelphia sentiments in some parts of Pennsylvania if it helped his Republican Party to maintain a majority in the state capital. He was even known to target his legislative enemies in various parts of the state by running ads that accused them of being too friendly to Philadelphia.

In 2000 Perzel almost lost his seat to a Democratic opponent. That close call convinced him he needed to invest more in his home district to protect his own seat. In that year Perzel and his supporters established the Mayfair Community Development Corporation to serve his political base in the Mayfair neighborhood. From 2000 to 2010 Perzel funneled $10.6 million into that one organization through a steady stream of WAMs. That extraordinary state largesse helped the CDC to buy a former adult movie house and renovate it as a multipurpose facility specializing in live theater productions, to undertake $2 million in streetscape improvements on the main commercial corridor, and to build a community center for athletic and other civic associations. The funding stream dried up abruptly in 2010, when Perzel lost an election after being indicted for misusing government funds for campaign purposes (a charge that was completely unrelated to his use of WAMs). Ultimately Perzel pleaded guilty and was sentenced to thirty months in prison. Subsequently the Mayfair CDC continued to operate with a much-reduced staff and budget, and the restored theater closed. The business model had assumed a continuing stream of state grants that was no longer available.

In another neighborhood known as West Oak Lane, the Ogontz Avenue Revitalization Corporation (OARC) is a nonprofit founded by State Representative Dwight Evans to rebuild declining residential blocks and commercial strips in this northwest section, whose housing stock looks similar to Mayfair's but is occupied predominantly by African American families. By the 1970s that housing had begun to decline, and community leaders pressed the city for loans and grants to help residents make repairs and improvements. The city's housing officials denied those requests because federal officials had warned that Philadelphia was already spreading its housing dollars too thin (Peters 1978). So when Evans was elected as a young politician in 1981 to represent the district in the state House of Representa-

tives, he established a new CDC to undertake neighborhood improvements
in his district with support from the state. Evans became an especially effective champion for OARC once he ascended to the chairmanship of the House
Appropriations Committee, where he was the ranking Democrat for twenty
years and chaired the committee from 2006 to 2010. He built OARC from
an informal neighborhood association to a large, professionally staffed nonprofit. During the ten years from 2000 to 2010 Evans secured an astonishing
$29 million in WAMs for programs and activities sponsored by OARC—a
sum far larger than any other organization in the state received from that
program during the same decade.

OARC used these funds for elderly homeowners to weatherize their
homes, for children's recreation, for small business loans, and to operate a restaurant and nightclub owned by the community organization, along with an
annual jazz festival and street fair. Even critics who questioned whether
nonprofit organizations should own nightclubs or restaurants conceded that
this legislator had succeeded in bringing resources to a declining district
that badly needed investment. Ultimately he lost his leadership position on
the Appropriations Committee when his fellow Democrats ousted him,
largely because of his blatant favoritism in dispersing WAMs to his own
OARC. His opponents were especially critical of state support for the jazz
and arts festival that the organization sponsored each year starting in 2004,
a project that received WAMs of close to $1 million annually during its last
few years. Once Evans lost his leadership position, the state subsidy dried up
and the jazz festival was discontinued. In fact the state government froze
all funding to OARC in late 2012 and restored it only after OARC agreed to
return $1.2 million in public funds and accept tighter spending controls
(Martin 2013).

A third powerful legislator who secured state funds for CDCs in his district was Vincent Fumo, who was first elected to the state Senate in 1978
and rose to become the ranking Democrat on the Senate Appropriations
Committee from 1984 to 2007. He represented a district extending north
from the southern tip of Philadelphia through downtown and into a few
gentrifying areas above downtown. Since senatorial districts are larger than
house districts, Fumo represented more varied neighborhoods than the
other two politicians. He created two nonprofit organizations while building his career in the state capital. In the southern part of his district he
founded Citizens' Alliance for Better Neighborhoods in 1993, with a stated

mission of rebuilding South Philadelphia communities. In the northern section of his district he created the Spring Garden Community Development Corporation in 1994 to help revitalize a section of the city near the Parkway Museums District.

Both of those organizations benefited from WAMs, although at lower dollar amounts than the CDCs cited earlier. From 2000 to 2010 Citizens' Alliance received $1.3 million, about the same amount received by Spring Garden CDC. If he was less active in seeking WAM dollars for his nonprofits, Fumo was far more aggressive than his legislative colleagues in tapping other sources of funds. In 1998 Fumo played a central role in negotiating the terms by which PECO Energy Company would relinquish its monopoly and begin competing against other utility companies in Pennsylvania. During those negotiations Fumo persuaded PECO to secretly donate $17 million to Citizens' Alliance. Fumo also used his political influence to pressure the Delaware River Port Authority (a bistate nongovernmental authority described in chapter 1) to spend some of its community development funds to support his two nonprofits; a total of $15 million was split between the two CDCs in Fumo's district (Kurland 2010). These financial manipulations eventually attracted the attention of law enforcement, and Fumo was convicted in 2009 on federal corruption charges, including misusing state funds and appropriating money from Citizens' Alliance for his personal use. He was sentenced to five years in prison.

In her Brooklyn study Marwell interpreted the patronage relationship as a voluntary exchange between a state legislator and a Brooklyn CDC that made effective use of neighborhood votes to secure government resources that would otherwise not come into a disadvantaged community. But in the Philadelphia examples state legislators literally created nonprofit CDCs as their instruments to pursue pet projects. Granted, most of those projects benefited constituents, while only a few were purely self-serving and illegitimate. Yet they prompted deep suspicion that the nonprofits served as a convenient place to park funds over which the legislative patron would then exercise control. And they raised questions about the disproportionate disbursements of state funds without reasonable standards of accountability for the money. These high-profile cases prompted newspapers, public interest groups, and legislators to demand reforms. The *Philadelphia Inquirer* editorialized about them, pointing out that these nonprofit community organizations "serve as political juice for legislators, fostering goodwill, patronage jobs, and contracts through tax dollars" (Editorial Board 2010). In response, the upper house of the legislature amended its rules in 2012 to establish stricter standards for senators involving themselves in operating nonprofits (Rules of the Senate of Pennsylvania 2013). The new rules prevented any senator from starting a nonprofit for the purpose of drawing down state grant money. They also prohibited senators from exercising sole control over nonprofits or assigning legislative staff members to provide services to nonprofits.

The public pressure for reform led Governor Tom Corbett to eliminate WAMs from his budget for the 2011–12 fiscal year, an action that played well to an outraged public but had troublesome consequences for his ability to form legislative coalitions. Afterward the governor candidly admitted that his legislative agenda had suffered from the absence of the kind of grants that had helped previous governors to forge coalitions: "You know, there were some bills, and I'm not going to go into which ones, all I needed was five votes . . . but I had nothing to negotiate with without the WAMs" (quoted in Wilson 2012). Some in the state capitol believe the governor and key legislators quietly reintroduced a form of WAMs into a $2.3 billion transportation bill that passed in 2013. Buried in that bill was a set-aside of $60 million each year to be divided among modest-size "transportation-related" projects across the state, at the discretion of the Commonwealth Financing Authority. That body is controlled by legislative leaders. In addition the bill assigned a separate pot of $40 million for the state transportation secretary to distribute for worthy purposes. Capitol watchers saw these moves as signals that political leaders have recognized their need for discretionary resources they can deploy to build legislative support for their agenda (Couloumbis 2013).

The public outrage over individual legislators funneling major dollars to their favored organizations, combined with a general trend toward cutbacks, also led Corbett to rewrite the rules governing Redevelopment Assistance Capital Program, a program I discussed in chapter 2. The governor had promised during his campaign to reform RACP, and once in office he introduced new guidelines to limit spending to $125 million a year. (The program had averaged more than $500 million a year during Governor Rendell's administration, subject to various ups and downs in funding levels.) Governor Corbett also changed the emphasis to give priority to large regional economic development projects; he established a defined application process and revamped the evaluation and selection system, promising transparency and thorough monitoring and reporting.

Community Reinvestment Has Not Fundamentally Reshaped the City

As noted earlier, Philadelphia CDCs have invested over $2 billion during the past twenty years. That is an impressive sum. The question this chapter raises is whether there is any evidence that those considerable investments were intended to address the competitive challenges facing the broader region. Thought leaders in rebuilding inner cities have stressed the importance of "linking the possibilities of the inner city to the regional economy," that is, positioning urban neighborhoods to both contribute to and take advantage of regional economic growth (Nowak 1997, 7). The neighborhoods with the most obvious potential are those located near ports, highways, central business districts, and other nodes where the region connects with the world. Had community development funds been strategically spent to bolster Philadelphia's role as a regional hub, we would expect to see disproportionate improvements in neighborhoods near employment centers like the airport or neighborhoods near transportation that could carry passengers to employment centers in the suburbs. In short, we might discern some strategic design underlying the pattern of community reinvestment.

Alert to external designs on urban neighborhoods, certain scholars studying community development corporations have actually posited that CDCs have become the agents of large external forces, carrying out the strategic intent of outsiders. Perhaps the strongest statement of this view is Silverman's (2001, 241) assertion that "these organizations [CDCs] primarily exist to implement projects and programs for larger institutions. . . . In effect, CDCs act as subcontractors in the broader community development industry system. In this capacity they relieve larger public, private and nonprofit organizations of many of the risks associated with neighborhood revitalization efforts."

It is easy to see the reason for these worries. This chapter has shown that the dollars that finance CDC construction projects come increasingly from outside the city, through a complicated financial system that channels CRA-related loans and grants through CDFIs and arranges corporate tax credits through syndicators. Corporate funds are critical components in the financial packages put together by CDCs, but it is difficult to conclude that corporations deploy their contributions to impose specific development agendas on recipients. In fact, as the urban scholars Todd Swanstrom and Julia Koschinsky (2000, 80) have observed, "the corporate sector is largely indifferent to policy priorities within community development as long as they do not impinge on private sector profitability." Resources also flow to community development through political patronage. Yet looking at Philadelphia it is hard to see any geographic pattern being imposed on the city's territory by these external forces. The complex system of financing produces no pattern reflecting any particular strategic intent for the city.

Nor does Philadelphia's government impose a strategic template for revitalizing neighborhoods. Despite the presence of over forty thousand vacant parcels of land in parts of North, South, and West Philadelphia near central Philadelphia, city officials have had only limited ability to guide community development. A traditional obstacle has been the difficulties the city has faced in turning vacant properties over to CDCs. Most vacant properties are privately owned, and the system for transferring vacant and abandoned properties to new owners has proven to be byzantine, time-consuming, and frustrating to renovators trying to acquire derelict parcels. A typical story is that of Habitat for Humanity Philadelphia, which took three years to assembly twenty parcels in North Philadelphia that it needed to build fourteen houses (Graham 2012). For years city staffers have worked—until recently without success—to streamline the property acquisition process (Econsult Corporation 2010; LISC 2010). A decade ago the Philadelphia Association of Community Development Corporations proposed a land bank as a solution to the problem: "Philadelphia must change the way it handles vacant land. Under the current system, which has put a wet blanket on redevelopment for years, it can take 54 separate steps by 12 different city agencies for the city to acquire a vacant property and turn it over to a redeveloper. A key solution is a Land Bank . . . which would put all vacant land in the city under one administrative roof, assemble developable sites, and set up straightforward procedures for CDCs and other redevelopers to withdraw land on which to build" (PACDC 2003, 3). We will return to the topic of the land bank in the concluding chapter, to consider whether the recent establishment of a city land bank may offer planners greater leverage on broad development patterns.

Other factors also discourage city administrators from pursuing a strategic plan for neighborhood reinvestment. That is not because city planners doubt the benefit to be gained by a strategic approach. In fact the comprehensive city plan "Philadelphia 2035" set forth specific criteria that should govern the location of public investments in neighborhood revitalization: "The location of new housing, particularly housing supported by government funding, should be prioritized based on adjacency to existing community assets and strengths." The specific factors that should determine reinvestment priorities, city planners argued, are "educational and medical institutions, thriving commercial corridors, rail transit stations, highway interchanges, major arterials, airport-noise zones, the 100-year floodplain, open space, preservation areas, and compatible land uses" (PCPC 2011, 47, 74). The trouble with that planning exercise was that it resulted in identifying as many as 1,800 acres of underutilized land suitable for residential reinvestment and three hundred more acres suitable for commercial redevelopment, but rather than rank those locations in any way, the city planners chose to draft eighteen separate neighborhood plans, assigning no timetables or priorities within or between neighborhoods. That was a politically safer course than selecting a few sections of the city to be given priority for city resources while other areas were told to wait.

The bottom line is that the city government does not control CDC production because it simply does not control enough resources to do so. City officials don't even try very hard to concentrate their limited funds strategically. The city's housing director during the 1990s openly acknowledged that he sometimes had difficulty knowing which of the CDC projects proposed for city funds would actually get built. Not being able to predict with certainty, the city government deliberately promised to contribute more dollars than it could deliver, and then paid only those CDCs whose projects actually materialized. The housing director estimated that promises exceeded payouts by four to one. The pattern of construction that resulted was not determined by a strategic plan but simply by which CDCs could ultimately deliver on construction (Kromer 1999, 76–79).

Nor does the state government, which *does* control significant resources in the form of tax credits, distribute those credits to influence land-use patterns. At least it has not done so yet. Interestingly some state officials have argued for trying to consciously use LIHTC decisions to create a different geographic distribution of affordable housing in the Philadelphia region.

Their effort echoes concerns voiced nationally that LIHTCs are distributed across the United States in ways that reinforce racial and economic segregation by favoring inner-city neighborhoods instead of building affordable housing in neighborhoods farther away from inner cities (Neuwirth 2004). That same point was made by Pennsylvania critics of LIHTC. Their state-level report argued that the criteria adopted by Pennsylvania for the distribution of its housing tax credits "inadvertently reward the placement of additional affordable apartments in concentrated poverty and often distressed neighborhoods and do not factor in the costs associated with ongoing (or worsening) economic and racial segregation—patterns that isolate lower-income families far from economic opportunity" (Buki et al. 2007, 15). That report recommended altering LIHTC distributions so as to provide affordable housing in areas with strong markets and close proximity to employment. Philadelphia's own housing director has expressed similar sentiments: "The last thing that highly-distressed urban communities need is more low-income housing" (Kromer 2010, 298). Although the state report called upon PHFA to use tax credits strategically to redistribute affordable housing from the poorest to more affluent communities, there is no evidence that PHFA has followed that advice, possibly because of the political hazards of adopting such a strategy. Higher income communities are notoriously unwelcoming to affordable housing being built in their neighborhoods.

The pattern in this chapter therefore differs from the one described in the previous two chapters. In chapter 2 we saw nonprofit institutions reshaping development districts of the city's core, creating new centers of development that have been incorporated into the city government's strategic land-use plan, "Philadelphia 2035." In chapter 3 we observed that the city's shift toward a portfolio model of education has significantly changed the geographic distribution of educational facilities, replacing neighborhood schools with charters clustered along commercial corridors. But neighborhood reinvestment by CDCs has not produced significant geographic shifts. As in those earlier chapters, this chapter identified an array of outside institutions determining the resources available to CDCs to invest in redevelopment: banks, foundations, corporations, CDFIs, the state PHFA, and governors and legislative leaders who distribute WAMs. These outside influences are not producing any consistent pattern of redevelopment. In the competition for dollars the winners are CDCs with a reputation for successful execution of projects or those with political patrons who have channeled government funds their way. The winning CDCs are not distributed in any intentional geographic pattern but rather have sprung up where effective leadership and community support have allowed them to flourish.

The result has not significantly altered the city's land-use pattern. Despite the very positive report on the performance of Philadelphia CDCs cited earlier (Econsult Corporation 2012), the researchers did not claim that CDCs had turned around property markets in neighborhoods. In fact when analysts described the effects of CDC investments on their surrounding neighborhoods, they spoke in terms of shoring up areas that would otherwise have slid further into decay: "If these projects had not been undertaken, property values within the city would be $680 million less" (11). The forty-four CDCs included in that impact study together produced an average of five hundred to six hundred new homes each year for twenty years spread across different parts of the city—not a large enough number to significantly alter land-use patterns. And it must be acknowledged that most CDCs do not really want to fundamentally alter the character of their communities. They are animated instead by a desire to preserve their neighborhoods for current residents.

The nonprofits discussed in this chapter are struggling against large-scale forces of decay and depopulation to preserve the homes, stores, schools, and playgrounds built by prior generations. In that process they must call upon resources controlled largely by outsiders—outsiders who are motivated by a wide variety of different goals: bankers trying to meet CRA obligations, state housing officials trying to pick CDCs with sufficient capacity to successfully complete tax credit transactions, CDFIs selecting projects that can pay back loans as well as improve communities, and politicians trying to channel funds to individuals and organizations that can help them win reelection. In this complex environment CDCs have done a remarkable job of leveraging support from many sources, putting together complicated financial packages to rebuild residential blocks and commercial corridors. Where successful, their efforts have shored up existing land-use patterns. But they have not fundamentally altered those patterns.

Chapter 5

WHO GOVERNS THE THIRD SECTOR?

Reliance on the Third Sector is not entirely new to Philadelphia. During the 1950s, for example, civic leaders who were interested in urban renewal employed Third-Sector institutions as an alternative to working through government machinery partly because they lacked influence in most of the political wards of the city. One historian of that period remarked on this challenge to the 1950s reformers, "To participate in politics in Philadelphia, you must reside in the ward. Early political reformers were concentrated in only a few neighborhoods—Center City, Chestnut Hill, West Philadelphia" (Petshek 1973, 290–91). Rather than relying on electoral campaigns, those midcentury reformers channeled their ambitions through nonprofit and quasi-public entities. What is new in the twenty-first century is that the geographic scale of the metropolis has expanded, even though traditional governmental boundaries have not. In this new context nongovernmental organizations offer regional elites an opportunity to help reshape central Philadelphia even though they are not citizens of the city. In this chapter I take a closer look at who governs the Third-Sector organizations featured in this book and what they are trying to accomplish.

Not long ago one might have assumed with confidence that the governing boards would be populated by the heads of Philadelphia's leading corporations. However, the past two decades have seen waning levels of participation by corporate leadership in U.S. cities (Gronbjerg et al. 1996). That observation certainly applies to Philadelphia, whose corporate leadership is less effectively mobilized to shape local policy than it was thirty or forty years ago. In the middle of the twentieth century the city's business elite was organized as the Greater Philadelphia Movement, a powerful alliance that the newspapers referred to admiringly as "the combat and control center of the city's movers and shakers." Yet by the early 1980s organized business had lost its grip on city development, and although they tried in 1983 to establish a new corporate coalition that would enlist the leaders of the largest suburban as well as city companies, that organization foundered, eventually consolidating in 2003 with the region's Chamber of Commerce, an organization that has a much broader membership, including many small businesses (Adams et al. 1991, 140–43).

Other cities have shown similar tendencies. A study of Atlanta found declining rates of social engagement from the 1960s to the 1990s among that city's corporate leaders and attributed the decline to the changing economy, as corporate leaders' interests became less tied to place. The author of that study observed that corporate control was not simply shifting from one location to another; rather he suggested that corporate elites were abandoning central cities because "delocalization" had eliminated place as an important variable in the new economy. That study argued that the civic withdrawal of business elites would have "cascading consequences for the philanthropic sector of cities and diminish the community's ability to sustain a dynamic associational life" (Heying 1997, 657).

Contrary to predictions that economic elites would abandon the city, the Philadelphia case shows a more complicated picture. It is true that much of the personal wealth that once was concentrated in the central city has migrated to the surrounding suburbs. Of the one hundred highest paid CEOs in the metropolitan Philadelphia region, seventy-six earned their enormous compensation packages (up to $28 million annually) at firms based in the suburbs (Philadelphia Business Journal 2013, 135). An increasing share of the region's wealthy residents both live and work in the suburbs. Yet they

Table 6. Governing board seats in selected Third-Sector organizations, 2012

	Major civic institutions	School choice organizations	Combined number	Combined percentage
Seats held by Philadelphians	234	11	245	31
Seats held by suburbanites	371	50	421	54
Seats held by residents from outside the region	109	3	112	14

have not altogether turned their back on the city. Those suburbs furnish volunteers who now occupy more than half of the board seats in the Third-Sector institutions leading the development projects discussed in chapter 2 and pursuing the transformation of public education outlined in chapter 3. Table 6 shows those numbers and percentages. It suggests that suburban elites have by no means abandoned the associational life of Philadelphia.

Consider the twenty-seven nonprofits that have led the way in the developments described in chapters 2 and 3. (Sixteen of them build and manage major facilities; eight more coordinate and promote districts; and three are proponents of restructuring public schools.) Each is governed by a board of directors or trustees that hires senior management, guides institutional strategy, plans construction projects, raises money, and approves operating and capital budgets. They are spearheading initiatives that will affect the city for generations into the future. Although a few of these boards give the governor, mayor, legislative leaders, and other public officials the prerogative to appoint some members, the vast majority of seats on these boards are occupied by people who have been recruited by the board members who preceded them. Except for the quasi-public authorities, these boards are largely self-perpetuating. Whom do they recruit?

A headcount in fall 2012 revealed that the governing boards of these organizations totaled 778 seats, or an average of twenty-nine seats per institution. Using public information sources, I collected residential addresses for all members of these governing boards to assess the extent of suburban participation, which turns out to be substantial. On only five of these twenty-seven boards did Philadelphia residents hold a majority of the seats. It is significant that all five have missions centered on planning and coordinating districts. They are the Avenue of the Arts, which promotes development on South Broad Street; the Delaware River Waterfront Corporation, formed to take over planning of the waterfront after several decades of failed planning efforts; the Fairmount Park Conservancy, which plans improvements to different sections of Fairmount Park; the Parkway Council, established to coordinate planning and promotion of the Parkway Museums District; and Philadelphia Industrial Development Corporation, which conveys land for development in many sections of the city and leads the planning effort at the Navy Yard. (The distinctive role played by these district development organizations affects board members' expressed motives, as noted later in this chapter.)

On twenty-two of the twenty-seven governing boards, Philadelphians were outnumbered by members who lived outside of Philadelphia. One reason is that many of these organizations build and operate large facilities, and they must raise the money required for the capital projects described in chapter 2. Their need to connect with personal and corporate wealth drives them to fill board seats with people from outside the city and even outside the region. Among the board members who lived outside of the region, two dozen were from New York City, while the others came from a variety of locations within and outside the United States, including California, Florida, Texas, Washington, DC, Hong Kong, and Singapore. Men occupied 72 percent of the board seats. Given how much public funding is entrusted to these boards, we might expect to see public officials occupying seats on these boards, but in fact only twenty-two out of 778 were elected or appointed government officials; the rest were private individuals.

Using the Third Sector to Channel Suburban Influence

Did suburban actors invent the Third Sector to help them influence city affairs? Hardly. As already noted, in Philadelphia the practice of employing Third-Sector organizations to manage major civic investments became commonplace in the mid-twentieth century before the great wave of suburbanization, and examples existed even in the nineteenth century. But the Third Sector has proven to be an ideal vehicle to incorporate suburban influence in the rebuilding of the city's culture and tourism infrastructure, its institutions of higher education, research, and medicine, and its waterfront development. Third-Sector institutions figured in each of the preceding four chapters, with each chapter showing Philadelphia drawing upon different funding channels to support redevelopment. The Third Sector offers a variety of institutional arrangements for connecting the providers of capital to the builders of urban infrastructure. Some of those arrangements give outsiders opportunities to move the city's development in directions favored by regional elites, while others do not. Specifically chapters 1 and 4 demonstrated that the institutional arrangements for investing outside dollars in the city's transportation infrastructure and in community redevelopment do *not* provide easy paths for outsiders to channel money strategically toward projects that reconfigure land-use patterns in Philadelphia. The reasons differ in the two policy domains.

In the case of transportation, the federal and state governments together provide a billion dollars each year to be allocated to projects across the metropolitan area through the Delaware Valley Regional Planning Commission, whose governing board is composed of equal representation from Philadelphia and each of the eight suburban counties. DVRPC decides the allocation of federal and state highway dollars, while it shares with the Southeastern Pennsylvania Transportation Authority the responsibility for allocating another portion of transportation dollars to mass-transit projects. Suburban seats far outnumber Philadelphia seats in both DVRPC and SEPTA, yet suburban members do not use their dominance to promote large transportation projects to reshape Philadelphia for the benefit of the suburbs. In the twentieth century, those suburban-dominated institutions had pursued such a strategy, backing the crosstown expressway for motorists and the commuter tunnel to benefit suburban rail riders. But these days the transportation dollars for both highways and mass transit are devoted almost exclusively to repair crumbling infrastructure. So dire is the need to fix the existing system that DVRPC and SEPTA spend virtually no money on new projects that would alter land-use patterns to enhance the city's value to the region. In the absence of any large city project that would serve suburban interests, the metropolitan planning organization is unlikely to channel disproportionate sums to the city, especially since the institutional framework lends itself to a share-out of transportation dollars across all nine counties rather than a disproportionate concentration of funds within the city, or within any member jurisdiction for that matter.

In the case of community development, federal policies have strongly encouraged private individuals and corporations to invest in projects benefiting low-income neighborhoods. However, channeling those outside investment dollars to community development corporations involves a complicated financial network in which dollars flow where the return on investment is assured, not necessarily where rebuilding the neighborhood is strategically important to the broader city and region. Consider the desirability of transit-oriented development, which DVRPC has identified as a planning approach that would generate regionwide benefits because it would assign priority for housing and commercial development to locations where mass transit is most easily accessible (DVRPC 2003). Concentrating investments in those locations would offer nearby residents convenient access to jobs in many parts of the region, increasing efficiency in deploying the regional labor pool. At the same time it would limit pollution in the region's air shed. Yet linking neighborhood reinvestment to regional transportation goals is nearly impossible, given that decisions about where to invest community development dollars are more often determined by financial performance criteria than by land-use planning criteria.

Chapters 2 and 3 focused on domains in which outsiders *can* and *do* exert significant influence on Philadelphia through Third-Sector organizations. Outsiders play a dominant role in leading the cultural, educational, research, and medical institutions that are creating new development districts and reconfiguring the metropolitan core of the region. Not just in Philadelphia but in many cities interest has developed in these so-called anchor institutions, a label adopted by planners and researchers to describe universities, hospitals, and cultural institutions with long-term fixed investments that have the potential to improve their surrounding neighborhoods. When that term was coined at an Aspen Institute Roundtable (Fulbright-Anderson et al. 2001) it spurred a national conversation about how the resources of large Third-Sector institutions might be leveraged to stimulate local redevelopment by supporting local businesses, hiring and contracting with local residents, enhancing educational and health services, and improving neighborhood environments. The Annie E. Casey Foundation, located in Baltimore, commissioned a report (Hahn et al. 2003) to encourage institutions of higher education to undertake their role as a community anchor in a cohesive and coordinated manner, integrating the activities and strategies being pursued by different parts of the university that engage with the community.

Policy discussions about anchor institutions are infused with an optimistic tone, emphasizing the potential that large, powerful Third-Sector institutions possess to assist their surrounding communities by adjusting their own employment and business practices and rethinking services they provide through health care and community schools. The hospitals and universities, with their large workforces, provide employment opportunities to neighborhood residents. One of the most often cited models of universities that have adopted an anchor institution mission is the University of Pennsylvania, whose Netter Center for Community Partnerships has worked energetically in University City to build alliances and support neighborhood projects. That Center sponsors meetings of a national network called the Anchor Institution Task Force, linking more than seventy institutions that are advancing an anchor mission.

The main message of the anchor institution movement is to encourage universities and hospitals to consciously and deliberately craft strategies to guide their impacts on the city. The reality is that big institutions inevitably have impacts, whether or not institutional leaders plan them consciously. Chapter 2 showed that major Third-Sector institutions are altering land-use patterns in the city, creating activity clusters that radiate outward from the historical boundaries of downtown. Major cultural initiatives like the Avenue of the Arts have spurred retail, restaurant, and real estate activity in the surrounding blocks.

At the northwest edge of the historic office center, the Parkway Museums District has enlivened the Benjamin Franklin Parkway to encourage pedestrians to visit multiple museums arrayed along that broad boulevard. There the Barnes Foundation has built a new museum to house the world-class art collection previously located in the suburbs. At the western edge of the office district, across the Schuylkill River, a half-dozen medical, educational, and research institutions have generated synergies sufficient to prompt Philadelphians to label University City a second downtown. Those institutions are so densely packed into University City that two of them (Children's Hospital of Philadelphia and the University of Pennsylvania) are now reaching east across the river to acquire major parcels of land for development on the eastern riverbank. Three institutions located at the historic fairgrounds of the city's 1876 Centennial Exhibition (the zoo, an outdoor concert venue, and a children's museum) have cooperated to create a family-friendly entertainment district in Fairmount Park. At the southern end of the office district, the Kimmel Center for the Performing Arts anchors a string of theaters, art schools, and smaller cultural venues now identified as the Avenue of the Arts. Several miles farther south, the Navy Yard is re-purposing a closed military base by developing a dense mixture of offices, research labs, and residences. And at the eastern edge of downtown, a non-profit waterfront development corporation has launched a plan to redevelop the Delaware River waterfront as a mixture of new structures and open spaces to make this natural amenity available to the public. Several miles north of downtown, Temple University is working against long odds to es-tablish a cluster of educational, arts, and medical activities that will attract ancillary land uses.

Development projects like these are crucial to the city's economic future. That is the rationale for supporting them with large government subsidies, even though they are built and maintained by nongovernmental organiza-tions. The result of nonprofit investments is to push outward from down-town, enlarging the core and creating private investment opportunities in the blocks surrounding these new districts. The Third Sector has created destinations where visitors from outside Philadelphia consume services as tourists and conventioneers, college students, and medical patients. It bears responsibility for bridges that carry suburban New Jersey commuters in and out of the city and for shipping nodes that bring freight from distant ports. In all these ways the Third Sector is connecting the city to the wider economy.

What Motivates Board Members?

When asked why they volunteer time and money to support the city, direc-tors of major cultural attractions, hospitals, and universities describe their motivation as institution building, not city building. They do not generally see their purpose as fundamentally reshaping Philadelphia. I found no evi-dence that suburban members join those boards with the intention of driv-ing the broader urban development agenda in particular directions. They express their purpose as building their institution's strengths, its clientele, and its reputation, including its national and even international profile. They take pride in its progress since they joined the board. Some of them report that their ambitions for the organization grew as they became social-ized into their board duties. That observation confirmed Clarence Stone's (2006, 26) work on urban regimes, which argued that people's intentions can be molded by participating in civic institutions: "Though an actor may carry a set of strongly held preferences into the formation of a community or association or into the joining of one, preferences are most appropriately seen as work in progress." Stone was echoing earlier work by Michael Cohen and James March (1986, 220), who also described intentions as changed by experience: "Human choice behavior is at least as much a process for discovering goals as for acting on them." Directors of major civic institutions sometimes mention upgrading their immediately surrounding neighborhoods as a goal. Yet even veteran board members of these established organizations do not describe their role as restructuring Philadelphia as a twenty-first-century city.

On the other hand, board members leading the organizations dedicated to developing whole districts (as opposed to free-standing institutions) expressed somewhat different attitudes. They are conscious of their role in revitalizing important sections of the city by developing positive connections among the institutions and businesses operating in those territories and mobilizing support for a shared agenda. The University City District sees its goal as promoting West Philadelphia as a research and technology hub whose presence and national profile affect the entire city's future. Directors of the Delaware River Waterfront Corporation are conscious of their responsibility for developing a strategic asset whose success affects not only the variety of business, tourist, residential, and manufacturing land uses located along its banks but the entire downtown area. Without question, directors of the Philadelphia Industrial Development Corporation regard the repurposing of the Navy Yard as a crucial component of the city's economic development strategy. This may be related to the fact that the governing boards of these district organizations contain higher proportions of Philadelphia residents than the other institutions in this study.

The clearest statements of intent to promote structural change in the city are expressed by the suburban directors who are promoting charters and school choice. They are determined to eliminate seats in underperforming schools and expand seats in high-quality schools. That requires closing schools and either opening new schools or expanding high-performing schools. Although they express their goals in purely educational terms, their agenda has spatial impacts, as it removes neighborhood schools and increases the number of charter schools serving a citywide catchment area.

Suburban board members do not necessarily join these Third-Sector institutions to advance the interests of their own companies, most of which sit

outside the city. My interviews with board members suggest they join because they perceive the intrinsic value of these institutions, and they gain
satisfaction from supporting them. In addition they gain the prestige that
board membership confers. Already in the 1950s giving to and serving major voluntary institutions was a way of identifying oneself as a "Philadelphia
gentleman" (Baltzell 1958). Francie Ostrower (1995, 140) has studied the importance of elite participation in philanthropy in recent decades and suggests that as regional elites have become more scattered, philanthropy may
become an increasingly important social marker of elite cohesion. Each
week the *Philadelphia Inquirer* reports on new members joining nonprofit
boards of directors. Both print and digital media provide ample coverage of
charitable fund-raising events, featuring photographs of prominent board
members pictured next to celebrities and award winners. For some people,
nonprofit board membership is a pathway to membership on the boards of
for-profit corporations, a coveted opportunity. Yet even for those who do not
seek media attention or directorships on business boards, the ability to associate with others of one's class within major civic institutions is an important benefit of serving on the boards.

Scholars who study corporate governance look for board members who
are serving multiple organizations as a way to understand structures of elite
influence. By that measure of overlapping memberships, there is a clear division between the elite networks that govern the civic institutions featured
in chapter 2 and the group of people governing the educational change
organizations described in chapter 3. Although there are many overlaps
among the twenty-seven boards I examined, there is only one person who
serves simultaneously on a board in both of those two domains. They appear to operate as separate realms of civic participation. However, we defi-
nitely find overlaps *within* the two domains, especially among the twenty-
four boards that govern major civic institutions (see table 7). Every single one
of the twenty-seven organizations shared a board member with at least
one of the others. At one end of the scale the Philadelphia Industrial Development Corporation shared board members with eleven other organizations. The next highest number of links belonged to the Philadelphia Art
Museum, which was connected to ten other organizations through shared
board members. At the low end of the scale seven institutions shared a
board member with only one of the other organizations. Some of these
interlocks occurred between sister boards, where there was a strong institu-

Table 7. Overlaps among organizations through sharing a board member

Number of boards linked to one other organization	7
. . . to 2 other organizations	3
. . . to 3 other organizations	3
. . . to 4 other organizations	5
. . . to 5 other organizations	4
. . . to 6 other organizations	2
. . . to 7 other organizations	1
. . . to 10 other organizations	1
. . . to 11 other organizations	1
Total boards linked to other organizations	27

tional connection between the two organizations. For example, the Center City District and the Central Philadelphia Development Corporation, which share an office and a staff, also shared five board members in common. Other instances of deliberate linkages could be seen at two large universities, Temple and Penn, each of which shared three board members with their affiliated health system. Among the three education nonprofits supporting school choice reforms in Philadelphia, I found three instances in which individuals served on two boards simultaneously.

Focusing attention on the individual board members rather than the institutions, I identified seven individuals (three from Philadelphia and four from the suburbs) who simultaneously held seats on three different boards. These were the six men and one woman who served as "superconnectors." Three of them held seats on the Philadelphia Industrial Development Corporation, the single best-connected institution among the group. Since PIDC is responsible for conveying land and giving nonprofits access to tax-exempt financing, it is obvious why other nonprofits would seek out board members who can connect them to PIDC. For some individuals, their job responsibilities make them important to advancing the agendas of multiple nonprofit institutions. For example, the president of the Center City District occupies a strategic position in development circles as one of the superconnectors. Similarly the city's commissioner of parks and recreation plays a key role in developing Fairmount Park and the Benjamin Franklin Parkway, and he sits on three boards that are focused on those areas.

In addition to the superconnectors, I identified forty-eight individuals who serve simultaneously on two of the boards I studied. Thirty of those connectors live in the suburbs, and eighteen are Philadelphians. At first glance forty-eight may not strike the reader as a large proportion of more than seven hundred individuals occupying board seats in these organizations. However, it is an impressive number when one considers that these organizations actually have reasons to avoid sharing their board members with other nonprofit institutions. When boards recruit new members, nominating committees look particularly for colleagues who will direct their donations and use their contacts in the service of their institution. They value business leaders as board members not only for their personal donations but also because executives can provide access to corporate contributions. Companies are more likely to contribute to institutions if their CEOs hold seats on the board (Useem 1988). Nominating committees also offer board seats to philanthropists who are willing to make donations from their personal wealth. They do not favor members with simultaneous commitments to multiple institutions. In fact the fund-raising imperative discourages deliberately seeking out individuals with multiple board memberships. Board members I interviewed described a practice common within nominating committees: seeking wealthy and/or well-connected board members who are finishing their term of service to another organization, so that there will be no competing loyalties. In this respect nonprofit boards operate differently from for-profit corporations. For-profit boards do not solicit board members for donations, and therefore they do not have to worry about divided loyalties. Indeed for-profit boards often value interlocks with multiple other corporations to advance shared agendas (Useem 1984). Nonprofits are less likely to select a board member based on his or her other nonprofit affiliations. When faced with replacing a board member who connected his or her institution to another nonprofit, nominating committees do not necessarily try to recruit another director with that same affiliation. This suggests that the substantial number of interlocks among the Third-Sector institutions I studied resulted from the preference of the board members, not by choice of the institutions they were serving.

Scholars who study nonprofit trusteeship regard boards of directors as the bridge between the internal organization and the community environment (Abzug & Simonoff 2004; Middleton 1987; Pfeffer 1973; Zald 1969). As members of the community in which the institution operates, board members stand in for the larger community, holding the paid staff accountable for advancing the public purpose that justifies their tax exemption. Looking at the board's function in this light prompts a question: To which part of the larger environment are board members supposed to link the organization? To the geographic community that surrounds the institution? To the patrons and clients who consume their services? To donors who provide resources that enable the organization to build and grow? The answer is all of the above. When they undertake major capital projects, however, these institutions are focused mostly on their donor base, which includes both wealthy individuals and politicians who can direct government grants to their projects.

When nominating committees select new colleagues, they often tap their personal connections. This is a highly personalized process that yields highly skewed results. Traditionally observers have assumed that the homogeneous composition of boards results from shared social status and political connections. My study suggests an additional, geographic dimension that helps explain who gets selected for board service in major civic institutions. As noted earlier, over half of all seats on these boards were occupied by residents of the suburbs around Philadelphia. But not just any suburbs. Figure 6 shows they hailed disproportionately from a set of suburbs that stretch west from Philadelphia, along the historic path of the Main Line of the Pennsylvania Railroad. That part of the region spawned the region's most affluent and fashionable suburbs of the twentieth century, made famous by the Kathryn Hepburn film of 1940, *The Philadelphia Story*. The pattern is one that the geographer John Adams identified in the early 1990s, when he observed that many metropolitan areas in the United States have a "favored quarter," that is, a quadrant of the metropolitan region containing the most high-end commercial and residential development (Adams et al. 1991). In Chicago it is the northwestern suburbs around Schaumberg, while in Atlanta it stretches outward through the Buckhead area of North Atlanta into Cobb County.

In metropolitan Philadelphia the favored quadrant had its origin in the Main Line but was reinforced dramatically when the highway interchanges around King of Prussia spawned a center of retail services, financial services, and technology. This confluence of major highways has attracted a concentration of employers in financial, insurance, and business services, along with a cluster of new technology firms. They offer well-paid employment that

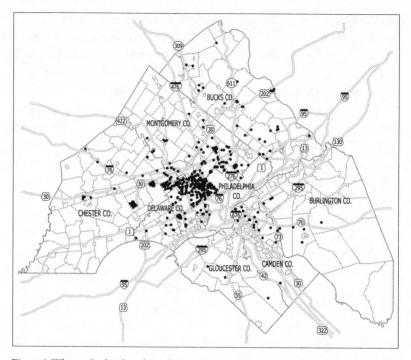

Figure 6. Where suburban board members live. (Each dot represents one board member.)

has spawned high-end residential development. Easy highway access has made this a location of choice for high-income households that want a convenient ride to central Philadelphia. They are "cosmopolitans" who make frequent use of the city's culture, dining, high-end medical services, airport, and rail connections to New York and Washington. They do not want to live at a great distance from the city, on the far edge of the region, and are willing to pay high housing prices for the combination of amenities and access that these mid-distance communities offer.

This is where the New Economy meets Old Money. *Forbes* magazine ranked two Main Line neighborhoods among the top two hundred most expensive zip codes in the nation in 2012: Gladwyne, with a reported median home price of $1.3 million, and Villanova, where the median home cost $1.2 million. These two communities sit squarely within a collection of seven townships that constitute the heart of the favored quadrant. Among those seven townships the single largest contingent of board members leading our twenty-seven organizations live in Lower Merion Township, whose residents hold an amazing 121 seats. Scattered through six additional townships (Easttown, Haverford, Narberth, Newtown, Radnor, and Tredyffrin) are ninety-two more board members. That is an amazing concentration when one considers that they make up only seven out of 350 townships and boroughs in the Pennsylvania and New Jersey portions of the metropolitan area. Their disproportionate representation doubtless reflects the extraordinary affluence of the population living in these seven suburban communities. But it also suggests that living in close proximity to people who already hold board seats increases one's chance of being offered a seat.

Board directors report that they often seek members who possess useful political connections. Many of the affluent individuals who join these boards have strong ties to state political officials—ties that they cultivate by making regular campaign contributions. Chapter 2 focused on the importance of state government grants to building projects undertaken by the city's major cultural, educational, and medical institutions. Some of those grants were awarded through the patronage of the governor, while others were secured through the influence of powerful legislators. Still others came to the city's cultural and creative sector through the Delaware River Port Authority, a nongovernmental body whose resources are subject to political pressure from both governors and legislative leaders. Suburban board members often possess strong connections to state officeholders. They maintain those connections by becoming reliable campaign donors. In Pennsylvania politics, while such contributions do not guarantee political favoritism, they often give donors access to elected officials in the form of telephone calls, e-mail connections, or face-to-face meetings. Since state funds are crucial to the capital projects of many institutions, state political connections are extremely important to boards. The organizations look for directors who have those connections and encourage board members to use them on behalf of the organization.

Consider the political contributions made during the 2010 campaign cycle (the most recent gubernatorial year, as of this writing) to three powerful state officials: Republican governor Tom Corbett, Republican senate majority leader Dominic Pileggi, and the Democrat who was then the house appropriations committee chair, Dwight Evans. Arguably these three represented the leading politicians capable of helping Philadelphia in the state capitol at that time. While Corbett hailed from the western side of the

Table 8. Political contributions by governing board members, 2010

Recipients	Philadelphia residents	Suburban residents
Governor Tom Corbett	$116,500	$714,508
State Senator Dominic Pileggi*	$ 32,000	$161,100
State Representative Dwight Evans	$110,550	$ 98,800

Source: http://www.followthemoney.org.

*Since 2010 was not a year when Senator Pileggi stood for election, he collected fewer and smaller contributions than he has collected in election years.

state, Pileggi was based in the Philadelphia suburbs, and Evans represented a district inside the city. A sizable number of the governing board members in our twenty-seven institutions made contributions to one or more of those three politicians in fall 2010. Table 8 shows the dollars contributed by board members to each of the three candidates, dividing the dollars according to whether the contributor lived in the city or the suburbs.

The figures in table 8 result from matching the politicians' donor lists against the list of individuals occupying the 778 seats on the boards of the two dozen institutions featured in chapter 2 plus the three nonprofit educational groups featured in chapter 3. The table includes only contributions of a significant size, that is, large enough to bring the contributor to the candidate's notice. In the governor's race the total includes only contributions of $1,000 or more; in the two state legislative races, the table includes only contributions of $500 or more. In the election cycle of 2010 larger dollar amounts came from the pockets of suburban supporters than from board members residing in the city. Altogether the board members of our selected nonprofit institutions gave $1.2 million in contributions to these three elected politicians. Predictably city board members contributed more to the legislator representing a city district than to the state senator who represented a suburban Philadelphia district. However, the fact that both city and suburban board members reached out to make contributions beyond the jurisdiction where they lived suggests that they were not motivated purely by matters related to their legislative district but were making the contribution for other reasons. One likely reason was that in fall 2010 all three of these politicians had the potential to influence future state grants and therefore drew support from donors outside their district whose institutions might be affected by state decisions and actions.

The Goal Is Serving Outsiders

Some researchers who study high-profile cultural and educational institutions have argued that they serve primarily the needs and interests of the affluent board members who govern them (Odendahl 1990). The logic is that since elite households are more likely than other segments of the population to patronize concerts, museums, universities, and high-end medical centers, the wealthy and powerful serve on those boards in order to sustain the institutions for their own benefit and that of their class. Predictably board members themselves offer quite different explanations for serving as directors. The board members I interviewed for this study reported that they were attracted by the opportunity to build important institutions. For example, board members serving cultural institutions emphasized the value created by those institutions for the community as a whole, offering education and enrichment to local residents. Interestingly none of the respondents said they supported the institution because it directly served their own needs or those of family and friends. They did not explain their membership on boards based on their own consumption of the services produced by these organizations. This is consistent with research done in New York showing that donors to cultural institutions did not display higher-than-average attendance at the institutions they supported. That study concluded that their participation was based not on ensuring that the arts would be available for their own enjoyment but rather on the social prestige attached to board service (Ostrower 1998).

Suburban directors who help lead major museums, universities, and hospitals are influenced by a strong sense that their institutions are important to the future of the region. Even if board members and CEOs do not talk or think about this in terms of employing an "export" model that links Philadelphia to the national and global economy, they share a cosmopolitan perspective. They are ambitious for the institutions on whose boards they sit. They want to create a national profile for such institutions. That leads them to try to attract a market for their institution beyond the city. Increasingly these institutions spend their efforts and budgets to draw outsiders.

For example, in 2011 the Kimmel Center inaugurated the first Philadelphia International Festival of the Arts, a month-long arts festival combining the efforts of dozens of performing and visual arts organizations. The centerpiece was an eighty-one-foot Eiffel Tower installed *inside* the atrium lobby of the massive performing arts center. Again in 2013 the Kimmel Center became the venue for a similar month-long festival showcasing dozens of artistic groups, this time by installing a massive Time Machine in its lobby. The goal each time was to offer a concentration of performances and exhibitions that could bring outside visitors to Philadelphia who might not be attracted by any single one of the offerings.

The Philadelphia Museum of Art has adopted the widespread practice of regular "blockbuster" exhibits that cater to out-of-town patrons. Shows that focus on impressionists and postimpressionists have been among the most successful, for example, a 1996 postimpressionist exhibition featuring the work of Paul Cezanne. After opening in Paris the show went to the Tate Gallery in London and later moved to its only U.S. venue, the Philadelphia Museum of Art. Even during the economic recession in 2010, an exhibit of the paintings of Renoir drew large numbers of visitors from out of town. In addition to boosting ticket sales, blockbuster exhibits increase sales at museum shops and grants from corporate sponsors.

A comprehensive study of how Philadelphia cultural institutions have used their marketing dollars to build audiences concluded that they exerted far greater efforts to bring suburban patrons to their performances and exhibits than to lure attendees from lower income, less educated, younger, and nonwhite communities within the city's boundaries (Martin 2012, 191). Critics of this emphasis on attracting art patrons from outside the city point out that it does not serve local citizens and can even divert resources away from projects that yield more direct benefits for local residents (Strom 1999, 2002; Eisinger 2000; Judd 1999).

Moving the Barnes Museum away from its traditional location outside the city to the Benjamin Franklin Parkway in downtown Philadelphia was based on the desire to make its collection more accessible to visitors. Planting the collection in the museum district made it a convenient destination for out-of-towners who might also visit the Philadelphia Art Museum, the Rodin Museum, and other nearby attractions during the same visit. Within a year of its 2012 opening the Barnes had served over a quarter of a million visitors, exceeding even its own projections. That number was especially surprising since the Barnes strictly controls the number of patrons who can view the collection at any one time because of the small size of its galleries. This is not an attraction that people can visit on impulse; it requires advance reservations. Yet that has not deterred visitors from other cities and other countries.

Cultural institutions are not the only nonprofits whose business model depends on drawing customers from outside the city. The same is true of the large, nationally prominent hospitals in the city. They are increasingly focused on suburban and even more distant markets. The Introduction made the point that government funding for health care and many other services increasingly takes the form of subsidies to individual consumers, as opposed to subsidies for the institutions that provide services. That shift, which induces competition among providers, has affected the shape of the region's health care market. The suburbs surrounding Philadelphia have experienced a virtual explosion in medical care since the mid-1990s. Suburban hospitals and ambulatory care centers are increasingly competing against downtown medical centers by specializing in the most lucrative procedures and treatments. Those money-making procedures (such as knee surgeries that are popular among well-insured older patients) have traditionally helped big downtown hospitals subsidize their most expensive departments, such as burn units, ICUs, and emergency rooms. To compete for well-insured patients, city hospitals have begun to establish suburban medical offices that can refer patients downtown. When Congress expanded health insurance through the Affordable Care Act, Temple University Health System began opening suburban urgent care centers, a new style of clinic that offers an alternative to expensive emergency rooms to treat relatively minor ailments and accidents. A handful of Philadelphia hospitals have reached even farther to draw patients; in 1999 several hospitals banded together to form Philadelphia International Medicine (PIM) to attract international patients, a trend labeled "medical tourism." Most of these patients come to PIM for cancer care, neural sciences, pulmonary care, and specialty procedures like bone marrow transplants. PIM provides the international patients with translators, transportation, hotel accommodations, even grocery shopping and other concierge services. In 2012 PIM served about six hundred patients from thirty-eight nations ("Taking Region's Health Care Worldwide" 2013).

At the same time, residents who live within blocks of the city's major medical centers lack many types of basic health care, for example, maternity care. Philadelphia's infant mortality rate is well above the national average and has been relatively constant in recent years at more than ten deaths per one thousand births. Observers tie this grim statistic to the deep poverty in some parts of the city and explain its persistence by the fact that Philadelphia has seen a steady drop in the number of city hospitals offering maternity services, from nineteen in 1997 to only six at present. That drop means not only fewer hospitals to deliver babies but also less prenatal care.

Similarly the presence of higher education institutions in the city does not necessarily translate into educational opportunity for city residents. Consider the city's major publicly supported university, Temple. Although structured as a nonprofit institution, Temple receives significant funding from the state government each year, about 12 percent of its budget. In Pennsylvania's higher education system, Temple is not a state university but rather is classified as a "state-related" institution. It is governed by its own board of trustees. In the 1990s, facing enrollment declines and tight finances, those trustees endorsed a plan to market the university more aggressively, increase admission requirements, recruit only students who could meet those higher requirements, and reduce the amount of remedial instruction that had been provided for students who entered the university unprepared to do college-level work (McCoy & Mezzacappa 1997). That meant casting a wider net to recruit new students, far into the suburbs and well beyond Pennsylvania. While some of that shift toward suburban students could be attributed to the tilt of the region's population toward the suburbs, another important reason was that fewer students graduating from city high schools met Temple's higher admission standard (Snyder 2009). Table 9, showing the change in geographic composition of the student body from 1989 to 2009, makes clear how dramatically the student body has been transformed.

Table 9. Geographic origin of Temple University student body, 1989–2009

City of Philadelphia	−27%
Pennsylvania suburbs	+56
Rest of Pennsylvania	+192
New Jersey	+94
Rest of U.S.	+83
International	+57

Source: Snyder 2009.

Mayor Michael Nutter, elected to his first term in fall 2007, announced that one of his main goals was to double the city's college attainment rate. In 2007 the U.S. Census Bureau reported that Philadelphia was ranked ninety-second out of the one hundred largest cities in the country in college degree attainment, with the rate for newcomers moving into Philadelphia significantly higher than the rate for young adults who had grown up in the city. Among youths who were ninth graders in the Philadelphia School District in 1999, only about 10 percent had graduated from college by summer 2009, attaining either a two- or four-year degree (Shorr 2010). As distressing as these numbers were, they were not surprising since graduates of Philadelphia high schools have difficulty getting admitted to colleges in their own city.

These examples show that across the domains of the arts, education, and medicine, Third-Sector institutions are working to attract outside audiences, in essence exporting their services to wider and wider markets. Board members I interviewed said this is because the limited incomes of many Philadelphians force local institutions to seek more affluent customers to support their growing budgets. An alternative explanation is that their governing boards naturally gravitate toward serving more affluent consumers whose tastes and preferences resemble their own. Both are likely to be true. Whatever the mixture of motives, the result is the same: as these institutions increase their physical investments in the city, they increasingly serve an audience that comes from outside the city limits.

To serve that audience, they have sometimes imposed significant costs on city residents. Some large-scale building projects, like those that established the University City Science Center and the Convention Center, involved the city in exercising eminent domain, dispossessing both residents and small businesses. Investments in major cultural and educational institutions have in some cases spawned gentrification in surrounding blocks. Even when they have not directly dispossessed property owners, they have unquestionably driven up property values. In 2013, as the city government completed a comprehensive reassessment of properties to capture those increased values in the tax base, city council members had to scramble to introduce homestead exemptions that could protect long-term residents from dramatic spikes in their tax bills.

Chapter 2 reported that the Third-Sector boards of development districts have sometimes found themselves in conflict with the most disadvantaged residents of the city, for example, the poor and hungry who line up for free meals at outdoor feeding stations on the Benjamin Franklin Parkway and homeless people who panhandle on the city streets. The Parkway Museums District, the Central Philadelphia Development Corporation, and the Convention Center have all urged the city government to police public behavior in areas where visitors congregate. "We're not trying to bully homeless people out," the director of the hotel association said. "But we can encourage the city to enforce sidewalk-behavior ordinances. We're trying to curb aggressive panhandlers because that really makes a lot of people uncomfortable" (Ed Grose quoted in Parmley 2011).

The most dramatic example of unintended costs created by Third-Sector initiatives is the negative impact the school choice movement has had on some city neighborhoods. As I explained in chapter 3, nonprofit organizations are transforming the landscape of public schooling. The establishment of over eighty charter schools has drawn tens of thousands of enrollments out of neighborhood school buildings, forcing the district to close dozens of schools. Many of those abandoned buildings are difficult to sell for reuse and too expensive to demolish. They sit vacant, adding blight to an already long list of burdens borne by local residents. At the same time the district is closing neighborhood schools, nonprofit charter operators have chosen to locate their schools along major commercial corridors. Those locations have numerous advantages for the school managers, the most important being easy access by car or mass transit. Yet the result is to remove important community institutions from residential blocks, weakening neighborhoods.

Holding the Third Sector Accountable

Wealthy individuals and religious denominations have always built nonprofit institutions in cities. Andrew Carnegie was famous for building libraries, providing many cities with important civic landmarks that serve a public purpose. The difference between those earlier nonprofit projects and the ones featured in this book is that Carnegie was using his own personal wealth, whereas now substantial tax dollars are being channeled to Third-Sector institutions to be invested by these essentially private, nongovernmental bodies. An important justification for these public subsidies is that the institutions serve functions that are essential to the new economy, such as mass transportation, health care, higher education and research, tourism, and the arts. They serve as anchors for redeveloping the urban spaces around them, bringing real estate investment back into neighborhoods where housing markets had stagnated, and they provide employment. While all of this is laudable, their liberal use of taxpayer support raises the issue of their accountability to the citizenry.

Accountability is difficult to ensure when so many Third-Sector organizations operate beyond the reach of the electorate. In fact there are observers of Philadelphia politics who think that lack of political accountability is actually a good idea, given the city's long history of municipal corruption. In some cases these nongovernmental bodies were established deliberately to remove them from political influence. Recall, for example, that the Delaware River Waterfront Commission was established to guide the revitalization of one of the city's most valuable stretches of real estate because civic leaders thought that elected politicians operate in time frames too short to accomplish long-term planning. One seasoned public administrator who was both a managing director of the city government and an interim CEO of its school district offered this observation about the propensity to assign the public's business to a crowded field of quasi-public and nonprofit organizations: "Philadelphia is brilliant at blurring lines of responsibility" (Goldsmith 2011). Since their governing boards are not popularly elected, directors of these organizations do not risk losing their position if citizens object to their decisions. They are frequently more concerned about the opinions of their funders. Observers have criticized nonprofits of all sizes, from small community development corporations to major institutions, for being more beholden to investors than to the citizenry.

By and large Third-Sector organizations are accountable only to their own governing boards. This became painfully apparent to the region's commuters when the Delaware River Port Authority chose to rely on the revenue from their bridge tolls to fund grants for economic development projects instead of bridge maintenance (described in chapter 1). DRPA demonstrated how much autonomy it possessed by ignoring media and public criticism as commuting motorists protested against using toll revenues for these ancillary purposes. DRPA even enjoyed a certain amount of autonomy from state control, despite the fact that it was created by the combined governmental actions of the two states. One researcher who compared DRPA to port authorities operating in other big cities argued that it exercises more autonomy than other port authorities because it is controlled by two states and it plays them off against each other (Brown 2009).

An important barrier to accountability is that citizens have a hard time obtaining information about the operations of these entities. Third-Sector organizations have less rigorous rules on public disclosure of information than government agencies must observe. That is a feature of nonprofit law that Philadelphia officials tried to use to their advantage, for example, when they solicited donations through a nonprofit to buy out the contract of a school superintendent who had lost their trust (described in chapter 3). Nonprofits do not have to disclose the names of donors. In that instance, however, public relations considerations outweighed legal requirements. The scheme was scrapped when news of the plan leaked out and citizens demanded to know the identity of private donors deploying their wealth to help terminate the superintendent's contract.

Recent hearings in the Pennsylvania state legislature have revealed confusion about whether charter schools must disclose information requested by the public, as is the case for agencies of government. Some legislators flatly assert that charter schools are public schools and as such must respond to public requests for information about budgets, payrolls, and student rosters. Yet the director of the state's Office of Open Records testified that charter schools routinely ignore such requests. She reported that her office had received over two hundred appeals from people who had been denied such information by charter school operators in Pennsylvania (Worden 2013). One might assume that quasi-governmental authorities have an inherent obligation to operate with public transparency since they are established by acts of democratically elected governments at the city, state, or federal level. But that is not necessarily the case. Penn's Landing Corporation, the quasi-public predecessor to today's Delaware River Waterfront Corporation, drew sharp criticism in 2005 for voting in secret to approve the construction of a waterfront casino without public knowledge, much less public input. The board chair unabashedly defended closed-door meetings, noting that a nonprofit corporation was not legally bound by the same sunshine laws as government (Gelbart & Sullivan 2005).

A similar stance was taken by the Delaware Valley Regional Planning Commission, a multicounty body whose members regard themselves as accountable mainly to the county governments they represent rather than to the broader public (see chapter 1). DVRPC declined repeated requests for information from a citizens' advocacy group called the Pennsylvania Transit Expansion Coalition, which pressed the regional planning commission for information about its spending decisions. DVRPC refused, saying the commission's nonprofit status exempted it from normal sunshine laws applied to government bodies. After more than a year of litigation, a state court in 2012 upheld DVRPC's refusal, ruling that the planning organization was not performing "an essential government function" and therefore did not have to open its records. Research in other U.S. cities has confirmed that metropolitan planning organizations elsewhere share DVRPC's resistance to involving organized stakeholder groups like the Pennsylvania Transit Expansion Coalition. A national survey of regional transportation planners found that they preferred not to give such groups any greater access than they give to individual citizens, mostly because organized coalitions have a greater ability to use information against them (Goldman & Deakin 2000, 64).

One political consequence of relying on the Third Sector is that it shifts the locus of citizen engagement from the level of governmental systems to individual institutions. Sometimes that is a conscious goal of the designers, for example, when the War on Poverty sought to shift citizen participation in neighborhood reinvestment away from local government (where poor and minority citizens consistently lost battles) and into community-based nonprofits (see chapter 4). Proponents of maximum feasible community participation during the 1960s reasoned that the experience gained by participating in their own communities would equip inner-city residents to engage in broader, citywide politics. As far back as the early 1800s Tocqueville (2000) had observed that voluntary associations served as "schools for democracy," where people developed civic virtues and learned citizenship skills they could subsequently use to hold government responsible. In that same vein more recent commentators have credited nonprofits with promoting civic awareness, making them particularly well suited to promoting participation by underrepresented groups (Leroux 2007). Some even argue that nonprofits can serve as effective alternatives to traditional political institutions (Hula & Jackson-Elmoore 2001; Kluver 2004). But there is a less optimistic way to judge the effects that the Third Sector may have on citizen participation in democratic processes. Philadelphia's experience demonstrates that assigning a civic function like schooling to nonprofit organizations does not necessarily give citizens greater opportunities for participation. The portfolio model of school governance disperses authority across a wide field and encourages reform-minded community members to channel their energy into individual schools as an alternative to fighting the hidebound school district bureaucracy. That is characteristic of portfolio models around the country (Henig 2010, 46), a pattern that may actually make it less possible for citizens to participate effectively in broad policy and resource decisions.

Sadly one reason for automatic public suspicion of Third-Sector organizations that hold closed-door meetings or refuse to disclose information is that Philadelphia has witnessed high-profile instances of mischief and malfeasance involving nonprofits and nongovernmental organizations. Chapter 4 showed how some leaders in the state legislature funneled extremely large sums of money to CDCs they created in their districts. One of them, Senator Vincent Fumo, was sentenced to prison in part because of the way he used his district CDC as a place to park funds for his personal spending. Following that scandal the governor commissioned a Pittsburgh accounting firm to investigate another Philadelphia CDC that had received disproportionate sums from the state's economic development programs, the Ogontz Avenue Revitalization Corporation established by Representative Dwight Evans (described in chapter 4). The investigators charged OARC with mismanaging portions of state grants, violating bid rules, and overpaying for real estate purchases (Martin 2013). The governor's administrators responded to the report by withholding $2 million they had promised and demanding that OARC return almost $3 million the state had already disbursed to the CDC. Nonprofit charter schools have also been accused of serious malfeasance, as we saw in chapter 3. They have been cited for inappropriate business ties to related corporations, paying excessive salaries to executives, paying exorbitant fees to management companies whom they hire to run the day-to-day operations of the school, and in some cases actually misappropriating funds for personal use by school leaders. Some charter officials have been convicted of those offenses and sent to prison, while others are awaiting trial.

At least some of the responsibility for irregularities and corruption rests with the government offices that oversee nonprofits. That was the conclusion reached by the state auditor general after he conducted an audit of the state's Redevelopment Assistance Capital Program, which has channeled state funds to many nonprofit institutions (discussed in chapter 2). That audit found that the agency responsible for administering RACP did not know why the state selected projects for funding, allowed applicants to miss deadlines (sometimes for years), failed to enforce reporting requirements, and failed to monitor the projects' economic impacts, which were presumably the reasons for awarding the funds in the first place (Wagner 2012).

Philadelphia's city controller reached similar conclusions about the inadequate performance of the school district's Charter Schools Office, which is supposed to continuously monitor more than eighty charter schools (Butkovitz 2010). While operating as independent nonprofits, the charter schools receive and disburse large amounts of government funds. The district would have to devote considerably greater resources to the Charter School Office (resources that the cash-strapped district does not possess) to assure citizens that tax dollars are being effectively and honestly spent. Ongoing revelations about charter school fraud have prompted some state officials periodically to suggest moving responsibility for monitoring charter schools upward to state government, out of the control of the local school district (Woodall 2010b, 2013b).

Citizens have no easy way to hold Third-Sector enterprises accountable. Admittedly the immediate neighbors of large institutions can often mobilize to address what they see as problems generated by institutions operating in their backyard. Neighbors can oppose zoning variances, permits, and licenses sought by the institutions, and they can mobilize public opposition to embarrass the institution. Community groups have periodically forced universities and colleges to negotiate policy changes or modify construction projects that threatened nearby residences. Institutions that bring students, patrons, patients, and other outsiders to their facilities do not want their visitors met with antagonism from neighborhood residents, so they have a strong motivation to maintain harmonious relations in their surroundings. On occasion residents have even organized to oppose actions by community development corporations that were planning projects in their neighborhoods. Beyond the immediate neighborhood, however, the broader citizenry of the city faces greater difficulty exercising any control over the actions of what are essentially private enterprises, albeit enterprises that serve the public. Since their boards are not elected, citizens cannot reach them through democratic politics. And since the decision-making processes of these institutions and authorities are not well understood, many ordinary citizens do not even know which responsibilities are assigned to which organization or who the board members are.

Investigative journalists are among the few people who understand the confusing organizational field of nonprofit organizations in Philadelphia. It has always been the responsibility of the press to expose corruption and mismanagement of public resources. As power steadily disperses across a wider spectrum of Third-Sector organizations, strong investigative journalism is more important than ever to the city. Unfortunately the weakened financial condition of the city's traditional newspaper industry has compromised its ability to produce investigative reporting. As newspapers decline, new web services have sprung up to provide in-depth coverage in specific policy domains; for example, PlanPhilly provides news and commentary on land development, and the Philadelphia Public School Notebook covers education. These web-based reporting services represent a new model of investigative reporting (Lewis 2007). To succeed, however, these new media sources must court corporations, foundations, and other funders because their business model depends upon grants secured from philanthropists along with support from readers and small donors. That business model could compromise coverage of institutions or agendas that the funders favor, since asking donors to finance investigations that might criticize their own operations is tricky at best.

Even in instances when a good deal of information is publicly available about the operations of the Third Sector, it is not easy to judge the contributions that these institutions are making to the city's development and civic life. At a time when the resources available to local government have diminished in relationship to growing need, the support that outsiders can bring has been critical to building and maintaining educational, medical, and cultural facilities. Suburban board members are employing personal and corporate wealth and political connections to help rebuild a metropolitan center that has drawn new downtown residents, employers, and increasing numbers of visitors. In the process it has become a stronger anchor for the regional economy.

At the same time, however, these institutional leaders have assigned a lower priority to serving city neighborhoods and residents. As direct government support diminishes for universities, hospitals, and the arts, cultural, and performing organizations, governing boards are designing their programs to attract consumers and patrons from outside the city. When they succeed in winning large grants from philanthropists, that money is often intended to help them make their mark in regional and national arenas.

To cater to those broader audiences, they are increasingly marketing peak experiences that cost money to produce. The example of the Barnes Foundation is emblematic. To shore up the finances undergirding that world-famous collection of postimpressionist art, the trustees moved it out of its original suburban home to a central location in the city. The cost of maintaining their expensive new building on the Benjamin Franklin Parkway along with constant programming has pushed the ticket price beyond the reach of residents in nearby North Philadelphia neighborhoods.

In the introduction I used the term *stealth regionalism* to describe growing outsider influence in the redevelopment of central Philadelphia because it has happened beyond the notice of most citizens. The trend is occurring under the radar for all but the most dedicated watchers of civic life. I did not use the term to imply a deliberately orchestrated campaign by suburban elites to wrest control of the development agenda from city residents. In fact my interviews suggest that those who join these governing boards are generally motivated by an opportunity to associate themselves with prestigious institutions and with fellow board members from important social spheres. The fact that so many board members reside in the most favored quadrant of the Philadelphia suburbs may help to explain how governing boards fill their seats, but it does not necessarily imply that they share a coordinated plan for the city. In fact in the conclusion I argue that the city would actually benefit from greater coordination among these institutional boards.

CONCLUSION

Harnessing the Third Sector to Benefit the City

Elected city leaders see the Third Sector as a set of institutional arrangements that help them mobilize outside resources to redevelop the city. The most notable example is Ed Rendell, who, as both mayor of Philadelphia and governor of Pennsylvania, promoted, cajoled, and fund-raised to help create the Avenue of the Arts and the Kimmel Performing Arts Center, the National Constitution Center, and the Please Touch Museum; to relocate the Barnes Museum to central Philadelphia; to massively expand the Convention Center in the heart of downtown; and to spur a host of other smaller projects.

Once Third-Sector institutions are up and running, politicians tend to treat them much as they treat for-profit corporations. That is, they assume these nonprofit corporations are entitled to pursue their own missions, independently defined by their governing boards. Yet these institutions are not private in the same sense that profit-seeking corporations are private. They benefit from a combination of one-time and ongoing subsidies provided by taxpayers at all levels of government, from local to national. In return democratically elected officials are entitled to expect Third-Sector institutions to display some accountability to the body politic, not merely to the patrons, students, medical patients, and other "customers" whom the institutions serve. In particular the citizens and taxpayers of Philadelphia, who make major contributions to the Third Sector in the form of tax exemptions, deserve more consideration than they now get from these institutions. Mayors must not regard them as the equivalent of private enterprises, the only difference being that they do not distribute profits to shareholders. Public officials must adopt a different stance if they are to gain full benefits from the presence of major Third-Sector developers in the city.

Nonprofit versus For-Profit Developers

Traditionally in U.S. cities the politics of urban redevelopment have been based on the common interest that city officials and developers share in seeing land values increase. Rising land values yield profits for private developers and at the same time expand tax bases for city services (since taxes on real estate constitute one of the largest sources of tax revenue for U.S. cities). This spontaneous convergence of interest between government and business means they often collaborate in efforts to draw population and investment into the city. So important is that convergence of interest that researchers in the field of urban studies have virtually identified urban politics with the politics of land development. Harvey Molotch (1976, 310) called attention to that equivalence in his writing about the urban growth machine: "A common interest in growth is the overriding commonality among important people in a given locale, [and therefore any given locality is] an aggregate of land-based interests." Molotch and other urban researchers have assumed that the urban growth coalition works constantly to develop and change the urban landscape in ways that boost the value of urban land by intensifying land use and increasing population, both of which increase the demand for the city's land.

Private developers maintain a keen interest in the city government's tax and regulatory policies, many of which may affect their cost structure and also affect the appeal of the city to new investors, thereby influencing the demand for land. Real estate developers whose fortunes depend on the market value of the properties they buy and sell can be counted on to be constantly active in urban politics, lobbying city government for regulations and especially tax policies that will be favorable to them. Nonprofit developers, however, tend *not* to be continuously engaged in political coalitions. One reason is of course that nonprofits must refrain from engaging in electoral politics as a condition of their tax-exempt status. (That does not stop individual trustees from serving as major campaign donors to politicians in a position to help their institutions.) Nonprofits have less motivation to stay continuously in the political game than for-profit enterprises because their stake in the land they occupy is different. Unlike businesses, Third-Sector institutions have limited interest in the rates of property, business, and sales taxes because they are exempt from these. Furthermore nonprofits operate with a different calculus than for-profit enterprises regarding the value of the land and property they own. They are not motivated by a desire to see land prices constantly rising since they are unlikely to sell property to realize a profit. In fact rising land prices in their vicinity actually increase the cost of institutional expansion, which is not an advantage to them. Nonprofit land developers are mainly motivated to protect the "use value" of their land, as opposed to the land's "exchange value." That is a distinction widely recognized by urban scholars regarding whether property represents a place where one lives and/or produces one's livelihood (use value) or instead represents a commodity that one can buy, sell, or rent to somebody else (exchange value; Logan & Molotch 1987, 1–2). Nonprofit institutions value their properties because they house the cultural, medical, educational, or other community activities that the institution pursues. Hence they tend to take a defensive role in the arena of urban politics: "Without a financial incentive to participate in local land use politics, most potential members of use value coalitions pay little attention except when threatened. So their mobilization capacity is almost entirely for purposes of defense. . . . They rarely constitute an alternative basis for positive or enduring political leadership" (Altshuler & Luberoff 2003, 259).

The city government actions that institutional leaders care about involve their own buildings and campuses: zoning, licensing and permitting, and the quality of municipal services (e.g., public safety, street repair) and amenities delivered to their immediate surroundings. To create what Dennis Judd (2003) calls the "infrastructure of play," institutions are relying on place-making as a redevelopment strategy. That is, they are working to refurbish the districts surrounding their facilities to provide a more appealing experience for consumers (Judd 1999). Broader municipal policies to increase the city's population and intensify land use are less relevant, especially as these institutions increasingly tailor their programs and plans to out-of-town visitors rather than local residents.

Some of these refurbished places have strategic importance for the region as a whole. Those are the ones that engage the interest, efforts, and money of regional elites. Other places within the city have to work hard, with only limited success, to interest outsiders in their revitalization. Some inner-city neighborhoods described in chapter 4 have tried to create food and shopping destinations that can draw visitors. Recall, for example, the restaurant and jazz festival created with state funds by the Ogontz Avenue Revitalization Corporation. The emphasis on place-making as an urban redevelopment strategy, combined with the inherent differences between places that have strategic value for the region and those that do not, is fracturing the urban landscape into zones with different development trajectories. Those differences in "urban fortunes" contribute to fracturing city politics instead of producing citywide development coalitions, much less regional coalitions.

The Third Sector as a Competitive Arena

In a city that is in dire need of reinvestment, the wisest course of action for public officials would seem to be careful planning and coordination to make the best use of every available dollar. Instead city and state governments are channeling dollars into organizational fields where the recipients use those public resources to compete rather than cooperate with one another. Lodging responsibility for public purposes in a growing welter of independent corporations and authorities makes the planners' task more difficult. Nevertheless local government officials are actively promoting reliance on the Third Sector as the future of the city. In the words of the head of the Philadelphia City Planning Commission, who is also deputy mayor for development, "This is what's going to happen all over the city in the near future. . . . You're going to see these quasi-public and quasi-private partnerships . . . all in the mix to make things happen" (Alan Greenberger quoted in Thompson 2011, 11).

Throughout this book I have emphasized that government furnishes a substantial share of the resources supporting Third-Sector organizations, through grants and contracts of many varieties, tax exemptions to nonprofit institutions, charitable tax deductions granted to donors who contribute to nonprofit institutions, and tax credits granted to investors who provide capital for nonprofits to build housing and commercial developments in low-income communities. The Congressional Research Service has estimated that government grants furnish about 12 percent of annual revenues for nonprofit institutions in education (including higher education) and the arts and about 37 percent of revenue for health care nonprofits (Sherlock & Gravelle 2009, 19). But those estimates include only direct grants; they do not count the additional subsidies that nonprofits gain through tax concessions from governments at all levels. The Pew Charitable Trusts' initiative Subsidyscope (n.d.) has estimated that the federal government's tax concessions claimed by all U.S. education and health nonprofits, their donors, and the investors who loaned them money to build facilities added up to almost $15 billion in 2012. It is more difficult to estimate the total cost of state and local government tax concessions to nonprofits and their donors and investors because of the multiplicity of data sources. One broad estimate for 2008–9 put those tax expenditures for all nonprofit organizations between $31 billion and $48 billion. By far the largest component of that total was the property tax exemption for nonprofit facilities (Sherlock & Gravelle 2009, 46).

Despite the high level of public funding that the Third Sector receives, that largesse has not meant that its institutions automatically fall in line with governmental objectives. In fact public officials impose only limited requirements in exchange for government support. One important reason is that a large share of the public subsidy to nonprofits takes the form of tax credits, tax deductions, and tax exemptions. Those are awarded more or less automatically to investors or donors who qualify, leaving little room for government to impose extra conditions on the nonprofit organizations that are benefiting. Another reason is that the policy environment in the United States strongly favors funding approaches that foster competition between organizations delivering services to the public as a spur to greater efficiency. Hence a good share of government support has transferred from supporting institutions to supporting consumers and asking institutions to compete for their patronage. The preceding chapters offered numerous examples of that policy shift.

The Pennsylvania state legislature created charter schools with the clear intent of fostering competition, in the hope of spurring both charter and traditional neighborhood schools to improve K–12 educational services. The result is that increasingly government funds are following students out of traditional public schools and into the competitive charter marketplace. The same may be said for government support for higher education. Federal aid follows college students in the form of grants and loans for tuition. Although state government historically provided operating subsidies to colleges and universities, the trend in Pennsylvania since the 1990s has been to offer less support to the institutions and more to student financial aid, pushing colleges to compete for enrollments (Adams 2003).

Similarly in health care, government subsidies follow medical patients via insurance schemes instead of supporting hospitals as institutions. Before the 1990s the state of Pennsylvania had forced a degree of coordination among health care institutions through a "certificate of need" law that obliged hospitals to ask the state for permission to add new procedures requiring expensive equipment. The certificate was intended to prevent unnecessary duplication of services between hospitals operating in the same geographic area and therefore to hold costs down. But in the mid-1990s the opponents of the process managed to eliminate the requirement by arguing that facilities developed in a free market would increase competition and thereby keep prices low without burdensome regulation. Since 1996 hospitals across the Philadelphia region have jumped into previously regulated specialties and into new locations. That Philadelphia trend is reflected nationally, as detailed in a 2012 study funded by the Robert Wood Johnson Foundation which showed that across the United States the competition for well-insured patients leads city hospitals to expand into suburban markets by building new facilities, acquiring physician practices, and establishing outpatient services (Carrier et al. 2012).

Not only do Third-Sector organizations compete for patrons; they also compete for capital funds to support ambitious building projects. Perhaps counterintuitively the recession appears to have spawned *larger* capital expenditures, because boards and institutional leaders believe new facilities will strengthen their competitive position. The Cultural Policy Center at the University of Chicago studied 725 cultural construction projects (museums, concert halls, and theaters) undertaken across the United States from 1994 to 2008 and found that cultural building increased even faster than construction in the health and education sectors. The multiple motivators for all of this building emerged from closely studying fifty-six of the projects.

Particularly important was the fact that they injected nonlocal money into the local economy. The researchers found that for those fifty-six projects, 68 percent of the funds came from sources outside the city, including foundation and corporate contributions, state and federal funds, and major individual gifts (Woronkowicz et al. 2012, 31). Philadelphia ranked among the top ten spenders on cultural facilities during those years, leading to what the study described as a "supply of cultural facilities that may have exceeded the demand for them" (3). An expanding supply of cultural facilities leads to fierce competition for both audiences and dollars. This is especially problematic at a time when the city's philanthropic foundations are shifting. Chapter 2 showed that over the past fifteen years a small group of foundations and wealthy individuals, particularly the Annenberg, Lenfest, Pew, and William Penn foundations, contributed disproportionately to major civic projects. Annenberg has now moved its headquarters and its focus to California following the death of Leonore Annenberg; the Pew Charitable Trusts have shifted much of their operation to Washington, DC, in order to concentrate on national and international issues; and the Lenfest Foundation has announced that it will spend down its dollars and close its doors within a decade. Only the William Penn Foundation will remain committed to Philadelphia, and the competition for its support will be fierce.

Community development corporations operate in a financing environment that has been labeled "contest federalism" (Bockmeyer 2003, 183) since they compete with each other for Low Income Housing Tax Credits, corporate funds prompted by Community Reinvestment Act requirements, allocations from Community Development Financial Institutions, foundation grants, and largesse secured through political patrons in the state and federal legislature.

Quasi-public organizations also compete for government grants. A classic example was the contest in 2010 between SEPTA, the region's mass-transportation authority, and the Center City District. SEPTA submitted an application to the U.S. Department of Transportation to begin building a smart card system that would eliminate its antiquated system of tokens, tickets, and passes, and establish a streamlined card system of the kind used in many other cities. SEPTA found itself competing against the Center City District, which applied for the same pool of capital funds to support the renovation of the pedestrian plaza connecting City Hall to a major downtown rail station. Since the funds had been advertised specifically as transportation funds, SEPTA was confident it would win, but in the end the federal funders picked the plaza renovation, forcing SEPTA to begin renovating its rail station ahead of its own schedule in order to align its work with the plaza reconstruction.

Given a funding framework that increasingly calls forth competition for paying patrons, students, patients, and others, it is hardly surprising that the leaders of Third-Sector institutions tend to see other nonprofits as rivals for resources rather than coalition partners. Competition in all the forms just enumerated drives the directors and CEOs of Third-Sector organizations to focus primarily on the welfare of their own institution or facility, and only secondarily on how they relate to broader planning for the city. The proliferation of nonprofit organizations in cities like Philadelphia is likely to exacerbate this tendency.

Unfortunately, when Third-Sector organizations operate in isolation they can create civic dysfunction. Particularly unfortunate examples in Philadelphia are the conflicting effects of the charter school movement and neighborhood reinvestment efforts. Community development corporations are working to rebuild some of the city's poorest neighborhoods, even while charter schools are drawing enrollments away from those same areas, and in some cases saddling them with vacant school buildings that create blight. Pursuing these contradictory strategies simultaneously defies a logic that has long been recognized by urban planners, namely, that effective strategies to strengthen inner-city neighborhoods must address both school improvement and neighborhood improvement. That dual focus on school and community revitalization is the central idea animating the Obama administration's Neighborhood Revitalization Initiative, launched by the White House in 2010 to align the place-based investments being made by separate federal agencies working on education, housing, health, safety, and human services "while busting silos and prioritizing public-private partnerships" (http://www.whitehouse.gov/administration/eop/oua/initiatives/neighborhood-revitalization). Sadly neighborhood planners at the city level have a hard time achieving that kind of alignment, not just because the local government is organized into bureaucratic silos but also because a multitude of independent nonprofit organizations are involved.

Like governments, philanthropic foundations have had trouble inducing cooperation among organizations that receive their grants, although they have certainly tried. A survey by the Urban Institute of 1,192 grant makers across the United States reported that 69 percent of them said they actively encouraged collaboration among their grantees, and 42 percent even said they sometimes required collaboration as a condition of receiving grants (Ostrower 2004). A large-scale example of this pressure for collaboration is the Bill and Melinda Gates Foundation grant received by Philadelphia and other U.S. cities, which specifically required cooperation among the city's school system, charter schools, and parochial schools to improve student outcomes. Many smaller foundations also press their grantees to collaborate with each other. Francine Ostrower (2005, 40), who analyzed the Urban Institute survey, offered this explanation of the foundations' motives: "Foundations seemed to encourage, and sometimes mandate, partnerships not necessarily because partnering was the best way to achieve a particular set of objectives given a specific context and problem, but because partnership fulfilled the foundations' view of how the social sector should operate." When Ostrower asked grantees (as opposed to grant makers) to assess the benefits of partnerships, she found a very different perspective. Grantees saw collaboration as time-consuming and costly, and they reported that once the funding ended, they had little desire to continue the partnerships that had been required by the grant (38).

Transactional Politics

Faced with a fragmented institutional landscape, Philadelphia's mayors have intervened on a project-by-project, place-by-place basis. Recent mayors have tended to engage the Third Sector not through comprehensive planning but transaction by transaction. Ed Rendell is the leading example, as seen in chapter 2. A couple of examples may help to convey the hands-on approach that Rendell and his senior aides took in order to secure deals with and for Third-Sector partners.

In 1995, when Temple University proposed building a major new arena, recreation, and retail complex on Broad Street, neighborhood leaders extracted a promise from the university to donate $5 million for housing construction and rehabilitation. However, that deal almost fell through because neighborhood representatives demanded that control over spending the $5 million be removed from the university and lodged in a newly created community corporation. When university leaders refused to cede control over the funding, Mayor Rendell and his chief of staff brokered a compromise in order to salvage the construction project. Instead of handing the $5 million to a brand-new community corporation, Temple University ceded control of the funds to the city government's Office of Housing and Community Development, an arrangement that both sides could accept (Goodman and Kaufman 1995).

Rendell's hands-on approach to shepherding Third-Sector projects was apparent even after he moved from City Hall to the governor's office. The relocation of the Barnes Foundation collection to Philadelphia's Museum District was already under way when Rendell was elected governor in 2002. But the project stalled at one point because of objections from Lincoln University, the institution that controlled nominations to the foundation's governing board. Rendell personally intervened to rescue the project, promising that he would seek $80 million from the state legislature that the university could use to build a science and technology building, an international center, and other projects; he would work to increase annual operating support from the state; and he would help Lincoln in its endowment campaign to raise $100 million. Standing in front of an audience of trustees, faculty, and students on the Lincoln University campus, Rendell assured listeners he could make good on his promise: "Those here who are from Philadelphia will tell you that I am a pretty good fund raiser. . . . Of the $275 million raised for the Kimmel Center for the Performing Arts, I probably raised $180 million of that" (quoted in Horn 2003). Soon after Rendell's promise, the trustees allowed a reconfigured board to push forward with moving the Barnes.

Rendell's mastery of the art of the deal spurred countless projects, some of which would never have come to fruition without him. Yet critics of his administration agree that he approached each deal as an individual transaction rather than following a broader city plan. The head of Rendell's city planning commission put it diplomatically: "The mayor is more interested in the here and now. . . . He has been less concerned with long-range planning because he has been very enthusiastic in taking advantage of opportunities presented to him" (Barbara Kaplan quoted in McCalla 1999).

Can Mayors Get More from the Third Sector?

Nonprofit organizations cherish their ability to operate autonomously. Perhaps that is why these organizations often refer to themselves as the "independent sector." In fact that is the name adopted for the national association of non-profits, foundations, and corporate giving programs that helps staff, boards, and volunteers to improve their performance. The organizations I have examined share this fundamental characteristic: their investment decisions are driven by organizational imperatives rather than city planning consid-erations. They do not shoulder responsibility for the public welfare de-fined in a larger framework than their own institutional mission. The broader public welfare is the responsibility of government. It therefore falls to state and local governments that have lodged so much responsibility in the Third Sector to align the work of these independent actors with the public interest.

Mayors of cities like Philadelphia should treat major nonprofit institutions more as public-purpose entities than as private corporations. That means asking those institutions to shape their programs and operations with the citizens of the city in mind. It also means pressing the institutions to see themselves operating within a larger civic sphere. Institutional leaders need to appreciate how their investment decisions influence broad development patterns and try to align themselves with the city's planning agenda. At present in Philadelphia the relationship between city planning and nonprofit agendas seems to work the other way around. As we saw in chapter 2, the city's most recent comprehensive plan, "Philadelphia 2035," appears to be a compilation and ratification of development plans being pursued by Third-Sector organizations rather than a bold statement of the government's agenda.

Mayors should ask the city's colleges and universities to see themselves not purely as competitors for student enrollments but as a critical sector of the city's and region's development, with public responsibilities that stem from the self-proclaimed "public purpose" that justifies their tax-exempt status. Higher eds must do more to emphasize fields of study that will sup-port future economic development in the city, and they should work in co-ordination to develop strategies to share responsibility for providing much broader college access to local high school graduates. An analysis of fresh-man classes at eleven colleges and universities located within Philadelphia's city limits showed that in fall 2013 only 13 percent of all freshmen came from the city (Bergman 2013). While a handful of institutions have set aside limited numbers of scholarships for Philadelphia students who qualify for admission, these efforts appear largely symbolic. They do not seriously ad-dress the college access problem for Philadelphia youth.

Charity care is another important contribution that nonprofit hospitals should be making as a requirement for nonprofit status. As in other U.S. cities, hospitals vary in their provision of uncompensated care to residents unable to pay for treatment, but not always in the way one would expect. In fiscal year 2012, for example, the nonprofit hospitals of the University of Pennsylvania and Children's Hospital of Philadelphia both provided less charity care as a percentage of their total care than did one of the city's big for-profit hospitals, Hahnemann Hospital (PHC4 2013, 27). In 2009 the *Boston Globe* published a study jointly undertaken with Harvard researchers showing that the value of tax exemptions to Boston's nonprofit hospitals exceeded the amount they spent on charity care and other community benefits (Allen & Bombardieri 2009). In 2011 the *Atlanta Journal-Constitution* reported similarly that some of that city's nonprofit, tax-exempt hospitals were providing less charity care than the for-profit hospitals that were paying taxes (Pell 2011). Mayors should call on urban nonprofit hospitals to provide, at a minimum, charitable care at a rate that is equivalent to their for-profit competitors. (As of this writing, Pennsylvania has not expanded Medicaid in response to the Affordable Care Act, so Philadelphia hospitals expect to continue serving many uninsured working poor who qualify for neither Medicaid nor the federal insurance exchange.)

In the domain of nonprofit housing development, the mayor should encourage the Philadelphia Association of Community Development Corporations to become a more robust force for coordinating the work of neighborhood development organizations. Currently the Association acts mainly as a trade organization promoting the importance of the work done by community development corporations and lobbying government for helpful legislation (e.g., a municipal land bank). But it does not function as a planning and coordinating body that would enable CDCs in different neighborhoods to coordinate the staging of their projects with each other and with city government.

In sum, city officials should work to induce greater sectoral coherence and concern for serving Philadelphians, to see that the city gains the greatest possible benefit from its concentration of tax-exempt institutions.

What kind of leverage do elected leaders have at their disposal to induce cooperation among institutions that have jealously guarded their independence? Leaders in a number of cities have focused on the tax-exempt status of nonprofits, particularly hospitals and universities. In 2013 the mayor of

Pittsburgh sued the prestigious University of Pittsburgh Medical Center to revoke its nonprofit tax-exempt status after the medical center closed hospitals in poorer neighborhoods, citing underutilization, and then opened facilities in more affluent areas. The mayor and his supporters criticized the hospital's lavish spending on a state-of-the-art pediatric center for high-paying patients at a time when the hospital was providing minimal charity care for members of the community. He also complained that the medical center paid its CEO almost $6 million a year. These practices, he argued, are not those of a charitable institution deserving tax exemption.

In Philadelphia and other cities mayors have tried to extract payments from nonprofits to compensate the city for such municipal services as safety, roads, and infrastructure. In Philadelphia that idea surfaces publicly at least once a decade, usually when the municipal budget is stretched thin. Currently 31 percent of all the value represented by real estate in Philadelphia is exempt from the city's property tax (see table 10). About one-third of all that exempted property is owned by nonprofit organizations; a little more than one-third is owned by government, including the school district; and slightly less than one-third is in the hands of private property owners to whom the city has granted generous tax abatements. Of the twenty most populous U.S. cities, only New York and Washington grant exemptions to a larger share of their property tax base than does Philadelphia.

During the 1990s Mayor Rendell announced that he would start asking for cash payments from nonprofits that the city believed did not meet the standard for "purely public charities" (Glancey 2002). Under Pennsylvania law at that time organizations seeking nonprofit status had to demonstrate that they (1) advanced a charitable purpose, (2) donated a substantial portion

Table 10. Percentage of property value exempted from taxation in selected cities, FY2012

Boston	29
Dallas	23
Houston	26
New York	42
Philadelphia	31
Washington, DC	37

Source: Governing Magazine, November 2012, 57.

of their services, (3) benefited persons who are legitimate subjects of charity, (4) relieved the government of some of its burden, and (5) operated entirely free from private profit motives. Nonprofit organizations objected to this standard because of its uncertainty and subjectivity. For example, what precise portion of an organization's service is it expected to donate? And what kinds of persons must be served to qualify?

When demanding payments in lieu of taxes, known as PILOTs, the mayor targeted hospitals, universities, and colleges, many of which strongly resisted. After more than a year of negotiation, the city ultimately gained agreement from forty-two nonprofits that they would contribute PILOTs, which collectively produced about $9 million in cash contributions in 1996— not an impressive sum compared to the size of the city's budget problem (Joint Committee of the Pennsylvania General Assembly 2009). But even that amount disturbed opponents to PILOTs, especially because the city's health care industry was going through a restructuring that included mergers, bankruptcies, and some hospital closures. The state legislature responded in 1997 with a bill that was favorable to nonprofits across the state (Act 55 of 1997), clarifying and broadening criteria for organizations to qualify as "purely public charities." While Act 55 encouraged nonprofits to make voluntary contributions in lieu of taxes to local government, it did not require them to do so.

Unexpectedly in 2012 the Pennsylvania Supreme Court issued a decision that changed the test of "purely public charities" back to the more stringent form that had predated the legislature's 1997 action. Philadelphia city council members were quick to respond to the state's reversal by reopening the issue of PILOTs. They called for hearings and even introduced legislation requiring nonprofits to prove they meet the Supreme Court's standards (Brubaker 2013). In reopening the issue, these public officials uncovered yet another instance of government's failure to hold nonprofits accountable. An enterprising journalist requested copies of documents that the city's Office of Property Assessment is required to keep for all nonprofits that qualify for tax exemption. When she requested records for more than one hundred tax-exempt properties owned by the University of Pennsylvania, municipal bureaucrats could not find such records for sixty-seven of them. Nor could they furnish documentation for a half-dozen other properties, ranging from a medical center to a housing group. Philadelphia's chief assessment officer explained that the files had disappeared in a move some years ago. When asked for his comment, the city controller responded sarcastically, "They lost the data in the move? Seriously? The dog ate their homework? What kind of explanation is that?" (Alan Butkovitz quoted in Otterbein 2013). That comment was somewhat disingenuous, since the city controller knew better than most Philadelphians how frequently government offices fail to provide proper oversight for nonprofits that are benefiting from taxpayer subsidies.

The rekindled interest in PILOTs appears to be related to the growing emphasis these institutions place on serving outsiders. The city's elected officials, like many other Philadelphians, have become increasingly aware that many of the college students, medical patients, and museum- and concert-goers who are served by major tax-exempt institutions come from beyond the city limits. As these institutions reach out to the suburbs and more distant markets, they are increasingly seen as serving outsiders at the expense of local residents. That leads local taxpayers to wonder whether and how much they should be subsidizing such enterprises with tax exemptions. Even the *Philadelphia Inquirer*, traditionally a staunch supporter of the city's Third-Sector institutions, editorialized in favor of the city council's move to revisit PILOTs, adding only this caution: "But if it asks nonprofits to pay more, it must be careful not to damage that sector of the local economy" (Editorial Board 2013). That statement reflects the vexed relationship that municipal officials have with the Third Sector. While it represents a solution to some difficult policy problems, it is a solution that creates its own set of problems.

In response to suggestions by city council members that the city's big nonprofits should resume paying PILOTs, a dozen of the city's universities and colleges banded together and hired a consultant to estimate their collective contributions. That group, which included the University of Pennsylvania, Drexel University, Temple University, and nine smaller institutions, hoped to forestall PILOTs by demonstrating that Philadelphia already receives more benefits from the voluntary activities of its higher education institutions than it would reap by imposing PILOTs. In fact the fifty-six-page glossy publication issued a thinly veiled warning that efforts to impose PILOTs could generate hostility between government and the city's higher education institutions, "turning partners in a common cause into adversaries by expending time and resources in conflict rather than in mutual service. It can also result in a reduction in community services and employment due to offsetting cuts made in response to the required payments" (Econsult Solutions 2013, iv).

PILOTs represent a "stick" that mayors can wield to gain cooperation from nonprofit institutions to support a citywide planning agenda. But mayors can also hold out "carrots" to gain cooperation. The most important inducements available to public officials stem from their ability to influence land use. Land disposition is important to the institutions featured in this book because they are intent on improving the place quality in the new development districts they have spawned. Figure 3 in chapter 2 showed that nonprofit institutions are establishing those new districts beyond the historic boundaries of downtown, moving into the zone of transition that surrounds the central business district. That zone includes many derelict properties that serve as blighting influences. Granted, a good number of those properties have attracted private developers, who buy them to rehabilitate as loft apartments and trendy restaurants and bars for affluent residents. Even well-financed developers, however, often cannot acquire vacant and abandoned properties in strategic locations because of Philadelphia's slow and ineffective system for dealing with tax-delinquent properties.

Until recently the process of transferring a tax-delinquent property to new ownership has started when the court ordered the Philadelphia sheriff to auction the property to prospective buyers. Since the sheriff's sale has mainly aimed at recouping unpaid taxes for the city treasury, the properties have been selected for auction based on their marketability, not on any strategic planning considerations. Rather than placing the abandoned property under the control of city government, the sheriff's sale has merely transferred the property from one private owner to another, with the city collecting the sale price to cover the tax arrears. The city has exercised almost no control over who purchases properties at auction. In blighted neighborhoods where some future development appeared possible, speculators have bought these buildings and allowed them to remain vacant, exacerbating neighborhood decline. In other locations already undergoing renewal, private developers have snatched up attractive parcels for projects that will make money for them but may not advance the public agenda for the area. This fragmented process for tax-delinquent properties has traded long-term redevelopment agendas for the short-term settling of tax obligations. It has offered no significant role for neighborhood associations or CDCs, much less any opportunity for the city planning commission to pursue smart growth at the city level.

Philadelphia recently acquired new tools to improve the disposition of vacant and abandoned properties. Following the example of Atlanta, Cleveland, St. Louis, and other U.S. cities, in December 2012 the state of Pennsylvania granted cities and towns the authority to establish municipal land banks. A year later Philadelphia took advantage of that opportunity to create a land bank that is empowered to take ownership of tax-delinquent properties ahead of private investors and decide when and how to sell the properties so they do not sit vacant, undermining surrounding communities. The creation of the land bank can make it faster and easier to move vacant properties into the hands of responsible owners who will invest in them to improve neighborhoods. Managers of the land bank can also assemble individual properties into larger parcels in order to promote coordinated development. This new power removes long-standing obstacles that have prevented developers, both for-profit and nonprofit, from acquiring continuous stretches of land, with the result that many blocks in the city have experienced "gap tooth" development.

Proponents of creating the land bank placed relatively little stress on its potential for allowing public officials to exercise strategic control over land development. That is probably because advocates for the land bank knew how suspicious Philadelphia citizens are about ceding greater control to government. They did not want to call attention to this planning potential because they thought that might actually hinder its adoption. Used wisely, however, this new power could help the city government balance the power of private developers to acquire strategic parcels and assert the public interest in the process of redevelopment. For example, it could enhance the city's ability to guide the development of affordable housing toward areas near jobs and transportation, that is, locations that are likely to become attractive targets of for-profit developers as higher energy costs and changing lifestyles increase the appeal of transit-oriented development. The land bank can help hospitals, universities, and other nonprofit facilities by working systematically to upgrade neighborhoods surrounding those institutions. A land bank can help spur upgrading in the blocks adjacent to major institutions by managing the transfer of land to encourage compatible uses. In that way the land bank gives city officials an important tool to use in negotiating with the institutions.

A More Coherent Third Sector

The report commissioned by a dozen colleges and universities in reaction to the threat of PILOTs estimated the direct economic impact on the city of higher education operating expenditures at $8.3 billion annually, supporting sixty-eight thousand jobs (Econsult Solutions 2013, 11). In addition the higher eds spend $800 million per year on construction, which supports 4,900 more jobs. Finally, the report claimed another $641 million per year that the higher eds contribute to the city in the form of public safety, community services, and scholarships for city residents. The institutions portrayed their ties to constituencies outside the city as a plus, noting that their sizable economic and in-kind contributions to the city are "made possible in large part by funds imported into the city from across the country and around the world in the form of tuition dollars from non-Philadelphia students, alumni donations, and research grants. Hence outside dollars are used to support Philadelphia" (ii).

To demonstrate the combined contributions to the citizens of Philadelphia, the report provides a lengthy compendium of all the discrete projects, initiatives, and on-campus and outreach programs undertaken by the twelve sponsoring colleges and universities. The aggregate contribution of these nonprofits represents a straightforward tally of the separate contributions of each institution. Nowhere does the report describe coordinated strategies orchestrated across the city in collaboration with city government. That is because these independent institutions do not see themselves as an integrated sector. To gain the greatest benefit from its Third Sector, the city needs a more coordinated approach.

To mobilize universities, hospitals, CDCs, and other nonprofit institutions as sectors rather than dealing with them one by one on a transactional basis, mayors in a few U.S. cities have created offices to improve their relationships with the Third Sector (Wolk & Ebinger 2010). For example, Denver opened an Office of Strategic Partnerships in 2004 as a liaison between city government and nonprofit organizations. New York City established the Nonprofit Assistance Initiative in 2009 to help nonprofit service providers weather the economic downturn. Those two examples are mainly aimed at increasing the effectiveness of social service provision in the city, much of which is carried out by nonprofit contractors. Those offices focus on improving contracting procedures, reducing costs, standardizing data collection, and other system changes. A second kind of initiative, exemplified by the Los Angeles Office of Strategic Partnerships, ties city government more closely to major foundations and philanthropists in order to raise private money for city programs and services. What Philadelphia needs, in addition to effective partnerships with nonprofit service providers, is a more coordinated approach to Third-Sector institutions as *developers* whose plans and investments are restructuring the city's built environment in ways that will influence its future for many decades.

In 2012 the U.S. Conference of Mayors adopted a resolution endorsing these offices and urging mayors around the country to "promote and model a more engaged culture of civic philanthropy, actively partnering with foundations and their associations, as well as public and nonprofit leaders in this effort" (USCM 2012). Ironically it was at that meeting that Philadelphia's mayor Michael Nutter was installed as president of the Conference, and he was one of the nine mayors who submitted the resolution. Nutter's hometown needs to make a stronger, more strategic effort to deal productively with the kind of Third-Sector organizations featured in this book. Perhaps Philadelphia officials will be more strongly motivated to undertake that difficult work if they bear in mind that in dealing with these Third-Sector institutions, they will be engaging powerful sources of money and influence from the suburbs. They will, in effect, be engaged in a form of regionalism.

References

Abzug, R., and J. Simonoff. 2004. *Nonprofit Trusteeship in Different Contexts*. Burlington, VT: Ashgate.

Adams, C. 2003. "The Meds and Eds in Urban Economic Development." *Journal of Urban Affairs* 25: 571–88.

Adams, C., D. Bartelt, D. Elesh, and I. Goldstein. 2008. *Restructuring the Philadelphia Region: Metropolitan Divisions and Inequality*. Philadelphia: Temple University Press.

Adams, C., D. Bartelt, D. Elesh, I. Goldstein, N. Kleniewski, and W. Yancey. 1991. *Philadelphia: Neighborhoods, Division and Conflict in a Postindustrial City*. Philadelphia: Temple University Press.

Adams, J. 1991. "Housing Submarkets in an American Metropolis." In *Our Changing Cities*, edited by J. Fraser, 108–26. Baltimore: Johns Hopkins University Press.

Allen, S., and M. Bombardieri. 2009. "Much Is Given by Hospitals, More Is Asked." *Boston Globe*, May 31.

Altshuler, A., and D. Luberoff. 2003. *Mega-Projects: The Changing Politics of Urban Public Investment*. Washington, DC: Brookings Institution Press.

Anderson, J. 2003. *Art Held Hostage: The Battle over the Barnes Collection*. New York: Norton.

Annie E. Casey Foundation. 2008. *Closing the Achievement Gap—School, Community, Family Connections*. Baltimore: Annie E. Casey Foundation.

Archdiocese of Philadelphia. 2012. "2012 School Report," June 30. http://www.catholic schools-phl.org/uploads/School-Report.pdf.

Argott, D., director. 2009. *The Art of the Steal*. Documentary film. Sheena Joyce, producer.

AsianWeek Staff. 2000. "Philadelphia Chinatown Wins Stadium Fight." *AsianWeek*, November 24–30. http://www.asianweek.com/2000/11/24/philadelphia-chinatown -wins-stadium-fight/.

Axelroth, R., and S. Dubb. 2010. *The Road Half Traveled: University Engagement at a Crossroads*. College Park: University of Maryland, The Democracy Project, December.

Baker, M., Jr. 2011. "422 Corridor Plus: A Better Ride. Synopsis and Findings." Study commissioned by the Delaware Valley Regional Planning Commission, September. http://www.422plus.com.

Baltzell, D. 1958. *Philadelphia Gentlemen: The Making of a National Upper Class*. New York. Free Press.

Bang-Jensen, L. 1984. *New York State's Other Government: The Long Shadow of Public Authorities*. Albany: Rockefeller Institute.

Barbour, E. 2002. *Metropolitan Growth Planning in California, 1900–2000*. San Francisco: Public Policy Institute of California.

Barnes, W., and L. Ledebur. 1998. *The New Regional Economies*. Thousand Oaks, CA: Sage.

BCG. 2012. "Transforming Philadelphia's Public Schools: Key Findings and Recommendations." Boston Consulting Group, August. http://webgui.phila.k12.pa.us/up loads/v_/IF/v_IFJYCOr72CBKDpRrGAAQ/BCG-Summary-Findings-and-Rec ommendations_August_2012.pdf.

Bear, L.A. 1990. *The Glass House Revolution: Inner-City War for Interdependence*. Seattle: University of Washington Press.

Benjamin, S., et al. 1994. "MPOs and Weighted Voting." *Intergovernmental Perspective* 20: 31–36.

Bergman, J. 2013. "Reality Check: Do Philly's Colleges Accept Philly Students?" *AXIS/ Philly*, October 11. http://axisphilly.org.

Birch, E. 2009. "Downtown in the New American City." *Annals of the American Academy of Political and Social Science* 626: 134–53.

Bishoff, K. 2008. "School District Fragmentation and Racial Residential Segregation: How Do Boundaries Matter?" *Urban Affairs Review* 44, no. 2: 182–217.

Bissinger, B. 1997. *A Prayer for the City*. New York: Random House.

Blue Ribbon Commission. 2012. "Faith in the Future: Sustainable Catholic Education for All Who Desire It." Archdiocese of Philadelphia, January. http://cbsphilly.files .wordpress.com/2012/01/commission-report.pdf.

Bockmeyer, J. 2003. "Devolution and the Transformation of Community Housing Activism." *Social Science Journal* 40: 175–88.

Bounds, A. M. 2007. "Philadelphia's Avenue of the Arts: The Challenges of a Cultural District Initiative." In *Tourism, Culture, and Regeneration*, edited by M. Smith, 132–42. Cambridge, MA: CABI.

Brennan, C. 2009. "Mayor Nutter Appoints Delaware River Waterfront Corporation." *Philadelphia Inquirer*, January 30.

Briffault, R. 1996. "The Local Government Boundary Problem in Metropolitan Areas." *Stanford Law Review* 48: 1115–71.

Brill, S. 2011. *Class Warfare: Inside the Fight to Fix America's Schools.* New York: Simon and Schuster.

Brinig, M., and N. Garnett. 2010. "Catholic Schools, Urban Neighborhoods, and Education Reform." *Notre Dame Law Review* 85: 887–954.

Brown, P. H. 2009. *America's Waterfront Revival: Port Authorities and Urban Redevelopment.* Philadelphia: University of Pennsylvania Press.

Brubaker, H. 2013. "Nonprofits Eyed for City Revenue." *Philadelphia Inquirer,* March 5.

Buki, C., et al. 2007. "Rethinking Community Impacts: An Analysis of the Deployment of Low-income Housing Tax Credits in the Commonwealth of Pennsylvania and Recommendations for Change." PA Housing Finance Agency, January. http://www .phfa.org/forms/housing_study/2007/czb_PHFA_mar2007.pdf.

Bulkley, K., J. Christman, and E. Gold. 2010. "One Step Back, Two Steps Forward: The Making and Remaking of Radical Reform in Philadelphia." In *Between Public and Private: Politics, Governance, and the New Portfolio Models for Urban School Reform,* edited by K. Bulkley, J. Henig, and H. Levin, 127–64. Cambridge, MA: Harvard Education Press.

Butkovitz, A. 2010. "Review of Charter School Oversight: A Fraud Vulnerability Assessment." Philadelphia, Office of the Controller, April. http://www.philadelphia controller.org/publications/other%20reports/CharterSchoolinvestigation_FullRe port.pdf.

———. 2011. "Review of Vacant School District Facilities: Neighborhood Nuisances and Hazards." Philadelphia, Office of the Controller, December. http://www.philadel phiacontroller.org/publications/SchoolFacilitiesReview_December2011.pdf.

Byers, R. 1996. "Big Donor Aims to Call Shots: Pew's $8.8M Reform Is Not without Strings." *Philadelphia Daily News,* February 13.

Caro, R. 1974. *The Power Broker: Robert Moses and the Fall of New York.* New York: Vintage Books.

Carrier, E., M. Dowling, and R. Berenson. 2012. "Hospital Geographic Expansion: The New Medical Arms Race?" *Health Affairs* 31: 827–35.

Casey, R., Jr. 1997. "Performance Audit of the Community Revitalization Program Administered by the Dept. of Community and Economic Development, July 1, 1996 through May 9, 1997." Harrisburg, Office of the Auditor General.

CCD. 2010. *State of Center City.* Philadelphia: Center City District.

CEO Council for Growth. 2006. "Thinking outside the Box: Addressing Greater Philadelphia Transportation Investment Needs through Public-Private Partnerships." Select Greater Philadelphia, March. http://www.selectgreaterphiladelphia.com/wp -content/uploads/2013/03/thinking-outside-box.pdf.

Chai, J. 2002. *Should California Revisit SB 45?* San Jose, CA: San Jose State University, Mineta Transportation Institute.

Clark, A. 2012. "Can Nonprofits Run Cities?" *Next City,* July. http://nextcity.org/fore front/view/welcome-to-your-new-government.

Cohen, M., and J. March. 1986. *Leadership and Ambiguity.* 2nd ed. Boston: Harvard Business School Press.

Commonwealth of Pennsylvania Transportation Funding and Reform Commission. 2007. "Operational Audit of SEPTA." Pennsylvania Department of Transportation, January 31.

Couloumbis, A. 2013. "Walking Around Money Is Back, Critics Allege." *Philadelphia Inquirer,* December 1.

Countryman, M. 2006. *Up South: Civil Rights and Black Power in Philadelphia.* Philadelphia: University of Pennsylvania Press.

CPDC. 1990. *South Broad Street—A Vision of the 1990s.* Philadelphia, Central Philadelphia Development Corporation.

CREDO. 2011. "Charter School Performance in Pennsylvania." Stanford University Center for Research on Education Outcomes, April. http://credo.stanford.edu/re ports/PA%20State%20Report_20110404_FINAL.pdf.

Dahl, R. 1961. *Who Governs?* New Haven, CT: Yale University Press.

Davidson, J. 1978. "Fresh Darts at Rizzo." *Evening Bulletin* (Philadelphia), April 5.

Dear, M., and S. Flusty. 1998. "Postmodern Urbanism." *Annals of the Association of American Geographers* 88: 50–72.

Delaware Riverkeeper Network. 2010. "Comment to U.S. Army Corps of Engineers regarding Southport Resolution." Philadelphia, September 21. http://www.delaware riverkeeper.org/resources/Comments/drn%20to%20army%20corps%20sept%2023 %202010.pdf.

Denvir, D. 2012. "Money Talks." *Philadelphia City Paper,* July 5–11.

Dilger, R. J. 2012. "Federalism Issues in Surface Transportation Policy: Past and Present." Washington, DC: Congressional Research Service, July 27.

DiStefano, J. 2011. "Amid PA Cuts, $437M to Private Projects." *Philadelphia Inquirer,* June 30.

Dobrin, P. 1998. "Finally, the Center Gets Started." *Philadelphia Inquirer,* November 8.

———. 2011. "A Financially Squeezed Please Touch Is Reaching Out." *Philadelphia Inquirer,* January 31.

Dreier, P., J. Mollenkopf, and T. Swanstrom. 2004. *Place Matters: Metropolitics for the 21st Century.* 2nd ed. Lawrence: University Press of Kansas.

DRWC. 2011. "Transforming Philadelphia's Waterfront: Master Plan for the Central Delaware." Delaware River Waterfront Corporation, December. http://www.plan centraldelaware.com.

DVG. 2011. "Delaware Valley Grantmakers Education Funders Survey." Philadelphia, April. http://c.ymcdn.com/sites/www.philanthropynetwork.org/resource/resmgr/re search_reports/edfundersurvey2011_execsummf.pdf.

DVRPC. 2003. "Linking Transit, Communities and Development: Regional Inventory of Transit-Oriented Development Sites," vol. 2: "Station Area Profiles." Delaware Valley Regional Planning Commission, December. http://www.dvrpc.org/reports /03036.pdf.

———. 2009a. "Connections 2035: The Regional Plan for a Sustainable Future." Delaware Valley Regional Planning Commission, July. http://www.dvrpc.org/Connections/.

———. 2009b. "Pennsylvania's 2011 Transportation Program Financial Guidance." Delaware Valley Regional Planning Commission, August 25. http://www.dvrpc.org/tip /pafinal/2011/PA2011FinancialGuidance.pdf.

——. 2009c. Transportation Improvement Programs for Pennsylvania, FY011, FY2011, FY2013. Delaware Valley Regional Planning Commission. http://www.dvrpc.org/tip/.

——. 2012. "Connections 2040: Transportation Investment Scenarios." Delaware Valley Regional Planning Commission, October. http://www.dvrpc.org/asp/pubs/publicationabstract.asp?pub_id=13004.

Econsult Corporation. 2010. "Vacant Land Management in Philadelphia: The Costs of the Current System and the Benefits of Reform." Redevelopment Authority of the City of Philadelphia, November. http://www.may8consulting.com/publications/Vacant_Land_Reform-REPORT.pdf.

——. 2012. "The Economic Impact of Community Development Corporations within the City of Philadelphia and the Commonwealth of Pennsylvania." Philadelphia Association of Community Development Corporations, October 29. http://www.pacdc.org/CDCImpactReport.

Econsult Solutions. 2013. "The City of Philadelphia and Its Higher Eds: Shared Goals, Shared Missions, Shared Results." Philadelphia, October. http://pgrophilly.org/wp-content/uploads/2013/10/PGRO-REPORT-2013-10-17.pdf.

Editorial Board. 1995. "Good Tidings: A New Poll on City-Suburban Attitudes Hints at a Growing Willingness to Cooperate." *Philadelphia Inquirer*, February 5.

——. 2010. "Taxpayers Pick Up the Tab." *Philadelphia Inquirer*, December 19.

——. 2013. "Tapping Nonprofits Is Worth a Discussion." *Philadelphia Inquirer*, March 15.

Eichel, L., with C. Zukin. 2010. *Suburbanites Value Philadelphia as a Place to Visit but Not to Live*. Philadelphia: Philadelphia Research Initiative of the Pew Charitable Trusts.

Eisinger, P. 2000. "The Politics of Bread and Circuses." *Urban Affairs Review* 5: 316–33.

Elkin, S. 1987. *City and Regime in the American Republic*. Chicago: University of Chicago Press.

Eshleman, R. 1997. "Creativity Did the Trick for Charter Schools: Some Unconventional Friends Helped Win Passage of the Revolutionary Measure." *Philadelphia Inquirer*, June 15.

Etienne, H. 2012. *Pushing Back the Gates: Neighborhood Perspectives on University-Driven Revitalization in West Philadelphia*. Philadelphia: Temple University Press.

Fainstein, S. 2001. *City Builders: Property Development in New York and London, 1980–2000*. 2nd ed. Lawrence: University of Kansas Press.

Fairmount Ventures, Inc. 1998. "South Broad Street Initiative." Status report prepared for William Penn Foundation, March 5.

Ferrick, T. 2011. "Real School Reform Finally?" *Philadelphia Inquirer*, December 25.

Ferrick, T., and L. Horwitz. 2010. *Philadelphia's Changing Schools and What Parents Want from Them*. Philadelphia: Philadelphia Research Initiative of the Pew Charitable Trusts.

Fiedler, E. 2012. "St. Martin de Porres Leads the Way toward Independent Catholic Schools in Philly." *Newsworks.org*, March 22.

Fischel, W. 2004. "An Economic History of Zoning and a Cure for Its Exclusionary Effects." *Urban Studies* 41: 317–40.

Forbes. 2012. "America's Most Expensive Zip Codes, 2012." October. http://www.forbes
.com/special-report/2012/1016_zip-codes_rank.html.

Franklin Institute. 2008. *Annual Report.* Philadelphia.

Frieden, B., and L. Sagalyn. 1991. *Downtown, Inc.: How America Rebuilds Cities.* Cambridge, MA: MIT Press.

Friedmann, J. "The World Cities Hypothesis." In *World Cities in a World-System,* edited by P. Knox and P. Taylor, 317–31. Cambridge, UK: Cambridge University Press.

Frisch, M., and L. Servon. 2006. "CDCs and the Changing Context for Urban Community Development: A Review of the Field and the Environment." *Community Development: Journal of the Community Development Society* 37: 88–108.

FTA. 2009. *Rail Modernization Study.* Washington, DC: Federal Transit Administration, April.

———. 2010. *National State of Good Repair Assessment.* Washington, DC: Federal Transit Administration, June.

Fulbright-Anderson, K., P. Auspos, and A. Anderson. 2001. *Community Involvement in Partnerships with Educational Institutions, Medical Centers, and Utility Companies.* Washington, DC: Aspen Institute Roundtable on Comprehensive Community Initiatives, January.

Gabriel, T., and J. Medina. 2010. "Charter Schools' New Cheerleaders: Financiers." *New York Times,* May 9.

Gamm, G. 2001. *Urban Exodus: Why the Jews Left Boston and the Catholics Stayed.* Cambridge, MA: Harvard University Press.

Gelbart, M., and J. Sullivan 2005. "A Powerful Agency Does Its Work in the Dark." *Philadelphia Inquirer,* December 18.

Gill, B., et al. 2007. *State Takeover, School Restructuring, Private Management, and Student Achievement in Philadelphia.* Santa Monica, CA: RAND Corporation, February.

Gittell, M., et al. 1999. *The Politics of Community Development: CDCs and Social Capital.* New York: Howard Samuels State Management and Policy Center, City University of New York, February.

Glaeser, Edward. 2011. *Triumph of the City: How Our Greatest Invention Makes Us Richer, Smarter, Greener, Healthier, and Happier.* New York: Penguin Press.

Glancey, D. 2002. "PILOTS: Philadelphia and Pennsylvania." In *Property-Tax Exemption for Charities: Mapping the Battlefield,* edited by E. Brody, 211–32. Washington, DC: Urban Institute Press.

Goldman, T., and E. Deakin. 2000. "Regionalism through Partnerships? Metropolitan Planning Since ISTEA." *Berkeley Planning Journal* 14: 46–75.

Goldsmith, P. 2011. "Finding the Right Stuff to Lead the System." Philadelphia Public School Notebook, December 14. http://thenotebook.org/december-2011/114303/finding-right-stuff-lead-system.

Goodman, H., and M. Kaufman. 1995. "City, Temple End Impasse on Apollo: Compromise on Money Clears Way for Arena." *Philadelphia Inquirer,* November 3.

Governor's Center for Local Government Services. 2002. "Municipal Authorities in Pennsylvania." Pennsylvania Department of Community and Economic Development. http://www.penntrain.net/NewFiles/Boards/munauthority.pdf.

Graham, K. 2011. "Bitterness over Buyout." *Philadelphia Inquirer,* August 25.

Graham, T. 2012. "Plan for a Philadelphia City Land Bank Is Taking Steps Forward." *Philadelphia Inquirer,* December 4.

Graham, T., and K. Graham. 2013. "100M for Philadelphia School Sites?" *Philadelphia Inquirer,* October 26.

Greenberger, A. 2011. "Vision Is Meeting Action in Philly." *Philadelphia Inquirer,* July 1.

Greenblatt, A. 2011. "Billionaires in the Classroom: How Bill Gates and Other Philanthropists Are Reshaping Public Education with Private Cash." *Governing Magazine,* October, 27–35.

Gronbjerg, K., A. Harmon, A. Olkkonen, and A. Raza. 1996. "The United Way System at the Crossroads: Community Planning and Allocation." *Nonprofit and Voluntary Sector Quarterly* 25: 428–52.

Gronbjerg, K., and L. Salamon. 2012. "Devolution, Marketization, and the Changing Shape of Government-Nonprofit Relations." In *The State of Nonprofit America,* 2nd ed., edited by L. Salamon, 549–86. Washington, DC: Brookings Institution Press.

Guthrie, D., and M. McQuarrie. 2008. "Providing for the Public Good: Corporate-Community Relations in the Era of the Receding Welfare State." *City and Community* 7: 113–40.

Gym, H. 2012. "Commentary: Put the Boston Consulting Group Where It Belongs—Before the Public." Philadelphia Public School Notebook, May 24. http://thenotebook.org/print/4881?page=show.

Hahn, A., C. Connerty, and L. Peaslee. 2003. "Colleges and University as Economic Anchors: Profiles of Promising Practices." Annie E. Casey Foundation. http://www.aecf.org/upload/publicationfiles/colleges.pdf.

Hannigan, J. 1998. *Fantasy City: Pleasure and Profit in the Postmodern Metropolis.* New York: Routledge.

Hanson, R., et al. 2006. "Corporate Citizenship and Urban Problem Solving: The Changing Civic Role of Business Leaders in American Cities." Discussion paper. Washington, DC: Brookings Institution Metropolitan Policy Program, September.

Henig, J. 2010. "Portfolio Management Models and the Political Economy of Contracting Regimes." In *Between Public and Private: Politics, Governance, and the New Portfolio Models for Urban School Reform,* edited by K. Bulkley, J. Henig, and H. Levin, 27–52. Cambridge, MA: Harvard Education Press.

Henig, J., and J. MacDonald. 2002. "Locational Decisions of Charter Schools: Probing the Market Metaphor." *Social Science Quarterly* 83: 962–80.

Herold, B. 2013. "Nonprofit Gives $3.4 Million to Expand Two Philadelphia Charters." *Newsworks.org,* March 14.

Heying, C. 1997. "Civic Elites and Corporate Delocalization: An Alternative Explanation for Declining Civic Engagement." *American Behavioral Scientist* 40: 657–68.

Hill, P., C. Campbell, and B. Gross. 2012. *Strife and Progress: Portfolio Strategies for Managing Urban Schools.* Washington, DC: Brookings Institution Press.

Hill, P., et al. 2009. *Portfolio Districts for Big Cities: An Interim Report.* Seattle: University of Washington, Center on Reinventing Public Education.

Hilty, J. 2010. *Temple University: 125 Years of Service to Philadelphia, the Nation, and the World.* Philadelphia: Temple University Press.

Horn, P. 2003. "Lincoln Board Accepts Smaller Role in Barnes." *Philadelphia Inquirer*, September 21.

———. 2005. "The William Penn Foundation and The Reinvestment Fund: Shared Interests, Values, and Vision." Annual Report. William Penn Foundation. https://folio .iupui.edu/bitstream/handle/10244/184/2005_WPF_Annual_Report.pdf?sequence=1.

Hula, R., and C. Jackson-Elmoore. 2001. "Nonprofit Organizations as Political Actors: Avenues for Minority Political Incorporation." *Policy Studies Review* 18: 27–47.

Hurdle, J. 2013. "Education Dept. to Hear School Closing Complaints." *New York Times*, January 28.

Infield, T. 2001. "House Power." *Philadelphia Inquirer*, September 2.

Innes, J., and J. Gruber. 2005. "Planning Styles in Conflict: The Metropolitan Transportation Commission." *Journal of the American Planning Association* 71: 177–88.

Jablow, P. 2013. "A Coalition Wants to Stop Charter Expansion: District Chief Says He Does Too." Philadelphia Public School Notebook, January 25. http://thenotebook .org/blog/135551/charters-loom-large-school-closing-debate.

Jan, T. 2009. "Ivy's Growth Transforms a City: Penn's $500 Million Expansion Could Be Harvard's Model." *Boston Globe*, May 3.

Janofsky, M. 1998. "Philadelphia Neighborhood Reborn: Housing and Business Programs Create Stability and Optimism." *New York Times*, February 24.

Johnson, K. 2004. "Community Development Corporations, Participation, and Accountability: The Harlem Urban Development Corporation and the Bedford-Stuyvesant Restoration Corporation." *Annals of the American Academy of Political and Social Science* 594: 109–24.

Joint Committee of the Pennsylvania General Assembly. 2009. "Tax Exempt Property and Municipal Fiscal Status." Report to the Pennsylvania Legislative Budget and Finance Committee, March. http://lbfc.legis.state.pa.us/reports/2009/26.pdf.

Judd, D. 1999. "Constructing the Tourist Bubble." In *The Tourist City*, edited by D. Judd and S. Fainstein, 35–53. New Haven, CT: Yale University Press.

———. 2003. *The Infrastructure of Play: Building the Tourist City*. Armonk, NY: M. E. Sharpe.

Judd, D., and D. Simpson. 2003. "Reconstructing the Local State: The Role of External Constraints in Building Urban Tourism." *American Behavioral Scientist* 46: 1056–69.

Judd, D., and J. Smith. 2007. "The New Ecology of Urban Governance: Special-Purpose Authorities and Urban Development." In *Governing Cities in a Global Era*, edited by R. Hambleton and J. Simone Gross, 151–60. New York: Palgrave Macmillan.

Katz, B., and J. Bradley. 2013. *The Metropolitan Revolution: How Cities and Metros Are Fixing Our Broken Politics and Fragile Economy*. Washington, DC: Brookings Institution Press.

Kerkstra, P. 2012. "Will a PAC Pick Philly's Next Mayor?" *PhillyPost*, July 6. http:// blogs.phillymag.com.

———. 2013. "Ravaged by Neglect: Part Two: Everyone Loses, Except the Investors." PlanPhilly, March 11. http://planphilly.com/articles/2013/03/11/ravaged-by-neglect -part-two-a-broken-property-tax-system-where-everyone-loses-except-investors.

Kettl, D. 1988. *Government by Proxy: (Mis)Managing Federal Programs*. Washington, DC: Congressional Quarterly.

———. 2009. *The Next Government of the United States.* New York: Norton.

Kirk, P. 2011. "Developers Give Gen Y What They Want." Washington, DC: Urban Land Institute, June. http://urbanland.uli.org/industry-sectors/residential/developers -give-gen-y-what-they-want/.

Kirst, M. 2004. "Turning Points: A History of American School Governance." In *Who's in Charge Here? The Tangled Web of School Governance and Policy,* edited by N. Epstein, 14–41. Washington, DC: Brookings Institution Press.

Kluver, J. D. 2004. "Disguising Social Change: The Role of Nonprofit Organizations as Protective Masks for Citizen Participation." *Administrative Theory and Praxis* 26: 309–24.

Kromer, J. 1999. *Neighborhood Recovery: Reinvestment Policy for the New Hometown.* New Brunswick, NJ: Rutgers University Press.

———. 2010. *Fixing Broken Cities: The Implementation of Urban Development Strategies.* New York: Routledge.

Kurland, A. 2010. "Report of Investigation: Citizens Alliance for Better Neighborhood and Spring Garden Community Development Corporation." Office of the Inspector General of the City of Philadelphia, May. http://www.phila.gov/ig/Report/PPJOC _report_Grant.pdf.

Landis, S. 1998. "A Comparison of Tax Effort for Local Government Functions in Philadelphia and Pittsburgh." Greater Philadelphia First, September.

Ledebur, L., and W. Barnes. 1992. *Metropolitan Disparities and Economic Growth.* Washington, DC: National League of Cities.

Leigland, J. 1995. "Public Infrastructure and Special Purpose Governments: Who Pays and How?" In *Building the Public City,* edited by D. Perry, 138–68. Thousand Oaks, CA: Sage.

Leroux, K. 2007. "Nonprofits as Civic Intermediaries: The Role of Community-Based Organizations in Promoting Political Participation." *Urban Affairs Review* 42: 410–22.

Lewis, C. 2007. "The Nonprofit Road: It's Paved Not with Gold, but with Good Journalism." *Columbia Journalism Review,* September/October, 32–36.

Lewis, P., and M. Sprague. 1997. "Federal Transportation Policy and the Role of Metropolitan Planning Organizations in California." San Francisco: Public Policy Institute of California, April. http://www.ppic.org/content/pubs/report/R_497PLR.pdf.

Liacouras, P. 1987. "Temple University Science and Technology Campus and Jobs Program." Philadelphia: Temple University, March.

LISC. 2010. *Improving Philadelphia's Vacant Property Programs: A Project of Philadelphia LISC and the National Vacant Properties Campaign.* Philadelphia: Local Initiatives Support Corporation.

Logan, J., and H. Molotch. 1987. *Urban Fortunes: The Political Economy of Place.* Berkeley: University of California Press.

Loyd, L. 2012a. "Penn's Building Boom Kicks into a New Phase." *Philadelphia Inquirer,* June 17.

———. 2012b. "Southport Marine Terminal Work Restarts at Navy Yard after Eagles' Nest Delay." *Philadelphia Inquirer,* February 24.

Lubienski, S., and C. Lubienski. 2005. "A New Look at Public and Private Schools: Student Background and Mathematics Achievement." *Phi Delta Kappan* 86: 696–99.

Mallett, W. 2010. "Metropolitan Transportation Planning." Washington, DC: Congressional Research Service, February 3.

Markusen, A., and A. Gadwa. 2010. "Arts and Culture in Urban or Regional Planning; A Review and Research Agenda." *Journal of Planning Education and Research* 29: 379–91.

Martin, J. 2012. "Marketizing the Arts: The Effect of Marketized Revenues on Constituency Size and Composition." PhD dissertation, Temple University.

——. 2013. "State Lifts Funding Freeze for OARC." *Philadelphia Inquirer*, July 17.

Marwell, N. 2007. *Bargaining for Brooklyn: Community Organizations in the Entrepreneurial City.* Chicago: University of Chicago Press.

Mccalla, J. 1999. "Planning Agency: A Disappearing Act." *Philadelphia Business Journal*, October 25.

McCoy, C., and D. Mezzacappa. 1997. "Temple Plans to Reorganize, Close a School: Enrollment Is Down, Finances Pinched." *Philadelphia Inquirer*, April 6.

McCray, R., and M. Friedlander. 2004. "Organizations Closely Affiliated with State or Indian Tribal Governments Reference Guide." Washington, DC: Internal Revenue Service. http://www.irs.gov/pub/irs-tege/eotopich04.pdf.

McGovern, S. 2008. "Evolving Visions of Waterfront Development in Postindustrial Philadelphia: The Formative Role of Elite Ideologies." *Journal of Planning History* 7: 295–326.

McLaughlin, J. P., Jr. 1999. "The Invisible Politics of Regional Cooperation: Philadelphia and Suburban Parties in the Legislature 1985–1996." PhD dissertation, Temple University.

Meyer, H.-D. 2010. "Local Control as a Mechanism of Colonization of Public Education in the United States." *Educational Philosophy and Theory* 42: 830–45.

MGA Partners. 2005. "The Centennial District Master Plan." Philadelphia: Fairmount Park Conservancy, June. http://www.fairmountparkconservancy.org/project/FPCD .MP.EXECUTIVE.SUM.pdf.pdf.

Middleton, M. 1987. "Nonprofit Boards of Directors: Beyond the Governance Function." In *The Nonprofit Sector: A Research Handbook*, edited by W. W. Powell, 141–53. New Haven, CT: Yale University Press.

Mollenkopf, J. 1983. *The Contested City.* Princeton, NJ: Princeton University Press.

Molotch, H. 1976. "The City as a Growth Machine: Toward a Political Economy of Place." *American Journal of Sociology* 82: 309–32.

Molotch, H., and S. Vicari. 1988. "Three Ways to Build: The Development Process in the United States, Japan, and Italy." *Urban Affairs Review* 24: 188–214.

MPIP. 2008. "Where We Stand: Community Indicators for Metropolitan Philadelphia." Philadelphia: Temple University, Metropolitan Philadelphia Indicators Project.

NAPCS. 2013. "A Growing Movement: America's Largest Charter School Communities." Washington, National Alliance for Public Charter Schools. http://www.public charters.org/wp-content/uploads/2013/12/Market-Share-Report-2013.pdf.

——. N.d. "Dashboard: A Comprehensive Data Resource." Washington, DC: National Alliance for Public Charter Schools. http://dashboard.publiccharters.org/dashboard /home.

NCCED. 2005. *Reaching New Heights: Trends and Achievements of Community-Based Development Organizations.* Washington, DC: National Congress for Community Economic Development.

NCRC. 2007. "CRA Manual." Washington, DC: National Community Reinvestment Coalition, September. http://www.community-wealth.org/_pdfs/tools/cdfis/tool-ncrc-cra-manual.pdf.

Nelson, A., T. Sanchez, and J. Wolf. 2004. "Metropolitan Planning Organization Voting Structure and Transit Investment Bias." *Transportation Research Record* 1895: 1–7.

Neuwirth, R. 2004. "Renovation or Ruin." *Shelterforce Online*, no. 137, September/October. http://www.nhi.org/online/issues/137/LIHTC.html.

New Jersey State Comptroller. 2012. "Investigative Report: Delaware River Port Authority." Trenton, March 29.

Newman, K., and R. Lake. 2006. "Democracy, Bureaucracy and Difference in Community Development Politics since 1968." *Progress in Human Geography* 30: 1–18.

Norris, D., D. Phares, and T. Zimmerman. 2009. "Metropolitan Government in the United States? Not Now . . . Not Likely." In *Governing Metropolitan Regions in the 21st Century*, edited by D. Phares, 11–38. Armonk, NY: M. E. Sharpe.

Nowak, J. 1997. "Neighborhood Initiative and the Regional Economy." *Economic Development Quarterly* 11: 3–10.

———. 2001. "Civic Lesson: How CDFIs Can Apply Market Realties to Poverty Alleviation." *Capital Xchange*, March. http://www.brookings.edu/research/articles/2001/03/metropolitanpolicy-nowak.

Nunn, S. 1990. "Budgeting for Public Capital: Reinterpreting Traditional Views of Urban Infrastructure Provision." *Journal of Urban Affairs* 12: 327–44.

Nussbaum, P. 2011. "$20 Million in Projects: DRPA's Vote Came amid Criticism from 2 PA Members." *Philadelphia Inquirer*, December 15.

———. 2012a. "DRPA Board Gives OK to More Changes." *Philadelphia Inquirer*, November 22.

———. 2012b. "Fix Road Funding, Agency Warns." *Philadelphia Inquirer*, October 26.

———. 2013. "What Pa. Transportation Bill Will Cost You." *Philadelphia Inquirer*, November 23.

O'Connor, A. 1999. "Swimming against the Wide: A Brief History of Federal Policy in Poor Communities." In *Urban Problems and Community Development*, edited by R. Ferguson and W. Dickens, 77–138. Washington, DC: Brookings Institution.

Odendahl, T. J. 1990. *Charity Begins at Home: Generosity and Self-Interest among the Philanthropic Elite.* New York: Basic Books.

O'Donnell, C. 2012. "Nonprofit with Business Ties: Where Is the Money Going?" *Philadelphia Business Journal*, December 14.

Orfield, M. 1997. *Metro Politics: A Regional Agenda for Community and Stability.* Washington, DC: Brookings Institution Press.

———. 2002. *American Metro Politics: The New Suburban Reality.* Washington, DC: Brookings Institution Press.

Orfield, M., and B. Gumus-Dawes. 2009. "MPO Reform: A National Agenda for Reforming Metropolitan Governance." University of Minnesota, Institute on Race and

Poverty. http://www.community-wealth.org/sites/clone.community-wealth.org/files /downloads/paper-orfield-gumus_dawns.pdf.

Ostrower, F. 1995. *Why the Wealthy Give: The Culture of Elite Philanthropy*. Princeton, NJ: Princeton University Press.

———. 1998. "The Arts as Cultural Capital among Elites: Bourdieu's Theory Reconsidered." *Poetics* 26: 43–53.

———. 2004. *Attitudes and Practices concerning Effective Philanthropy: Survey Report*. Washington, DC: Urban Institute Center on Nonprofits and Philanthropy.

———. 2005. "The Reality underneath the Buzz: The Potentials and Pitfalls of Partnering." *Stanford Social Innovation Review* 3: 34–41.

Otterbein, H. 2013. "Philadelphia Can't Prove Some Tax Exemptions Are Legit." *Newsworks.org*, May 22.

PACDC. 2003. "Invest in Neighborhoods: An Agenda for Livable Communities." Philadelphia Association of Community Development Corporations, May. http://www .pacdc.org/wp-content/uploads/2009/06/InvestIn.pdf.

———. 2008. "Expanding Economic Opportunities and Revitalizing Neighborhoods: A Report on the Philadelphia CDC Tax Credit Program." Philadelphia Association of Community Development Corporations, October. http://www.pacdc.org/wp-con tent/uploads/2009/06/CDCTaxCredit_2008.pdf.

PADOT. 2009. "General and Procedural Guidance for the Development of the 2011 Transportation Program." Pennsylvania Department of Transportation, August 25. ftp://ftp.dot.state.pa.us/public/Bureaus/Cpdm/LRTP/2011General&ProceduralGuid ance.pdf.

Pagano, M., and D. Perry. 2008. "Financing Infrastructure in the 21st Century City." *Public Works Management and Policy* 13: 22–38.

Parkway Council Foundation. 2014. Mission Statement. http://www.parkwaymuseum districtphiladelphia.org/Parkway-Council-Foundation/27/.

Parmley, S. 2011. "New Tactics for Handling Panhandlers." *Philadelphia Inquirer*, April 3.

PCPC. 1960. "Comprehensive Plan: The Physical Development Plan for the City of Philadelphia." Philadelphia: Philadelphia City Planning Commission.

———. 1963. "Center City Philadelphia Plan." Philadelphia: Philadelphia City Planning Commission.

———. 2011. "Philadelphia 2035." Philadelphia: Philadelphia City Planning Commission, June. http://phila2035.org.

Pedroni, T. 2007. *Market Movements: African American Involvement in School Voucher Reform*. New York: Routledge.

Peirce, N. 1993. *Citistates: How Urban America Can Prosper in a Competitive World*. Santa Ana, CA: Seven Locks Press.

Pell, M. B. 2011. "Charity-Care Hospital Regulations Scrutinized." *Atlanta Journal-Constitution*, August 7.

Penn Institute for Urban Research. N.d. "Anchor Institutions and Their Role in Metropolitan Change." University of Pennsylvania, Penn IUR Initiatives on Anchor Institutions. http://penniur.upenn.edu/uploads/media_items/anchor-institutions -and-their-role-in-metropolitan-change.original.pdf.

Pennsylvania Budget and Policy Center. 2010. "Missed Opportunities: An Analysis of 2010–11 Budget." Harrisburg, PA, July 8. http://pennbpc.org/missed-opportunities -analysis-2010-11-budget.

Pennsylvania Transportation Funding and Reform Commission. 2006. "Investing in Our Future: Addressing Pennsylvania's Transportation Funding Crisis. Final Report." Harrisburg, PA, November. ftp://ftp.dot.state.pa.us/public/pdf/STCTAC /TFRC/Reports/TFRC%20Final%20Report.pdf.

Perry, D. 1995. "Building the City through the Back Door: The Politics of Debt, Law, and Public Infrastructure." In *Building the Public City,* edited by D. Perry, 202–36. Thousand Oaks, CA: Sage.

——. 2003. "Urban Tourism and the Privatizing Discourses of Public Infrastructure." In *The Infrastructure of Play: Building the Tourist City,* edited by D. Judd, 19–49. Armonk, NY: M. E. Sharpe.

Peters, N. 1978. "West Oak Lane Losing Bid for Federal Renewal Funds." *Evening Bulletin* (Philadelphia), November 10.

Petshek, K. 1973. *The Challenge of Urban Reform.* Philadelphia: Temple University Press.

Pfeffer, J. 1973. "Size, Composition, and Functions of Hospital Boards of Directors: A Study of Organization-Environment Linkage." *Administrative Science Quarterly* 18: 349–63.

PGSC. 2011. "Philadelphia Great Schools Compact." Philadelphia, December 20. http://www.phila.k12.pa.us/greatschoolscompact/FinalCompact.pdf.

PHC4. 2013. "Financial Analysis 2012," vol. 1: "General Acute Care Hospitals.' Pennsylvania Health Care Cost Containment Council, May.

Philadelphia Business Journal. 2013. *Book of Lists.* Vol. 31. Philadelphia: Philadelphia Business Journal Inc.

Philadelphia Council of Neighborhood Organizations v. William T. Coleman, Jr., Secretary of Transportation of the United States. 1977. United States Court of Appeals, Third Circuit. 437 F.Supp. 1341, September 12.

Philadelphia Research Initiative. 2010. "Suburbanites Value Philadelphia as a Place to Visit but Not to Live." Philadelphia: Pew Charitable Trusts.

——. 2012. "Philadelphia: The State of the City—2012 Update." Philadelphia: Pew Charitable Trusts, March 31.

——. 2013a. "Philadelphia 2013: The State of the City." Philadelphia: Pew Charitable Trusts.

——. 2013b. "Shuttered Public Schools: The Struggle to Bring Old Buildings New Life." Philadelphia: Pew Charitable Trusts, February 11.

Pinsky, M. 2001. "Taking Stock: CDFIs Look Ahead after 25 Years of Community Development Finance." *Capital Xchange,* December. http://www.brookings.edu /research/articles/2001/12/metropolitanpolicy-pinsky.

Portland Metro. 2012. "A Synthesis of the Relationship between Parks and Economic Development." Portland, OR, March 28. http://library.oregonmetro.gov/files/parks _and_economic_development_report.pdf.

Puentes, R. 2011. "Transportation Reform of 1991 Remains Relevant." Washington, DC: Brookings Institution Up-Front Blog, December 19. http://www.brookings.edu /blogs/up-front/posts/2011/12/19-transportation-reform-puentes.

Puentes, R., and L. Bailey. 2005. "Increasing Funding and Accountability for Metro-politan Transportation Decisions." In *Taking the High Road: A Metropolitan Agenda for Transportation Reform*, edited by R. Puentes and B. Katz, 139–68. Washington, DC: Brookings Institution Press.

Puentes, R., and R. Prince. 2003. "Fueling Transportation Finance: A Primer on the Gas Tax." Washington, DC: Brookings Institution, March.

Ravitch, D. 2010. *The Death and Life of the Great American School System*. New York: Basic Books.

Reckhow, S. 2010. "Disseminating and Legitimating a New Approach: The Role of Foundations." In *Between Public and Private: Politics, Governance, and the New Port-folio Models for Urban School Reform*, edited by K. Bulkley, J. Henig, and H. Levin, 277–304. Cambridge, MA: Harvard Education Press.

Research for Action. 2012. "School District Portfolio Management." Pennsylvania Clearinghouse for Educational Research, July. http://www.researchforaction.org/wp-content/uploads/2012/07/RFA-PACER-Brief-on-School-District-Porfolio-Manage ment-Models.pdf.

Roeger, K., A. Blackwood, and S. Pettijohn. 2012. *Nonprofit Almanac 2012*. Washington, DC: Urban Institute Press.

Rohe, W., and R. Bratt. 2003. "Failures, Downsizings, and Mergers among Community Development Corporations." *Housing Policy Debate* 14: 1–46.

Rondinelli, D., J. Johnson Jr., and J. Kasarda. 1998. "The Changing Forces of Urban Economic Development: Globalization and City Competitiveness in the 21st Cen-tury." *Cityscape*. 3: 71–105.

Rosentraub, M., and W. al-Habil. 2009. "Why Metropolitan Governance Is Growing, as Is the Need for Elastic Governments." In *Governing Metropolitan Regions in the 21st Century*, edited by D. Phares, 39–53. Armonk, NY: M. E. Sharpe.

Rudenstein, N. 2012. *The House of Barnes: The Man, the Collection, the Controversy*. Philadelphia: American Philosophical Society.

Rules of the Senate of Pennsylvania. 2013. "Rule 37: Affiliation with Nonprofit Enti-ties." Harrisburg, PA. http://www.pasen.gov/rules/2013SenRules.pdf.

Rusk, D. 1999. *Inside Game/Outside Game: Winning Strategies for Saving Urban America*. Washington, DC: Brookings Institution Press.

——. 2013. *Cities without Suburbs: A Census 2010 Perspective*. 4th ed. Baltimore: Johns Hopkins University Press.

Saffron, I. 2006. "Psst! Did You Hear about This Riverfront Agency?" *Philadelphia In-quirer*, June 2.

——. 2011. "A Small Scale Blueprint for Philadelphia's Next 25 Years." *Philadelphia Inquirer*, June 10.

——. 2012. "Changing Skyline: Odd Silence on Options for Altering I-95." *Philadelphia Inquirer*, February 17.

——. 2013. "What Really Happened on South Broad Street." *Philadelphia Inquirer*, November 1.

Salamon, L. 1987. "Partners in Public Service: The Scope and Theory of Government-Nonprofit Relations." In *The Nonprofit Sector: A Research Handbook*, edited by W. Powell, 99–117. New Haven, CT: Yale University Press.

———. 1995. *Partners in Public Service: Government-Nonprofit Relations in the Modern Welfare State*. Baltimore: Johns Hopkins University Press.

———. 2012. "The Resilient Sector: The Future of Nonprofit America." In *The State of Nonprofit America*, 2nd ed., edited by L. Salamon, 3–86. Washington, DC: Brookings Institution Press.

Salisbury, R. 1964. "Urban Politics: The New Convergence of Power." *Journal of Politics* 26, no. 4: 775–97.

Salisbury, S. 2012. "Despite the Heat, Attendance Is Up at Most Major City Museums and Sites." *Philadelphia Inquirer*, July 28.

Sanchez, T. 2006. *An Inherent Bias? Geographic and Racial-Ethnic Patterns of Metropolitan Planning Organization Boards*. Washington, DC: Brookings Institution, January.

Sassen, S. 2009. "Cities Today: A New Frontier for Major Developments." *Annals of the American Academy of Political and Social Science* 626: 53–71.

Savitch, H., et al. 1993. "Ties That Bind: Central Cities, Suburbs and the New Metropolitan Region." *Economic Development Quarterly* 7: 341–57.

Scally, C. 2009. "State Housing Finance Agencies Forty Years Later." *Journal of Planning Education and Research* 29: 194–212.

School District of Philadelphia. 2013. "School Reform Commission Approves Facilities Master Plan." March 7. https://webapps.philasd.org/news/display/articles/1458.

Sciara, G.-C., and M. Wachs. 2007. "Metropolitan Transportation Funding: Prospects, Progress, and Practical Considerations." *Public Works Management and Policy* 12: 378–94.

Scott, J. 2009. "The Politics of Venture Philanthropy in Charter School Policy and Advocacy." *Educational Policy* 23: 106–36.

SDP. 2011. *Facilities Master Plan*. Philadelphia: School District of Philadelphia.

———. N.d. "Charter Fact Sheet." Philadelphia: School District of Philadelphia. http://webgui.phila.k12.pa.us/offices/c/charter_schools/charter-fact-sheet.

Shatkin, G. 1998. "Building Community Development Capacity in Philadelphia: A Report to the Ford Foundation." Rutgers University Center for Urban Policy Research, November. http://policy.rutgers.edu/cupr/ford/phila.pdf.

Sherlock, M., and J. Gravelle. 2009. "An Overview of the Nonprofit and Charitable Sector." Washington, DC: Congressional Research Service. http://www.fas.org/sgp/crs/misc/R40919.pdf.

Shorr, L. 2010. PowerPoint presentation by the chief education officer, City of Philadelphia, September 13.

Silverman, R. M. 2001. "Neighborhood Characteristics, Community Development Corporations and the Community Development Industry System." *Community Development Journal* 36: 234–45.

———. 2008. "The Influence of Nonprofit Networks on Local Affordable Housing Funding: Findings from a National Survey of Local Public Administrators." *Urban Affairs Review* 44: 126–41.

———. 2009. "Sandwiched between Patronage and Bureaucracy: The Plight of Citizen Participation in Community-Based Housing Organisations in the US." *Urban Studies* 46: 3–25.

Smith, J. 2010. "Re-stating Theories of Urban Development: The Politics of Authority Creation and Intergovernmental Triads in Postindustrial Chicago." *Journal of Urban Affairs* 32: 425–48.

Snyder, S. 2007. "District Gets New Feedback on Privatization." *Philadelphia Inquirer*, February 24.

———. 2009. "Tightening Standards, Striving to Be the Best." *Philadelphia Inquirer*, December 23.

———. 2011. "Collaborative School Effort Wins a Grant." *Philadelphia Inquirer*, December 21.

———. 2012. "Drexel Looks to Branch Out over Rail Yards." *Philadelphia Inquirer*, November 11.

Snyder, S., and M. Woodall. 2002. "Board's Vote Starts Plan for Privatization." *Philadelphia Inquirer*, March 27.

Steffens, Lincoln. 1903. "Philadelphia: Corrupt and Contented." *McLures Magazine*, July.

Steinberg, M., and R. Quinn. 2013. *Assessing Adequacy in Education Spending: A Summary of Key Findings from Pennsylvania and Philadelphia*. Philadelphia: University of Pennsylvania, November 20.

Stern, M., and S. Seifert. 2010. "Cultural Clusters: The Implications of Cultural Assets Agglomeration for Neighborhood Revitalization." *Journal of Planning Education and Research* 29: 262–79.

Sternlieb, G. 1971."The City as Sandbox." *Public Interest* 25: 14–21.

Stoecker, R. 1997. "The CDC Model of Urban Redevelopment: A Critique and an Alternative." *Journal of Urban Affairs* 19: 1–22.

Stone, C. 2006. "Power, Reform, and Urban Regime Analysis." *City and Community* 5: 23–38.

Stoutland, S. E. 1999. "Community Development Corporations: Mission, Strategy and Accomplishments." In *Urban Problems and Community Development*, edited by R. Ferguson and W. Dickens, 193–240. Washington, DC: Brookings Institution Press.

Strom, E. 1999. "Let's Put On a Show: Performing Arts and Urban Revitalization in Newark, New Jersey." *Journal of Urban Affairs* 21: 423–36.

———. 2002. "Converting Pork into Porcelain: Cultural Institutions and Downtown Development." *Urban Affairs Review* 38: 3–21.

Subsidyscope. N.d. "Tax Expenditures in the Nonprofit Sector." Pew Charitable Trusts. http://subsidyscope.org/nonprofits/tax-expenditures/.

Swanstrom, T. 1999. "The Non-profitization of United States Housing Policy: Dilemmas of Community Development." *Community Development Journal* 34: 28–37.

Swanstrom, T., and J. Koschinsky. 2000. "Rethinking the Partnership Model of Government-Nonprofit Relations: The Case of Community Development." In *Nonprofits in Urban America*, edited by R. Hula and C. Jackson-Elmoore, 65–91. Westport, CT: Quorum Books.

"Taking Region's Health Care Worldwide." 2013. *Region's Business: A Journal of Business and Politics,* February 28.

Teaford, J. 1979. *City and Suburb: The Political Fragmentation of Metropolitan American 1850–1970*. Baltimore: Johns Hopkins University Press.

Thompson, I. 2011. "The King of Center City." *Philadelphia City Paper*, October 6–12.

Tocqueville, A. 2000. *Democracy in America: The Complete and Unabridged Volumes I and II.* New York: Bantam Classic.

Toll, J., and M. Gillam. 1995. *Invisible Philadelphia: Community through Voluntary Organizations.* Philadelphia: Atwater Ken Museum.

TRF. 2013. *2012 Annual Report.* Philadelphia: The Reinvestment Fund.

Ung, E. 2003. "After $300 Million, DRPA Pump Going Dry." *Philadelphia Inquirer,* June 24.

Urban Partners. 2005. "The Centennial District Economic Development Strategy." Commerce Department of the City of Philadelphia. http://construction.basf.us/files /resources/Centennial%20District%20Economic%20Dev.%20Strategy%20-%20final %20report.pdf.

URS Corporation. 2011. "Long Range Facilities Plan." School District of Philadelphia, November. http://www.crpe.org/sites/default/files/Philadelphia_LongRangeFacili tiesPlan_Nov2011_0.pdf.

U.S. Census Bureau, Population Division. 2012. "Annual Estimates of County Resident Population: April 1, 2010 to July 1, 2012," December. http://factfinder2.census.gov /faces/tableservices/jsf/pages/productview.xhtml?src=bkmk.

USCM. 2012. "Endorsing Offices That Facilitate Close Collaboration between Local Government, Foundations, and Nonprofit." Resolution adopted June 2012 by U.S. Conference of Mayors, Orlando, FL. http://usmayors.org/resolutions/80th_Confer ence/metro14.asp.

U.S. Department of Housing and Urban Development. N.d. Community Planning and Development Program Appropriations Budget 1995, 2000, 2005, 2010, 2012. http://portal.hud.gov/hudportal/HUD?src=/program_offices/comm_planning /about/budget.

Useem, M. 1984. *The Inner Circle: Large Corporations and the Rise of Business Political Activity in the U.S. and U.K.* New York: Oxford University Press.

——. 1988. "Market and Institutional Factors in Corporate Contributions." *California Management Review* 30: 77–88.

USGAO. 2013. "Interstate Compacts: Transparency and Oversight of Bi-State Tolling Authorities Could Be Enhanced." Washington, DC: U.S. Government Accountability Office, August. http://www.gao.gov/assets/660/656956.pdf.

Vicino, T. 2010. "New Boundaries of Urban Governance: An Analysis of Philadelphia's University City Improvement District." *Drexel Law Review* 3: 339–56.

Wagner, J. 2012. "Poor Administration of the Redevelopment Assistance Capital Program." Harrisburg, Department of the Auditor General, June. http://www.auditor gen.state.pa.us/reports/performance/special/speRACP062712.pdf.

Walker, C. 2002. *Community Development Corporations and Their Changing Support Systems.* Washington, DC: The Urban Institute, December.

Warner, S. B. 1987. *The Private City: Philadelphia in Three Periods of Its Growth.* 2nd ed. Philadelphia: University of Pennsylvania Press.

Warren, M., and K. Mapp. 2011. *A Match on Dry Grass: Community Organizing as a Catalyst for School Reform.* New York: Oxford University Press.

Weiler, C. 1974. *Philadelphia: Neighborhood, Authority, and the Urban Crisis.* New York: Praeger.

Weir, M. 1996. "Central Cities' Loss of Power in State Politics." *Cityscape* 2: 23–40.

———. 2005. "States, Race, and the Decline of New Deal Liberalism." *Studies in American Political Development* 19: 157–73.

Weiss, M. 2002. *State Policy Approaches to Promote Metropolitan Economic Strategy.* Washington, DC: National Governors Association.

Westervelt, E. 2013. "Charter Schools in Philadelphia: Educating without a Blueprint." National Public Radio, *Morning Edition*, November 22.

Williams, O. 1967. "Lifestyle Values and Political Decentralization in Metropolitan Areas." *Southwestern Social Science Quarterly* 48: 299–310.

———. 1971. *Metropolitan Political Analysis: A Social Access Approach.* New York: Free Press.

Wilson, M. 2012. "WAMs: One Less Arrow in the Quiver, One More Scapegoat for Failed Negotiations." WITF, Harrisburg, PA, December 6. http://www.witf.org /state-house-sound-bites/2012/12/wams-one-less-arrow-in-the-quiver-one-more -scapegoat-for-failed-negotiations.php.

Wolfinger, R. 1974. *The Politics of Progress.* Englewood Cliffs, NJ: Prentice Hall.

Wolk, A., and C. Ebinger. 2010. "Government and Social Innovation: Current State and Local Models." In *Innovations.* Special Edition for the Tulane-Rockefeller 2010 Model City Conference, 135–57. New Orleans: Tulane University. http://www.isgim pact.com/wp-content/uploads/2012/04/Govt-and-Social-Innovation_MITInnova tionsJournal.pdf.

Wong, K., and F. Shen. 2003. "Measuring the Effectiveness of City and State Takeover as a School Reform Strategy." *Peabody Journal of Education* 78: 89–119.

Woodall, M. 2010a. "Michael O'Neill Launches Nonprofit to Raise Money for Successful Phila Schools." *Philadelphia Inquirer*, July 23.

———. 2010b. "Report Cites Questionable Charter School Practices." *Philadelphia Inquirer*, April 5.

———. 2012a. "Court: District Illegally Capped Charter's Rolls." *Philadelphia Inquirer*, April 5.

———. 2012b. "Feds Charge Philly Charter School Mogul in Massive Fraud." *Philadelphia Inquirer*, July 25.

———. 2013a. "Network to run 14 former parish schools." Philadelphia Inquirer, July 17.

———. 2013b. "Report Will Allege Abuses at Charters." *Philadelphia Inquirer*, March 19.

———. 2013c. "Well-Heeled Call for School Funding." *Philadelphia Inquirer*, May 30.

Worden, A. 2013. "Charters Abusing the Right to No?" *Philadelphia Inquirer*, May 14.

Woronkowicz, J., et al. 2012. *Set in Stone: Building America's New Generation of Arts Facilities, 1994–2008.* Chicago: Cultural Policy Center, University of Chicago.

Zald, M. N. 1969. "The Power and Function of Boards of Directors: A Theoretical Synthesis." *American Journal of Sociology* 75: 97–111.

Zimmer, R., et al. 2008. "Evaluating the Performance of Philadelphia's Charter Schools." Philadelphia: Research for Action, March.

Zimmer, R., et al. 2012. "Examining Charter Student Achievement Effects across Seven States." *Economics of Education Review* 31, no. 2: 213–24.

Index